Voices in Exile

A Study in Sephardic Intellectual History

by
Marc D. Angel

KTAV PUBLISHING HOUSE
BROOKLYN, NEW YORK

IN ASSOCIATION WITH
THE INSTITUTE FOR JEWISH IDEAS AND IDEALS
AND
THE SEPHARDIC EDUCATIONAL CENTER
2019

This book, originally published in 1991, is reprinted as part of the "Sephardic Initiative" sponsored by the Institute for Jewish Ideas and Ideals, and the Sephardic Educational Center. We thank Isabelle and Nugi Jakobishvili for their support of the "Sephardic Initiative" and we welcome others to join in supporting this important work.

Published by
Ktav Publishing House
527 Empire Blvd.
Brooklyn, NY 11225
Tel: (718) 972-5449 | Fax: (718) 972-6307
www.ktav.com | orders@ktav.com

ISBN 978-0-88125-370-2

Print year: 2019

Library of Congress Cataloging-in-Publication Data

Copyright © 1991, 2019 Marc D. Angel

Angel, Marc.
    Voices in exile : a study of Sephardic intellectual history / by
Marc D. Angel.
    p.   cm. — (The Library of Sephardic history and thought)
    Includes bibliographical references and index.
    ISBN 0-88125-370-7
    1. Judaism—History.   2. Sephardic—Intellectual life.   I. Title.
II. Series.
BM190.A54   1990
296-8'3—dc20   90-24764
                                                          CIP

Manufactured in the United States of America

Contents

Preface   vii

Acknowledgments   ix

1. Expulsion   1
   Historical Background   1
   Reactions to the Expulsion   4
   The Sephardic Diaspora   7
   The Expulsion: Why?   9
   Accepting Suffering   11
   Religious Understanding of History   13

2. Reactions to the Expulsion   16
   Anti-Rationalism and Rationalism   16
   Acceptance and Rebellion   22
   Halakhah   35
   Kabbalah   37
   Kabbalistic Ethics   40

3. The Conversos   42
   The Judaism of the Conversos   46
   Jewish Attitudes Toward the Conversos   49

4. Return and Reconciliation   56
   Spiritual Struggles   57
   The Western Sephardic Tradition   65

5. The Era of Sabbatai Sevi   68
   Philosophy versus Kabbalah   68
   Anti-Halakhic Tendencies   69
   Acceptance versus Rebellion   70
   Sabbatai Sevi   72
   Rabbi Moshe Hagiz   77

6. The Promised Land: Maintaining a Dream   85
   Preparing for Redemption in Israel   89
   The Shadarim   94
   Faith and Despair   97

7. The Folk Mind and Spirit 101
   Rabbi Yaacov Huli 103
   Folk Wisdom and Intellectual Wisdom 110

8. Musar: Ethics and Moral Guidance 117
   Musar Study and Musar Practices 120
   Musar Teachings 124
   Relationship with Hassidism 133

9. Acceptance and Rebellion: Prelude to Modernity 135
   A New Approach 138
   The Blood Libels in Damascus and Rhodes in 1840 144

10. Sephardic Haskalah 150
   Grace Aguilar: Jewish Spirituality 152
   Eliyahu Benamozegh: Jewish Ethics 155
   Rabbi Israel Moshe Hazan 157
   Rabbi Yehudah Yaacov Nehama: Defending Tradition 159
   Rabbi Henry Pereira Mendes 160
   Traditional Communal Framework 162

11. Secular Sephardic Literature 164
   Elia Carmona 166
   Angel Pulido 171
   La America 172
   Poetry 175

12. Religious Responses to Modernity 179
   Attitude Toward Secular Education 182
   Rabbi Elilyahu Hazan 184
   Rabbi Reuben Eliyahu Israel 187
   Halakhah and Modernism 188
   Rabbi Benzion Uziel 194

13. Israel and the Nations 197
   Israel and Humanity 200
   Maintaining Uniqueness and Universality 202
   Conversion to Judaism 204
   Zionism 205

Epilogue 209
   Notes 211
   Bibliography 225
   Index 233

Preface

This book is a study of the intellectual life of Sephardic Jewry from the period of the expulsion from Spain in 1492 through the first half of the twentieth century. More accurately, it is a series of studies of various aspects of the intellectual and spiritual creativity of the Sephardim of Spanish-language background. It deals primarily with thinkers and trends among the Sephardim of Turkey and the Balkan countries, the land of Israel, North Africa, and the Western Sephardic communities of Europe and the New World.

The field of Sephardic intellectual history since the expulsion from Spain has not received adequate attention. There are histories of various communities and biographies of some personalities; but this is the first book dedicated to tracing the course of intellectual life among Sephardim in a comprehensive way. It provides a panoramic view of nearly five centuries of Sephardic experience.

This book is an introduction to a vast field of Jewish thought which has been very much neglected by historians, scholars, and philosophers. I have written it in the hope that it will stimulate considerably more research, and many more books, to fill the void in our knowledge of Sephardic intellectual life.

I have entitled the book *Voices in Exile*. On one level, this refers to the fact that the Sephardic thinkers discussed in the book lived as Sephardim exiled from Spain. But it also suggests that the Sephardic thinkers are *still* in exile; their voices have still not been heard by most people, even highly educated students of Judaism and Jewish history. Their teachings and struggles have remained relatively unknown and, therefore, uninfluential in the general intellectual life of the Jewish people today. This book is an attempt to remedy this deficiency and to bring their voices out of exile. The Sephardic mystics and masters of past generations have much of value to teach us.

Acknowledgments

This book developed over the course of years. Many libraries and individuals were helpful in providing materials, insights, and useful advice. I am grateful to all who were of assistance to me in the preparation of this work.

Much of the material in this book was presented in a number of courses and lectures I gave at Congregation Shearith Israel, the historic Spanish and Portuguese synagogue in the city of New York. I thank those congregants, as well as members of Sephardic House, who attended these sessions and offered constructive responses to my presentations.

I thank Mr. Moshe Heller of Ktav Publishing House for his cooperation and commitment to this book. I am grateful to him and his staff, with a special thanks to Shira Atwood, for making this book available to the public.

My wife, Gilda, has provided the love, patience, and under-standing without which this work could never have been accomplished. To her—and to our children and grandchildren—I extend my love and sincere appreciation.

• 1 •

Expulsion

Historical Background

In the spring of 1492, shortly before Passover, the festival of freedom, King Ferdinand and Queen Isabella decreed the expulsion of the Jews from Spain. This was the culmination of over a thousand years of Jewish experience in that country.

The Jews of Spain, known in Hebrew as Sephardim, had a tradition that they were descended from the aristocracy of ancient Judea, who had been transferred to Spain (Sepharad in Hebrew) following the destruction of the First Temple in Jerusalem (586 B.C.E.). The prophet Obadiah had spoken of "the captivity of Jerusalem that is in Sepharad" (v. 20), and Spanish Jewry applied this verse to itself. The first definite historical evidence of Jewish life in Spain is a tombstone inscription dating back to the third century of the common era. During the many centuries of Jewish life in Spain, there were good times and bad. [1]

Moslem forces conquered much of Spain early in the eighth century. The Jews, who had been persecuted and forcibly converted by the earlier Christian rulers, welcomed the arrival of the Moslems. Under Moslem rule, Jewish life in Spain began to flourish and indeed came to enjoy a golden age. In the tenth century, Hasdai Ibn Shaprut was a leading Jewish personality who created a strong Jewish cultural center in Cordoba. He attracted great scholars and helped stimulate the development of an indigenous Spanish rabbinic leadership. Formerly, Spanish Jewry had relied heavily on the rabbinic scholars of Babylonia.

The tenth and eleventh centuries witnessed a flowering of Jewish intellectual life. Classic works were created in rabbinic literature, Hebrew poetry, biblical studies, philosophy, and ethics. This was the era of such luminaries as Rabbi Yitzhak

Alfasi, who headed the rabbinic academy in Lucena; Shelomo Ibn Gabirol and Bahya Ibn Pakuda, profound philosophers who flourished in Saragossa; and Yehudah Halevy, the premier poet of medieval Jewry, who flourished in Toledo. The accomplishments in poetry and biblical studies of Abraham Ibn Ezra and Moshe Ibn Ezra also were produced in this golden age.

During the eleventh century, Shemuel ha-Nagid, a Jewish scholar and poet, served as vizier and commander of the army of Granada. He also served simultaneously as the head of the Jewish community. He combined greatness in Jewish learning with active political and military involvement on behalf of the Moslem government of Granada. His son, Yosef, succeeded him upon his death, but anti-Jewish agitation among Moslems escalated, and Yosef was assassinated in 1066. At that time, there were general Moslem attacks against the Jews of Granada, and many fled to other locations, especially to Lucena.

In 1146, the Almohads, a fanatic Berber dynasty of Morocco, began their conquest of Moslem Spain. They were fiercely anti-Jewish and brought an end to the Jewish communities of Andalusia. A number of Jews accepted Islam outwardly but maintained Judaism in secret. Many Jews fled to portions of Spain under Christian rule. Others left the country altogether. Among them was the family of Moshe ben Maimon (Maimonides), who was to become the single most important figure produced by Sephardic Jewry. His works in Jewish law and philosophy remain classics to this day. His achievements as a doctor, logician, and mathematician were greatly respected by Jews and non-Jews alike.

The period of the Christian reconquest of Spain began early in the eleventh century. The Jews who lived in Christian Spain during the eleventh and twelfth centuries flourished. In Barcelona, for example, Jews were major landowners.

When Christian forces conquered Toledo in 1085, the Jews of the city did not flee. The Christian rulers offered them protection. This pattern was followed in other cities conquered by the Christians. Jews in Christian Spain rose to prominence, especially in Castile.

Early in the thirteenth century, the Jews in Christian Spain suffered a variety of legal disabilities. Anti-Jewish sentiment was rising. The kingdom of Aragon began a vigorous campaign to convert Jews to Christianity. The masses were incited to violence against them by fanatical Christian clerics. Public disputations were held in order to humiliate Jews and Judaism, the most famous of which took place in Barcelona in 1263, pitting Rabbi Moshe ben Nahman against a Jewish apostate, Pablo Christiani. Shortly after the disputation, Rabbi Moshe left Spain to settle in Israel.

In 1267, Pope Clement IV gave the Inquisition the freedom to pursue converted Jews who had returned to their former religion. The Inquisition was also empowered to act against Christians who converted to Judaism. Jews who were accused of having too much influence over Christians were also endangered.

During the thirteenth century, kabbalah blossomed. Rabbi Yitzhak the Blind (ca. 1160–1235) and his circle of mystics turned Gerona into a major center of Jewish mysticism. Rabbi Moshe ben Nahman spread the influence of kabbalah through his activities as teacher and author. Late in the thirteenth century, Rabbi Moshe de Leon issued the Zohar *(The Book of Splendor)*, a kabbalistic text attributed to the talmudic sage Rabbi Shimon bar Yohai.

Concurrent with the rise of kabbalah was a growing disillusionment with philosophy. The late thirteenth century witnessed a great controversy between those who favored the study of philosophy, adherents of Maimonides, and those who strenuously opposed the study of philosophy, attacking Maimonides' philosophical work. The leading rabbis of the time, such as Rabbi Asher ben Yehiel of Toledo and Rabbi Shelomo ben Adret of Barcelona, were drawn into the dispute. The controversy continued for many decades; even when it subsided, the essential differences of opinion continued among Spanish Jewry.

Life in Christian Spain became increasingly difficult for Jews during the fourteenth century. Anti-Jewish Christian fanatics preached hatred and incited violence against them. In June 1391, riots broke out in Seville in which many Jews were killed; many others were forcibly converted, and a number of Jewish women and children were sold into slavery. Synagogues were taken over and converted into churches. The anti-Jewish disorders spread to Andalusia, but the monarchy made no effort to protect the victims. In July, Jews were massacred in Aragon. On August 5, over four hundred Jews were killed in Barcelona. On August 10, many Jews were killed in Gerona.

During this horrendous period of persecution, a large number of Jews converted to Christianity in order to save their lives and property. At the same time, faithful Jews struggled to maintain and support their own communities. The relationship between the faithful Jews and those who had accepted baptism was complex. On the one hand, there was a sympathy for the conversos, who had been forced to accept Catholicism. On the other hand, there was a feeling that the conversos had betrayed their God and their people. Nevertheless, Catholic fanatics felt that the existence of a real Jewish community in Spain made it impossible for the conversos to adopt Catholicism fully. The fanatics thought the Jews were a pernicious influence on the Christianization process.

When Aragon and Castile were united in 1479, Ferdinand and Isabella were anxious to consolidate their joint kingdom as a Catholic entity. In 1480 two Dominicans were named inquisitors for the kingdom of Castile. A number of conversos were tortured and burned at the stake. In 1481 inquisitors were appointed for Aragon. In 1483, Jews were expelled from Andalusia. When the Christian forces conquered Granada in January 1492, the last stronghold of Islam in Spain fell. The inexorable process of purging the kingdom of all non-Catholics was reaching its climax. The decree to expel the Jews from Spain, issued in March 1492, was a cruel manifestation of this process.

Reactions to the Expulsion

The leading Jewish figure in Spain at the time of the expulsion edict was Rabbi Yitzhak Abravanel, whose family was believed to be descended from King David. In describing Sephardic Jewry, Rabbi Abravanel stated:

From the rising of the sun to its setting, from north to south, there was never such a chosen people [as the Jews of Spain] in beauty and pleasantness; and afterwards, there will never be another such people. God was with them, the children of Judea and Jerusalem, many and strong. [They were] a quiet and trusting people, a people filled with the blessing of God with no end to its treasures; a pure and upright people, revering the Lord. I am the man who saw this people in its glory, in its beauty, in its pleasantness.[2]

Since the Sephardim had such a tradition of nobility, the persecution they suffered was all the more painful, humiliating, and traumatic. Abravanel and other leading Jewish dignitaries sought to have the expulsion decree rescinded. But the king and queen held to their original decision. Those Jews who agreed to convert to Catholicism could remain in Spain. The rest were compelled to settle their affairs and leave the kingdom within three months.

Significantly, the date of the expulsion was set for the Jewish month of Ab, during the season of the fast of the Ninth of Ab. This saddest date on the Jewish calendar commemorates the destruction of both the first and second Temples in Jerusalem in antiquity. With the expulsion from Spain, a new national calamity was added to the Jewish memory of the Ninth of Ab.

There was great turmoil among Spanish Jews during those three fateful months. The pressures to abandon Judaism and to accept Christianity were enormous. Many Jews, including intellectuals and even rabbis, accepted baptism rather than face exile. Jews who intended to adhere to their faith had to determine what to do with their property, how to transfer possessions, where to find new homes, and how to travel. How would they be able to take the elderly and infirm? What about their young children and babies? And how could they make all these decisions and arrangements in so little time?

Abravanel described the reaction of Spanish Jews to the news of the decree.

The people heard this evil decree and they mourned. Wherever word of the decree reached, there was great mourning among the Jews. There was great trembling and sorrow the likes of which had not been experienced since the days of the exile of Jews from their land to the land of foreigners. The Jews encouraged each other: let us strengthen ourselves on behalf of our faith, on behalf of the Torah of our God. . . . if [our enemies] let us live, we will live; and if they kill us, we will die. But we will not profane our covenant [with God], and our hearts will not retrogress; we will walk forward in the name of the Lord our God.[3]

He estimated that three hundred thousand were expelled from Spain. While the figure may be too high, it nevertheless indicates that a considerable number of Jews chose to leave Spain rather than forsake their Judaism.

The physical hardships experienced by the exiles were overwhelming. A sixteenth-century historian, Yosef Hacohen, recorded that some of them were robbed and killed. Others were captured and sold into slavery. Disease was rampant. Ruthless ship captains filled their vessels with Jewish exiles seeking safe haven, then exploited and tortured them.[4]

Rabbi Abraham ben Shelomo Halevy Bacrat, among a group of Spanish Jews who went to Algeria, indicated that twelve thousand Jews arrived in Tlemcen. Three thousand died shortly after their arrival, due to their many sufferings. The remainder were destitute and further debilitated by famine. Many, unable to withstand the physical hardships, decided to return to Spain and accept conversion.[5]

Rabbi Eliyahu Capsali of Candia, a contemporary who chronicled the history of the period of the expulsion, indicated that tens of thousands of Jews converted to Catholicism at this time. But even many of those who had decided to leave Spain ultimately returned and were baptized. They had suffered so intensely in their exile that they simply could not withstand the pain.[6]

The spiritual sufferings of the exiles were excruciating. Jews who had had such pride in their aristocratic ancestry, their elevated status, and their many accomplishments in Spain were now reduced to wandering victims, scorned and despised. They were powerless against their oppressors. No one came to their assistance. God Himself seemed to have abandoned them. Reflecting the great spiritual despair of his people, Rabbi Abravanel wrote three messianic tracts in which he argued that the arrival of the Messiah was imminent. He felt compelled to publish these works because the exiles needed to be encouraged and consoled.

The Abravanel family suffered its own personal catastrophe in the explusion. Yehudah Abravanel, son of Rabbi Yitzhak Abravanel, had his older son, Yitzhak, sent to Portugal, where the family hoped he would be safe until they could reunite with him. But the child was kidnapped, probably in an effort to coerce the Abravanels into accepting Christianity in return for the child. But the family did not convert. They left Spain with the other Jewish exiles, and the child was lost to them.

Some years later, when the child would have been twelve years old, Yehudah Abravanel wrote a touching Hebrew poem to the son he had lost to Christian fanatics. In the poem, he told the youth that he was the child of sages and was a beloved son. He expressed the hope that his son would be able to escape from among the Gentiles and return to his family. Then they would thank God together, and all would be well.[7]

The experience of the Abravanels epitomizes the personal tragedies that befell countless Spanish Jews. Families were separated when some members chose to remain faithful to Judaism and leave Spain, while others preferred to accept baptism and remain there. These struggles separated husbands from wives, parents from children, siblings from one another. Faithful Jews prayed for a miracle to save them, some divine manifestation that would set things right for them. But no miracle came. God had hidden His face.

The Sephardic Diaspora

The period of the expulsion and the several generations thereafter was a time of profound transformation for Sephardic Jewry. Exiled from Spain, they nevertheless retained their Sephardic culture, character, language. Dispersed over a wide geographic area, they adapted themselves to new societies, new systems of government, new environments. Greatly reduced in numbers, they mourned their dead and those members of their families and communities who had remained in the Iberian Peninsula as forced converts. This was a period of intense physical, spiritual, and emotional duress, when Sephardic Jewry had to draw on all its strength in order to transplant itself and take on new life outside of Iberia.

After the fast of Ab in 1492, Spanish Jewry was radically transformed. Thousands of Jews converted to Catholicism in order to remain in Spain. Other thousands crossed the border into Portugal, where they hoped to continue to live openly as Jews. But that respite was short-lived: Judaism was outlawed in Portugal in 1497. The refugees in Portugal were compelled to give up Judaism or leave the Iberian Peninsula.

The benevolent and mighty Ottoman Empire welcomed Jewish refugees to its domains. Major centers of Sephardic Jewry emerged in such cities as Istanbul, Izmir, and Salonika. Sephardic refugees also found havens in the lands of the Middle East and North Africa.

A number of the exiles made their way to cities in Italy and other locations in Western Europe. The Catholic lands were not particularly hospitable to Jews in that age of church intolerance. During the sixteenth century, a vibrant Sephardic community emerged in Amsterdam, composed largely of Iberian Jews who had converted to Catholicism and then returned to Judaism. Other communities of former conversos came into being in Paris, Bordeaux, Bayonne, and Hamburg. During the seventeenth century, communities of ex-converso background were established in London and in various places in the New World, including Curaçao, Surinam, St. Thomas, Jamaica, and New York.

Clearly, the vast majority of Sephardic exiles found haven in Moslem lands. Islamic law allowed full civil rights and privileges only to Moslems. Jews (and Christians) were tolerated as infidels and placed in the category of *dhimmis*, or protected people. Generally, their religious autonomy was accepted and protected in return for the payment of special taxes.

The Koran teaches: "Fight against such of those to whom the Scriptures were given as believe neither in Allah nor the Last Day, who do not embrace the true faith, until they pay tribute out of hand and are utterly subdued" (9:29). But once they paid this tribute, the People of the Book—Jews and Christians—were allowed to live under Islamic rule.

The *dhimmis* were allowed certain basic freedoms, such as the right to own property and practice their religion freely. They were not permitted to build new houses of worship, although this restriction was often disregarded by Moslem rulers. Communities of *dhimmis* were self-governing. They operated their own educational systems, courts, welfare programs. Each community appointed its own tax collectors to raise funds, both for the needs of the community and for taxes that were due the government. The communities also designated leaders to direct their affairs as well as to represent them to non-Jewish officials.

Dhimmis were subject to a variety of legal disabilities. For example, their testimony was not accepted against that of a Moslem. Moslems could not be put to death for murdering a *dhimmi*. *Dhimmis* were restricted in their right to travel freely, and were generally not allowed to ride horseback or carry weapons. In order to make clear their subservient status to Moslems, they were obliged to wear distinctive clothing.

These requirements varied in different places and periods. As Professor S. D. Goitein has noted: "The yellow badge for Jews was known in Muslim countries many centuries before it was introduced into Christian Europe."[8] According to a seventeenth-century observer: "The Jews in Turkey dress like the Turks except that they may not wear green, nor a white turban, nor a red jacket. They are usually dressed in violet but they are obliged to wear a violet bonnet made in the shape of and the same height as a hat and those who have the means to own a turban wear it round the base of their bonnet. They must also wear socks and violet slippers."[9]

In general, the legal status granted to the Jews in Moslem lands made it possible for them to retain their own way of life. They lived in their own quarters, spoke their own language, operated according to Jewish law and custom. While they were obviously influenced by the cultures and economies of the Moslem lands in which they lived, the Jews continued to have a strong sense of their own identity.

The arrival of Sephardic refugees created a variety of tensions within existing Jewish communities. On one hand, the native Jews were eager to help the Sephardim, who had suffered enormously in an ordeal of unparalleled dimensions. It was felt that they were entitled to sympathy and practical assistance in their efforts to reestablish themselves. Moreover, Sephardim were regarded as highly cultured and aristocratic. It was considered an honor to associate with them and to marry into their families.

On the other hand, native Jews resented the newcomers' feelings of cultural superiority. They resented the fact that the Sephardim, who were accustomed to doing things in their own style, tended to impose their will on non-Sephardim. To complicate matters, the Sephardim formed a diverse group among themselves, with divisions based on the communities in Spain and Portugal from which they originated.

The expulsion from Spain in 1492 marked a critical turning point in the history of Sephardic Jewry. Sephardim of that generation had drawn on the centuries of spiritual and intellectual tradition that their people had acquired in the Iberian Peninsula. In Spain they had been guided by classic Jewish ideas and ideals as seen through the prism of the Sephardic religious experience. The generations that followed the expulsion had to integrate these traditions into new circumstances. Influenced by the new milieus in which they found themselves, they evolved distinctive new insights into Judaism in general and into the meaning of Jewish life in particular.

The Expulsion: Why?

The task of the spiritual leaders among the exiles was to interpret the bewildering circumstances in which they found themselves. Why had God allowed them to be expelled from Spain? Why were they forced to sacrifice so much because of their Jewishness? Was there purpose and meaning in their exile?

People are able to withstand a surprising degree of physical, spiritual, and emotional torment if they know *why* they are suffering. One can achieve a sense of heroism, even martyrdom, if one believes that his suffering has purpose and meaning.

Traditional Jewish thought contained the idea that suffering was the result of sin. The Jewish prayer book has long included a passage stating that "because of our sins we have been exiled from our land." This concept, in which the victim blames himself for his predicament, saw history as an ongoing relationship between humankind and God. Victims may not blame their oppressors, because the oppressors are in some way the agents of God's plan. Moreover, God cannot be blamed, since He is just and righteous. Therefore, the only one to blame is the victim himself.

This idea was expressed by Rabbi Yosef Yaavets, one of the leading rabbis among the expelled Spanish Jews. In his book *Or ha-Hayyim*, he told the exiles that their punishment was the result of their sins, for they had abandoned the ways of the Torah. To be sure, during the period preceding 1492, the religious academies of Spain had been filled with students, and the number of people engaged in Torah study had never been greater. Nevertheless, stated Rabbi Yaavets, these Torah students and scholars had such serious moral flaws that they were unable to protect their generation from God's wrath.

For example, some Torah students had devoted six or seven years to study with the great rabbis of Spain and then turned to secular studies. They had moved away from traditional religious faith, rebelling against the authority of Jewish tradition. In other cases, there were scholars who had devoted themselves entirely to Torah study but were more interested in showing off their intellectual prowess than in personal piety. Only a few scholars had truly studied Torah for its own sake, and these few had been unable to counterbalance the prevailing spiritual weakness of Spanish Jewry. The Jews had brought on their own punishment due to their sins, he concluded.[10]

In another of his works, *Hasdei Hashem*, Rabbi Yaavets argued not only that the Jews were sinful but that they were actually worse than the non-Jews! In antiquity, the Jewish people had been the first to have a true conception of One God; they had been chosen and loved by God. In contrast, the non-Jews had been pagans, steeped in primitive immorality. By the time of the expulsion, however, non-Jews had come to understand the central teachings of Jewish theology and had also learned to practice the ethical laws of the Torah. But the Jewish spiritual level had declined. God chose to have the Jews exiled as a lesson that would teach them to improve their ways. [11]

Rabbi Yaavets cited an analogy to the fifteenth-century exile in the experience of the biblical forefather, Jacob. The Bible taught that Jacob was forced to flee from his father's house, fearing that his brother Esau would kill him. He found himself abandoned and alone, and had to sleep on the ground with a rock as his pillow. Jacob dreamed of a ladder with its legs on the ground and extending to heaven. Angels ascended and descended the ladder. This dream was a message from God teaching him that heaven and earth were connected, and that God's providence extended over the totality of existence. The ascents and descents of the angels symbolized the ascents and descents of the Jewish people throughout history, under God's divine providence. In Rabbi Yaavets's view, the faith of the Jews was being tested by their sufferings and exile. Just as the angels in the dream ascended, so too the Jews were in a state of suspension. But just as the angels in the dream also descended, so the Jews would ultimately complete this test of their faith, return to their land, and reestablish their kingdom forever. [12]

Indeed, said Rabbi Yaavets, the exile actually provided the Jews with a unique opportunity to demonstrate their perfect faith in God.

The Almighty, may He be blessed, has placed us in exile because He wishes to forgive our sins, thereby enabling us to maintain the yoke of His Kingship over us. When He, may He be blessed, sees our strong love toward Him—that we bear so many hardships for the sake of His name with love—He will cover our sins and will fulfill His covenant with us. . . . [God will say] just as they uphold My divinity, so I will uphold them. It turns out that exiles are the reason for the maintenance of our souls before God; and they are an absolute good. [13]

Accepting Suffering

Jewish ethical literature had frequently referred to suffering as *yisurin*, or "chastisements." Personal and national tragedy can thus be interpreted as chastisements inflicted by God for the benefit of the afflicted party. *Yisurin* force a person to reevaluate his life, to clarify its meaning and redirect it in a spirit of repentance. Seen in this context, suffering has great value, and is in fact a sign of God's loving concern. After all, doesn't a parent sometimes chastise and punish his children? And don't these chastisements actually help the child to improve his character? At the time of his punishment, a child may resent his parents. But as he grows older, he will appreciate what they have done and be grateful to them. Likewise, we may not be eager to receive chastisements from God. Yet we know that they are for our own good.

Rabbi Yaavets extolled the virtue of receiving *yisurin* with happiness. One who rejoices in *yisurin* truly recognizes the unity of God. A pious person is obliged to acknowledge that all of God's actions toward him are supremely wise, regardless of whether they appear to be good or bad from a human perspective. The ultimate state of piety is to bless God even when receiving painful chastisements, since one should be more pleased by the cure for his soul than displeased by the pain for his body. *Yisurin* should be viewed as a spiritual opportunity and a true test of faith. [14]

The need to accept *yisurin* found expression in the writings of other authors of the generation following the expulsion. Rabbi Abraham Gabison, who was among the Jews expelled from Granada, settled in Tlemcen. The king of Algeria had invited Gabison to the city because he sought his services as a physician. Gabison wrote a commentary on the biblical Book of Proverbs in which he stated that a God-fearing person is one who accepts *yisurin* willingly. One should receive chastisements from heaven with a pleasant countenance, without becoming angry. The power of Torah does not fully take hold of a person until he has undergone pain and suffering. [15]

Rabbi Moshe Almosnino, who flourished in Salonika during the sixteenth century, commented on the verse "I am black and comely" (Song of Songs 1:5) that these words were uttered by the people of Israel to God. Even though I, Israel, am black from exile and suffering, nevertheless I am also comely in this exile and in my sufferings. Since my tribulations are an atonement for my sins, my beauty and inner purity are enhanced. [16] Elsewhere in his writings, Rabbi Almosnino praised the virtues of *yisurin*, maintaining that they cure all the soul's diseases and purify it from its deficiencies. *Yisurin* allow us to achieve the spiritual perfection of valuing the soul more than the body. [17]

Religious Understanding of History

For several generations after the expulsion, Sephardic intellectuals and the Sephardic masses sought ways of understanding and interpreting their existential condition. In attempting to respond to their particular dilemma, they looked for transcendent meaning in the exile—for hints of a divine plan. It was not just they who had a spiritual crisis: it was also God. His justice and His ways were also on trial.

The voices of the sages in those generations were to influence the Sephardic voices in exile for generations to come. They sought a religious understanding of history that would help them cope with the trauma of expulsion.

For example, the Talmud told the story of four great rabbis who lived in Israel during the period of Roman occupation after the destruction of the Temple in Jerusalem (Makot 24a–b). One day, as they were walking together, they heard the sounds of a large gathering of Romans in the distance. Three of the sages began to cry; but the fourth, Rabbi Akiba, laughed. They asked: "Why do you laugh?" He replied: "And why are you crying?" They answered: "These pagans who worship idolatry dwell safely and securely, while we are demeaned, the house of our Lord being burnt. Should we not then cry?" Rabbi Akiba answered: "That is the reason I am laughing. If God gives such wonderful reward to those who violate His will, does it not stand to reason that He will give even greater reward to those of us who follow His will?"

On another occasion, the four sages were walking toward Jerusalem. When they arrived at Mount Scopus, they rent their garments as a sign of mourning. Arriving at the Temple Mount, they saw a fox running through the ruins where the Holy of Holies used to stand. Three of the sages began to cry, but Rabbi Akiba laughed. Again they asked him: "Why are you laughing?" Again he replied: "Why are you crying?" They responded: "In this holiest of places, where only the high priest was allowed to enter, foxes run freely. Should we not then cry?" Rabbi Akiba said: "That is the reason I am laughing. Just as the prophecies predicting the destruction of the Temple were fulfilled, so will the prophecies predicting our ultimate redemption be fulfilled. Now that we have seen with our own eyes that the prophecies of destruction were true, we can be all the more confident that the prophecies of redemption are also true." His colleagues then said to him: "You have consoled us, Akiba, you have consoled us."

Similarly, the exiled scholars took comfort in the belief that God's providence revealed itself in the course of history, and was evidenced in the visions of prophets. God is not capricious; He is true to His word. If He has punished us for our sins, He will also reward us for our virtues. If He has inspired His prophets to describe accurately our punishments, He has also inspired them to describe truthfully our future redemption. Having experienced and survived the punishment, we should have abiding hope that healing and salvation are just ahead.

A sixteenth-century mystic and ethicist, Rabbi Eliyahu de Vidas of Safed, followed this pattern of thought in his explication of the phenomenon of exile. The Passover Haggadah records that in each generation enemies arise to destroy the Jewish people; but the Holy One, blessed be He, saves us from them. If the Almighty in fact despised us, then He would destroy us altogether. Since we see that He always saves a remnant of our people, it is clear that His goal is not to eliminate us altogether. Rather, the purpose of exile and destruction is to chastise us, to direct us to repentance. When we sincerely atone for our past sins, God has compassion on us. Therefore, when we are undergoing a period of suffering, we should repent our past sins. We may then be confident that God will be merciful to us.[18]

There was an efflorescence of Jewish historical works during the sixteenth century, following the expulsion of Jews from Spain. Far more comprehensive than earlier Jewish historical writings, these works attempted to present a coherent, consecutive survey of centuries of Jewish experience. A unique feature of these works was the importance they assigned to postbiblical and post-talmudic history. Professor Yosef H. Yerushalmi has observed that these historical works "bestow a new value upon the events that have transpired over the entire course of the Middle Ages. They seem to recognize implicitly that these events too have a meaning for the present and the future which cannot be grasped merely by focusing attention on ancient times, and they are therefore worth recalling. All this marks a significant change in outlook."[19] Yerushalmi notes that these works tended to record facts not for their own value, but for the hints they offered. Their authors generally attempted to interpret historical events as fulfillments of biblical prophecies, as examples of an unfolding drama that would culminate in the arrival of the Messiah. In short, these historical works can themselves be viewed as an attempt to understand the expulsion by placing it into a historical context, guided by the providence of God.

Some of these works recorded various tragedies that had befallen Jews throughout the preceding ages. Persecutions, pogroms, and other expulsions were presented in a litany of Jewish grief. Significantly, the historian Yosef Hacohen entitled his work *The Valley of Tears*. However, the goal of these books was not to make the Spanish Jews feel sorry for themselves but rather to encourage them in their faith. Samuel Usque, in his *Consolation for the Tribulations of Israel,* presented each tribulation and then suggested the prophecy that it seemed to fulfill. Following the teaching in the story of Rabbi Akiba and his three colleagues, Usque presented the case that just as the prophecies of misfortune proved to be right, so we must believe that the prophecies of our blessings will also come true. After all, both sets of prophecies emanated from God. [20]

The several generations following the expulsion were rich in creative Jewish thought. Sephardic mystics and masters struggled with the question of faith versus rationalism, the acceptance of God's will versus rebellion, and the emphasis on halakhah, Jewish legalism, versus kabbalah, Jewish mysticism.

•2•

Reactions To The Expulsion

Anti-Rationalism and Rationalism

Rabbi Yosef Yaavets believed that the root problem of pre-exilic Spanish Jewry had been its predilection for rationalism. The Spanish Jews' study of Greek and Arabic philosophy, in particular, had led to a corrosion of their religious faith. They had become skeptical of rabbinic tradition, critical of authority. Indeed, because of their commitment to rationalism and philosophy, their devotion to Judaism weakened. The fact that so many Spanish Jews accepted baptism rather than expulsion was clear proof of the deterioration of their religious faith.

Rabbi Yaavets observed: "Most of those who prided themselves on their wisdom and good deeds apostasized on that bitter day. But the common people sacrificed their lives and possessions to sanctify their Creator."[1] He noted that "it was the Sephardic women who left, and who brought their husbands to martyr themselves for the blessed God, while those who prided themselves on their wisdom, apostasized on the bitter day. This is a great proof that if they had not sought after wisdom but remained among the simple, their simplicity would have saved them, since God preserves the simple."[2]

The rabbi likened individuals who studied philosophy and other wisdom (but did not devote themselves deeply to Torah study) to trees with many branches but with weak roots. Such trees appear to be healthy, but once a strong wind comes they are easily overturned. Once the rationalists among the Sephardim were confronted with the winds of expulsion, they were easily uprooted from their faith and turned against their own God. On the other hand, those who retained their pure faith by rejecting philosophy

16

were able to preserve their loyalty to God. Their deep roots in faith were able to withstand the conversionary pressures.[3]

Rabbi Yaavets believed that philosophical study tended to undermine Jewish faith. It led the Sephardim to abandon or doubt the principles of reward and punishment, resurrection of the dead, and other Jewish concepts.[4]

Some Sephardic intellectuals argued that greater understanding of Torah could be attained through the study of philosophy, but Rabbi Yaavets rejected this claim altogether. He argued that the essence of religious life is devotion, humility, holiness, and fear of sin. These qualities cannot be attained through the study of philosophy. Rather, they are imbued through the study of Torah, Talmud, and the writings of the rabbinic sages. The purpose of life is to serve God humbly and righteously. Philosophy does not help in the fulfillment of this purpose, only Torah study does so. The more philosophy one studies, the further one departs from the proper goal. The more one studies Torah, the closer he comes to achieving the goal.[5].

A person who feels that he is very pious and will not be negatively influenced by the study of philosophy should recognize that he is mistaken. Little by little he will be drawn away from his faith. He will not even be aware of the transformation within himself. If he feels that all the wisdom of the Torah and the Jewish sages cannot fulfill his quest to understand God, he is choosing a course leading to personal turmoil and frustration. One should recognize that greater ultimate reward will be gained by means of faith than by rational inquiry. A righteous person lives in his faith, not in his rationalism. One should devote his life to serving God with a pure and full heart.[6] Those who seek to understand the Torah through philosophical methods, evaluating Jewish principles on the basis of rationalistic inquiry, create a counterfeit faith, said Rabbi Yaavets.

He spoke of "the little foxes which I saw in Spain," individuals who studied Talmud for seven or eight years and then became attached to philosophy. "They left their holy garments in order to wear filthy ones." Their religious observance declined; they became scoffers. He considered them even worse than the professed philosophers, because they had some Torah learning and camouflaged their philosophical heresies with references to classic Jewish sources. Rabbi Yaavets mentioned that even some scholars who devoted much of their lives to Torah study were seduced by philosophy. Ultimately they came to reject the Torah. It was clear, then, that only very exceptional rabbinic scholars could permit themselves the luxury of studying philosophy. For the masses, and even for the majority of scholars, "one should not learn from their books [philosophy] and not listen to their sages— even when they say the truth, one should not listen to them."[7]

There were several reasons for Rabbi Yaavets' opposition to philosophical speculation. Not only did philosophy undermine religious faith, it was essentially a creation of non-Jewish thinkers. The Jewish people had its own religious, intellectual, and spiritual tradition and did not need to graft non-Jewish wisdom onto its existing religious structure. Indeed, the wisdom of the non-Jews was insidious, because it clearly and consciously rejected Jewish tradition. How, then, could Jews strengthen their religious faith by drawing on the wisdom of those who were hostile to the Jewish faith?

Rabbi Moshe Almosnino of Salonika did not reject the wisdom of the non-Jews, but compared it to a fragrance which has no essence and is evanescent. On the other hand, Torah study is solid and real, the essence of genuine knowledge.[8] Rabbi Almosnino echoed the thought of Rabbi Yaavets that the wisdom of the non-Jewish world had enervated the Jewish people by dividing them and disrupting their tradition of service of God. Once Jewish spiritual unity was destroyed, the Jews were vulnerable to attacks from without and from within.[9]

Rabbi Yaavets' opposition to philosophy was based on yet another concern. Ultimately, religious tradition rests on the authority of its sages. Jewish tradition had been passed down intact since the time of Moses, with the chain of authority vested in the recognized sages of each generation. These sages had received the authentic tradition, interpreted and explained it to their contemporaries, and handed it on to the scholars of the following generation. Rabbinic authority was a basic precept in Jewish religious consciousness. Reliance on and respect for the sages was fundamental.

Rationalistic philosophy, on the other hand, called for the individual to utilize his own critical faculties to arrive at truth. Traditional authority in itself was not convincing; rational proofs and demonstrations were needed. Once an individual rejected rabbinic authority in one instance, he might come to reject it in others as well. Thus, rationalism contained the seeds of the destruction of a traditional, revelation-based religion.

Yaavets noted that the conflict between acceptance of traditional authority and reliance on the individual's reasoning had been a pervasive feature of the intellectual life of Spanish Jewry for centuries. The discussion often centered on whether one was obligated to accept literally all the teachings of the rabbinic sages, particularly those that were not specifically related to religious law. The Talmud and Midrash contained numerous rabbinic statements on a variety of topics, theological as well as general. The fundamentalist position was to accept all these statements as true. If a statement appeared to be in conflict with reason, the deficiency was attributed to reason, not to the rabbis. One should always suspect his own intelligence, not the intelligence of the sages, who spoke the truth.

This attitude was promoted not only by Rabbi Yaavets but by other leading Sephardic scholars of his generation. For example, Rabbi David Ibn Abi Zimra, a boy of thirteen when his family left Spain in 1492, became one of the leading rabbinic scholars of his generation. He served in Egypt and later in Safed. He taught that the Aggadah, the rabbinic homiletic literature, must be accepted as true. It was "given from heaven like the rest of the Oral Law. And just as the Oral Torah is interpreted with thirteen principles, so the Aggadah is interpreted with thirty-six principles. And these principles were transmitted to Moses our teacher at Sinai."[10]

The fundamentalist position is illustrated by the reaction to the words of Rabbi Moshe ben Nahman during his celebrated disputation with Brother Pablo Christiani in Barcelona in 1263. Brother Pablo, a Jewish apostate who had become a Dominican monk, confronted Rabbi Moshe with a rabbinic text (*Eikha Rabbati* 1:57) which stated that the Messiah had been born on the day the Second Temple in Jerusalem was destroyed. He used this rabbinic text to prove that the Messiah had already come, thus refuting the Jewish notion that the Messiah was still to be awaited.

In response to this charge, Rabbi Moshe ben Nahman, an outstanding mystic and legalist, stated: "I do not believe in this Aggadah at all." He explained that Jewish religious writings were divided into three traditional categories: Bible, Talmud, and Midrash.

The first we believe entirely . . . ; the second, we believe when it explains laws. We have yet a third book which is called Midrash, sermons so to speak . . . ; and this book, if one wishes to believe it he may, and one who does not believe it does not have to. . . . We call it a book of

Aggadah, which is to say discourses . . . it merely consists of stories which people tell one another.[11]

This statement shocked Jewish fundamentalists, who had regarded Rabbi Moshe ben Nahman as their champion and leading spokesman. But they decided that Rabbi Moshe did not mean what he said; he had taken this position only to deflect the argument of his opponent in the disputation. Rabbi Yitzhak Abravanel, in his discussion of the role of midrashic authority in disputations with Christians, disavowed Nahmanides' stance because "it opens the gate to the undermining of all rabbinic authority when we consider any of [the ancient rabbis'] words as errors or foolishness."[12]

However, the nonfundamentalist position had also been quite strongly held among the Jews of Spain. Rabbi Shemuel ha-Naggid, following in the footsteps of a number of great Babylonian Gaonim, wrote that the Aggadah reflected the individual opinions and interpretations of rabbis. Therefore, it need not be considered to be binding and authoritative.[13]

Rabbi Abraham, the son of Maimonides, argued that to accept something as true simply because it was stated by an important or great person is against both reason and the method of the Torah itself. He noted:

We, and every intelligent and wise person, are obligated to evaluate each idea and each statement, to find the way in which to understand it; to prove the proof and establish that which is worthy of being established, and to annul that which is worthy of being annulled; and to refrain from deciding a law which was not established by one of the two opposing opinions, no matter who the author of this opinion was. We see that our sages themselves said: If it is a halakhah [universally accepted legal tradition] we will accept it; but if it is a ruling [based on individual opinion], there is room for discussion.[14]

Maimonides himself contended that those who accepted the words of the rabbinic sages literally, without trying to understand deeper meanings in them, were "of impoverished understanding."

One must feel sorry for their foolishness. According to their understanding, they are honoring and elevating our sages, when in fact they are lowering them to the end of lowliness; and they do not even realize this.

By heaven! This group is dissipating the glory of Torah and clouding its lights, and they place the Torah of God against its own intention. [15]

The rationalist tradition was maintained after the expulsion from Spain. For example, Rabbi Abraham Ibn Migash, a sixteenth-century intellectual living in Turkey, argued forcefully on behalf of reason. "One must know that the ultimate human achievement is attained in the most honorable human power— the power of reason."[16] Those who think they can learn all wisdom from the Torah alone are mistaken. No one has been able to learn the various branches of wisdom, e.g., medicine, science, simply by studying Torah. On the contrary, each field of knowledge has its own specific books which must be mastered. Ibn Migash was sharply critical of would-be intellectuals who dabbled in kabbalah and did not use their powers of reason. He himself decided not to engage in kabbalistic speculation but to rely on wisdom, intelligence, and reason. [17]

A number of Sephardic intellectuals engaged in philosophic study and discussion. Salonika was the home of such thinkers as Rabbi Yosef Taitatsak, Rabbi Yitzhak Aderbi, and Rabbi Shelomo le-Bet ha-Levi. [18]

The intellectual ferment of the time is reflected in the work of Yehudah Zarco, a Hebrew poet who lived in Rhodes. In his *Lehem Yehudah*, published in 1560, Zarco revealed that he had been befriended by a patron from another city. He left Rhodes to join a group of young Jews in that city who discussed literature and philosophy. Like others in the group, he was plagued by religious doubts and inner spiritual turmoil. After going through a period when he all but lost his faith, Zarco returned to his original religious convictions.

Lehem Yehudah is an elaborate allegorical tale in which Zarco argued that reason should control emotion. He warned the reader not to be deceived by the trickery of the evil inclination. [19]

While respect for rationalism and philosophy persisted for several generations after the expulsion, the trend against these disciplines gained force and came to dominate Sephardic intellectual life. Philosophical inquiry was viewed as a threat to traditional faith. Kabbalah rose in popularity, among both the elite and the masses. Sephardim sought refuge in traditional Jewish sources; the allure of general philosophy and wisdom from non-Jewish sources faded.

The ascendant attitude was reflected in the writings of Rabbi

Meir ben Gabbai, a Sephardic exile who apparently found haven in Turkey. He argued that the study of philosophy was simply a waste of time. In each generation, philosophers presented new ideas and theories, rejecting the concepts of earlier philosophers. Obviously, philosophy could not be trusted, because what was considered true in one generation was rejected in the next. Gabbai was critical of Maimonides for giving credence to Aristotle and other philosophers. The Jewish people was wise and had no need to seek wisdom from others.

There is no wisdom nor understanding except in the study of Torah and in the keeping of its commandments. Those who keep the Torah call out to God and He answers them. This is their wisdom and their understanding in the eyes of the nations—not the inquiry into the various branches of philosophy. . . . Philosophy is forbidden to anyone who would call himself a Jew. [20]

Acceptance and Rebellion

The intellectual and spiritual life of Spanish Jewry following the expulsion was pervaded by a nagging question: Why does God, who is all good, allow evil to exist in the world? How could God, who chose Israel, now abandon the Jewish people and allow them to suffer so grievously? Theodicy was the conscious and subconscious dilemma of the Sephardim in exile.

A number of writers justified God's ways to humanity by positing that the all-perfect God does not create evil. God is absolutely just and righteous. Thus, that which seems evil is in fact necessarily good because it emanates from God.

Rabbi Moshe Almosnino evaluated the problem of evil by delineating three types of "good." Spiritual good is beneficial for the soul and includes such things as understanding, ethics, and free will. Bodily good refers to positive qualities, such as beauty and strength, which relate to the physical organism. The third category is extrinsic good, and this consists of (1) that which we call good fortune (luck), including such things as wealth, a happy marriage, nice children; and (2) honor.

Spiritual good belongs only to a person who is himself good. Everyone can attain spiritual goodness, and those who do not do so are at fault. Bodily good is hereditary. It is determined prior to one's having chosen to be good or evil. Individuals cannot claim

that their biological features are determined by their own goodness or wickedness. They are simply "givens."

The whole question of explaining why God allows the righteous
to suffer and the evil to prosper relates only to the category of
extrinsic good. When the two types of extrinsic good are exam-
ined the question is found to be irrelevant. It does not apply to
the category of honor, which is given by human beings of their
own free will. Honor is given only to one who merits it. A
righteous person does not honor a wicked person. If a wicked
person does not honor a righteous person, he is all the more
wicked. God does not determine whether a person merits and
receives honor: that is a human enterprise.

So the entire question comes down to the question of good
fortune or luck. Yet we must realize that things that come to us
by luck are not intrinsically good or evil. By the value ascribed to
these things, human beings determine whether they are to be
considered good or not. Indeed, some things that seem good
actually destroy the good of the soul and hence are not really
good. Precious stones have no intrinsic value. We do not need
them. But since people want them, they become valuable. So it is
with all other things. Their value is not intrinsic but is determined
solely by what people think about them. What appears to be good
luck may in fact be a great misfortune. On the other hand, what
seems to be unfortunate may in reality be beneficial to the soul.

Genuine good is always related to virtue, Almosnino argued.
Fortune cannot affect this type of good. Deprivation of extrinsic
good does not diminish the glory of virtue. Righteous people may
appear to suffer because of extrinsic evils, but this does not mean
that they are really suffering. If they have attained virtue, they
have attained the absolute good. Their extrinsic suffering is pe-
ripheral to their lives and may be for their own good in any case.
On the other hand, if wicked people prosper, this does not mean
that their situation is good. On the contrary, since they lack
virtue, they necessarily lack the real good in life. The extrinsic
benefits which they enjoy are really bad for them, lulling them
into a sense of security so that they do not have the opportunity
to repent their evil ways.

Thus, Almosnino concluded, the question of why God allows
the wicked to prosper and the righteous to suffer is not valid. God
judges everyone fairly and rewards everyone according to his
virtue. Extrinsic things, whether physical pleasures or sufferings,
are not objectively good or evil. They are so defined by human

beings, whose understanding of such matters is limited. God, whose understanding is unlimited, knows the real value of these extrinsic things, and all that God does is just and right.[21]

By explaining away the existence of objective evil, Rabbi Almosnino promoted an attitude of acceptance. He believed that God is the source of absolute righteousness, justice, and goodness. Any occurrence that seemed to contradict this truth had to be reevaluated in its light. From the perspective of God, which is the only true perspective, there is no problem of why the wicked prosper or the righteous suffer. This question is relevant only from the limited perspective of human beings who fail to understand that good and evil are subjective human terms, not descriptive of objective reality.

Rabbi Meir ben Gabbai offered another theory to explain away evil. He believed that God is the source of everything, and is good and perfect. Originally, before the existence of the physical world, there was only the unity and harmony of God. There were no opposites. This spiritual existence was the highest level of existence possible and is the goal to which human beings must still strive.

With the creation of the physical world, opposites appeared, creating struggle and inner turmoil. When the human soul, which contains perfect understanding of the true unity of God, is linked to a body, it must deal with the conflicts generated by contact with the physical world. Its goal is to guide a human being toward a unified understanding of God. The life of a perfect person is one that "strives to include evil in good until everything is encompassed in the category of good. This is the foundation of the commandment: 'And you shall love the Lord your God with all your heart,' with both your good and evil inclinations. One must encompass both of them with love, which is the foundation of unity."[22]

This approach had also been offered by Rabbi Yosef Yaavets in his *Hasdei Hashem*. Yaavets suggested that one who accepts exile willingly and happily is testifying to his own wisdom.

This demonstrates that he believes in the unity of his Creator, that He has no opposites within Him. Everything derives from Him, and all that comes from Him is absolutely good. . . . The evils which come from Him are in fact very good, better than the good things. There is no greater recognition of the unity of God than when one rejoices in his sufferings and admits the unity of God. . . . When you believe that God is absolute unity, you will recognize and understand that there are no opposites in His qualities; you will understand that no evil derives from Him. [23]

Rabbis Almosnino, Gabbai, and Yaavets formulated a spiritual worldview that explained away the problem of evil. They sought to transcend human limitations and to accept everything, including suffering and pain, as part of the divine harmony of the universe.

Yehudah Abravanel, son of Rabbi Yitzhak Abravanel, expressed a similar attitude quite vividly in his *Dialoghi d'Amore*, an important work of sixteenth-century Neoplatonism. Abravanel left Spain in 1492, going first to Naples. When the Jews were expelled from that city in 1497, he moved on to Genoa, Barletta, Venice, perhaps Florence. Ultimately he returned to Naples, where he served as court physician to the Spanish viceroy. Abravanel found spiritual kinship with Italian humanism and frequented the most cultured circles in Italy. His book, first published in Italian in 1535, went into numerous editions and eventually was translated into Spanish, French, Latin, and Hebrew.

The *Dialoghi* is a philosophical love-treatise. Its approach is universalistic, encompassing all experience in a harmonious framework of love. Abravanel drew on Greek myths as well as biblical passages. He discussed Jewish heroes and philosophers, and also drew on the teachings of Aristotle and Plato. The underlying thesis of his work was that the cosmos is infused with love, which originates with God. This idealistic and peaceful philosophy contrasts sharply with Abravanel's turbulent life. He had suffered expulsion and degradation, his son had been kidnapped and lost to him; he could not avoid recognizing the reality of hatred and evil. Indeed, in one passage, Abravanel noted that any theory of love does not and cannot completely explain human behavior.

Men naturally love one another, as do beasts of the same species; and especially so, men of the same country or land. But this love is not in men as sure and steadfast as in animals. For the fiercest and most savage beasts do not turn their savagery against others of their own kind: lions do not rend lions, nor snakes poison snakes. But men suffer more evils and deaths at the hands of their fellows than through all other animals and adverse forces of the universe; yes, more men succumb to the enmity, sneers and violence of other men than to all other accidental and natural ills together. This decay of the love ordained by nature between men is due to their greed and care for superfluities: which begets feuds not only between far-sundered habitants of different countries, but between those of a single province, a single city, a single household: between brother and brother, parents and children, husband and wife. And to this must be added other human superstitions which give rise to savage enmities.[24]

This passage, which expresses realistically Abravanel's own awareness of evil and bitterness, contrasts with the general pattern of the dialogues. For the most part, he suppressed feelings of bitterness in his Neoplatonic philosophy of love. He drew on the Platonic idea that the world operates on two different levels. The world in which we live is a world of illusions and shadows. The real world, the world of being, is a world of ideas that dwells beyond our mundane world.

Abravanel's philosophy of love was an attempt to transcend the physical realities of human existence by grasping at an explanation of the entire universe. He preferred to avoid the grossness of human social reality, and to operate instead on an idealistic plane. His focus was not on the dismal reality of this world but on the purer, truer world of ideas and ideals. Like Gabbai, Almosnino, and Yaavets, Abravanel attempted to understand the world from God's point of view, not from the point of view of human beings. From this transcendent perspective, the problem of evil receded into insignificance.

The flowering of mysticism throughout the Sephardic dispersion was another manifestation of the Jews' spiritual drive toward acceptance of God's decrees. Kabbalists viewed the activities of the temporal world as symbolic of higher spiritual realities. Thus, the exile of the Jews was in some way a symbol of the exile of God Himself. The fulfillment of God's commandments in this world influenced the spiritual world beyond and brought the physical universe into closer harmony with God's ultimate will. The kabbalah stressed the importance of the spiritual world. The reality of the physical world, grossly inferior to the qualities of the spiritual world, gained importance only as it brought itself closer to the latter.

But along with the calls for acceptance of God's decrees, there were also voices that questioned God's justice. They did not blame the sufferings of the Jews on the victims, and they did not attempt to explain away the existence of evil. Rather, they claimed that God had in fact acted against the rules of justice, and that He must rectify the Jews' desperate situation in order to redeem His own reputation.

These views are reflected in several elegies that came to be included in the Sephardic service for the fast-day of the Ninth of Ab. Written after the expulsion from Spain, the elegies are presented in the form of a dialogue between the people of Israel and God.[25]

I

Alas, our Father, is this the recompense we have sought?

Who is the father who raises children
to take vengeance on them,
to pour anger on them,
with great and fuming wrath?
   We have sat on the ground;
   We have also wept.

      Why do you all cry out against Me?
      Your murmurings have reached Me.
      In My kindness I have daily saved you from sufferings:
      you yourselves are my witnesses.
         But you have not kept to My ways, alas,
         My children, will you feud with Me?

      Your brothers went as exiles from Jerez and Seville.
      I saw their stubbornness.
      I brought on the expulsion from Castile
      and Sicily, Aragon, Granada, My children.

      But even if we have sinned, where are Your mercies?
      If in anger You expelled us, tell us wherein the children
         sinned,
      whose kindnesses we have seen
      with our own eyes.

      I took you from the Holy Land
      as exiles into bondage.
      I saw your stubbornness.
      You did not heed Isaiah or Jeremiah.
         Therefore, I had no mercy on you, My children.

         We have pondered Your mercies
         now that several years have passed.

But we, your witnesses, renew the question each day:
Is this the way a father treats his children?
We have drunk the dregs of gall and wormwood.

I examine the hearts of men,
their inner feelings and thoughts.
Before your days of misfortune came
I surely recognized your good deeds.
But did I not, My children,
seize you for your own sins?

You judged that our women be tortured,
young maidens and wives.
They were stripped of their clothes
and left naked for days and nights.
And we were shamed.

You have rebelled against My Torah
and have served other gods.
I was very jealous
so I made you drink the bitter waters.
You have strayed from My ways.

Is there no cure and healing
for all our pains?
Each nation has its kingdom;
but the glory of our honor is fallen:
our enemies have destroyed our stronghold.

See, My Presence is in the midst of the nation,
children of exile.
Throughout your dispersion, I have revealed My glory to you
each day and each night, My children.

If our sins and transgressions have increased,
yet we are Your people, the sheep of Your fold.
The hand of the Lord is against His flock's camp.
(We have rejected Your commandments and Your Torah.)

I know that My Name is profaned
among the nations and peoples.
The chosen of priests and Levites,
the righteous, upright, and pure
are laid waste.
And I do not spread My tent to shelter My flock.

Remember our ancestors; send us the Redemption.
Ignore our evil ways,
our defiled souls.
Greatness is Yours, our Master.
Our Father: this is the recompense we have sought.

I Myself in My majesty will hide a crown for this nation
and build the House of My Glory as it was in years past.
In pleasantness shall I awaken a song on My lute.

II

Who is the father who tortures his child
with afflictions of vengeance,
who violently pours his wrath on him?
　We have sat on the ground;
　we have also wept.

　How can you speak thus, My children?
　How can you shout against Me in anger?
　I gave the Torah at Sinai
　and you have brazenly abandoned it.
　　Was this not so?
　　Surely you are to blame, not I.

　We know, our Rock, that we have rejected
　the pleasantness of the teachings of the Torah.
　But remember: we are made of dust.
　This fact cannot have eluded You.
　If we have sinned, You have not forgiven us
　according to Your compassion.
　Relent for the sake of Your mercy,
　Merciful Lord of Hosts.
　Forgive our sins and errors
　in the abundance of your kindness.
Do this as a good omen,
for we trust in You.

　Your brothers went as exiles from the Holy Land into
　　captivity.
　I saw their stubbornness.
　I brought on the expulsion from Castile,
　and Sicily, Aragon, Granada, My children.

In Your wrath, You destroyed the strongholds of the
daughter of Judah,
You burnt Your land and Your Temple.
You did not accept thanksgiving offerings
from our hands.

I destroyed My Temples because of your sins.
As I have told My holy ones:
I will dwell among you—in your Temple services,
as the prophet explained. (Woe unto Me.)

But Zion said: what is my sin?
Even if the children have transgressed
You have uprooted the strength of my might,
the trees, the stones;
The neighbors raised their voices in our Temple.

Zion will be redeemed by justice
for she has prevailed in her suit with God.
No more will she be ploughed like a field.
The eyes of My congregation will see
the moment of Israel's salvation,
the building of the Temple Altar.

These elegies are powerful statements of protest. Even while
recognizing that Israel is not without sin, they fault God for not
acting as a compassionate and just Father. His punishments were
too severe. They affected innocent people along with the guilty.
They were not tempered by fatherly love. Israel's claims were
forceful. Although God offered His responses, Israel prevailed in
the argument. God was forced to concede that Israel's case was
just. He promised to redeem Israel and to restore the Kingdom of
Israel in the land of Israel.

In the mind of the poet who wrote the elegies, and in the minds
of those who chanted them, there was a clear challenge to God's
actions. Instead of accepting God's decrees, they rebelled against
them.

The spirit of rebellion was also evident in a prayer composed by
the great 16th-century mystic, Rabbi Shelomo Alkabets. In his
prayer, he told God that there were no words to describe the
horrible events that had befallen the Jewish people, who were
forced to wander from nation to nation, from one kingdom to
another. "And nevertheless, they have held firm to Your Torah

and have not abandoned it nor forsaken it. They freely spend their gold to glorify it, to establish it, and to uphold it. Even today, they eagerly observe it and rejoice in it, exceedingly happy to perform Your mitzvot, being modest and acting with loving-kindness." Alkabets noted the shocking discrepancy between the pious faithfulness of the Jewish people and the terrible treatment they had received from God.

Rabbi Alkabets's prayer noted that the Jewish people had spent their money and sacrificed much in order to return to Erets Israel, the Holy Land, which was barren and destroyed, ruled by non-Jews. Nevertheless, despite their suffering, Jews had returned to their sacred land. "Will You not take note of this and save them, O Lord? Have You completely despised them, have You come to loathe a nation like this? Heaven forbid that You should do so. For they are Your people and Your inheritance, whom you have liberated from the land of Egypt from the iron furnace." Rabbi Alkabets' prayer called on God to listen to the pleas of the Jews both in Israel and in the exile. They had suffered too much. Their faithfulness was pure and noble. It was simply unjust for God to abandon them. [26]

This spirit of rebellion against God's decrees of exile and suffering also underlay the powerful spiritual current of Jewish messianic thought during the aftermath of the expulsion. Messianism is often said to be the hope of helpless victims. But at root, it is a demand that God reward the righteous and punish the wicked, that He restore Israel to its kingdom, where the Israelites may live in peace, tranquility, and glory. The messianic trend during the period following the expulsion illustrates this point.

There had been a long-held belief among Jews, going back to antiquity, that the Messiah would appear only after a period of great tragedy. The expulsion from Spain seemed to be just such a tragedy.

Rabbi Joseph Shaltiel, son of Moshe Hacohen, writing in Rhodes in 1495, interpreted the historical events of his time as follows: "I think that the sufferings which the Jews have found in all the kingdoms of Edom [Christianity] from 5250 to 5255 [1490–95] constitute a period of sorrow for Yaacov [Israel] from which he will be saved; these are the pains which will usher in the Messiah. [27]

Other thinkers made the same point. Rabbi Abraham son of Eliezer Halevy, who settled in Jerusalem, attempted to prove that the travails of redemption had begun with the expulsion in 1492 and would end in full glory in 1531.[28]

An anonymous commentary on Psalms, *Kaf Haketoret*, stated:

According to the words of the sages, the Torah has seventy aspects, and there are seventy aspects to each and every verse; in truth, therefore, the aspects are infinite. In each generation one of these aspects is revealed, and so in our generation the aspect which the Torah reveals to us concerns matters of redemption. Each and every verse can be understood and explained in reference to redemption.[29]

Rabbi Yitzhak Abravanel observed that the horrors of the expulsion from Spain had caused widespread despair among the Jews. A spirit of defeatism had set in. The hope that the Messiah would soon come had faded. To counteract this negativism, Abravanel wrote three books which contended forcefully that the Messiah would indeed appear—and in the year 1503. This was a startling and bold assertion, since it placed the coming of the Messiah at a time when many exiles could still hope to witness him. In his first messianic book, Abravanel demonstrated that the biblical prophecies relating to the Messiah had not yet been fulfilled but would be borne out within several more years. In his second book, he demonstrated that the authoritative rabbinic homilies concerning the Messiah had not been fulfilled in the past, but referred to a period in the near future. His third book was a commentary on the Book of Daniel in which he interpreted passages to prove that the arrival of the Messiah was imminent.

Abravanel felt that he was obligated to sidestep the tradition that had generally discouraged individuals from calculating the date of the Messiah's arrival.

And if, according to my understanding, the time of redemption is here, and we today are at the end of our exile, and the salvation is near to come, as will be explained, therefore it is time to serve the Lord. This essay is to bring the good news and to make known the salvation. I do not claim that what is said in this essay is the absolute truth, because it did not come to me in prophecy, nor did I receive it from my teachers as a tradition going back to Moses at Sinai.[30]

Abravanel's messianic writings contained several major themes. First, there would be revenge on the enemies of Israel. All the nations that had perpetrated evils against the Jews during their long exile would come to Jerusalem with heads bowed. Second, Israel would be completely redeemed, having its own kingdom, living independently. The third theme was the resurrection of the dead. Abravanel argued that it was not only the faithful who would be resurrected; the wicked people who had persecuted the Jews in every generation would also be brought back to life, so that they could be made to suffer for their many crimes against Israel. These very strong sentiments for revenge must have found a sympathetic audience among the exiles from Spain.

In order to understand the power of the messianic idea, it is helpful to recall a biblical story about the patriarch Abraham that was, of course, known to all Jews. When God decided to destroy the cities of Sodom and Gomorrah, He first divulged His plan to His faithful servant, Abraham. But Abraham was not pleased. He protested: "Will You indeed sweep away the righteous with the wicked? . . . That be far from You to do after this manner, to slay the righteous with the wicked, so that the righteous should be as the wicked; that be far from You; will the Judge of all the earth not do justice?" (Genesis 18:23–25). Abraham assumed that God was not entitled to punish the righteous for sins which they had not committed. Abraham was not afraid to challenge God and to demand that He not only deal fairly but compassionately.

Certainly, as the Jews knew only too well, human history had not always conformed to Abraham's assumption. Often enough, the righteous suffered and the wicked prospered. Yet, following Abraham, Jewish messianic thought had refused to accept this situation as reality, and sought to correct the distortions of history. It began with the premise that God is just. If things occur in this world that appear to be unfair, God will rectify them in the world-to-come. Righteousness is always rewarded, and wickedness is always punished.

Seen in this light, the messianic idea as promulgated by the Sephardim during the period of the expulsion was not an empty and distant hope, but a demand. God was obliged to redeem Israel because the Jews had suffered enormously and unfairly. Justice demanded that the Jews be restored to freedom and independence, and that they be compensated for the abuse and pain which they had suffered.

Abravanel thought the Messiah would appear in 1503. Others also believed, and hoped, that the Messiah's arrival was imminent. This belief was based not only on the demand for justice but on the reality of deteriorating conditions among Jews.

Rabbi Yosef Hayun placed the following words in the mouth of the people of Israel as they implored God: "I lose hope of redemption since I see myself spread out among the nations . . . I fear lest I become lost among them and that I will behave as they behave . . . covered and absorbed among the nations."[31]

Another contemporary, Rabbi Abraham Saba, complained: "If God waits to redeem Israel until that day hinted at by the prophets . . . it isn't fair to Israel to wait such a long time. According to the sufferings which newly arise against them each day, when that time arrives [for the redemption], there won't be any of them left [to be redeemed]."[32]

Some Jews felt that they could force God's hand so that He would send the Messiah. Rabbi Yaacov Berav, who settled in Safed about 1535, initiated the process of granting semikhah, (rabbinic ordination). The ancient Sanhedrin, which had been Jewry's authoritative judicial body, had comprised seventy-one rabbis who were duly ordained. The ancient form of ordination had ceased with the exile of the Jewish people from the land of Israel. In seeking to reestablish the traditional semikhah, Rabbi Berav was in fact attempting to restore the Sanhedrin. Since it was generally believed that the Sanhedrin would only be restored in messianic times, Rabbi Berav was beginning the process of ushering in the messianic era. Among those ordained by him was Rabbi Yosef Karo, whose classic works in Jewish law made a lasting contribution to halakhah.

The process of semikhah continued for a period of approximately sixty years, in spite of the fact that there was strong opposition to it by Rabbi Levi ben Habib and others.[33] It should also be mentioned in this context that Don Yosef Nasi, a leading Sephardic Jew in the Ottoman Empire, sought to establish a Jewish colony in the vicinity of Teveriah (Tiberias) in the north of Israel. By creating industry there, he hoped that a Jewish community would be able to support itself. This, in turn, would lead Jewish exiles to return to their ancestral land, another development held to be characteristic of messianic times.

Those who challenged God's ways did so in prayer, literature, messianic belief, and symbolic premessianic action. They did not call on Jews actually to fight back against their oppressors. The Jews expelled from Spain apparently did not organize themselves to fight their enemies.

Rabbi Yosef ben Yahia, who lived in the second generation after the expulsion, wondered why the Jews had not fought against those who expelled them. He concluded that since the Jews had been scattered throughout Spain and were a small minority in the cities, they could not organize themselves to resist the expulsion. [34] To this can be added the fact that Jews in the diaspora did not often entertain the thought that they could fight back physically against their enemies. They viewed their exile as a punishment for their sins. Their salvation would come from God, not from their own resistance to their enemies' attacks.

Halakhah

Jewish law, halakhah, has universal application and applies to Jews wherever they live. The halakhah contains a set pattern of life that can be transferred from one place to another without major disruption. For example, the laws and customs of the Sabbath can be observed in the same manner whether Jews are living in Barcelona or Istanbul, Granada or Tangiers. The Jews who were expelled from Spain brought into exile their commitment to the comprehensive details of halakhah. The basic patterns of life as governed by Jewish law offered security and continuity.

Rabbi Moshe Almosnino commented on a verse in the Song of Songs (1:8) that when one is unable to arrive at truth through his own reasoning, he should follow in the footsteps of his ancestors, who were the shepherds of the Jewish people. Indeed, one who follows in their paths will retain his Jewish identity and distinctiveness. One should raise his children according to the traditions established by the holy ancestors of the Jews. Rabbi Almosnino also stated that when children studied Torah, they learned absolute truth directly. They were able to retain their pattern of life as they grew older, and the people of Israel could retain its own life-style, impervious to pressures for change. [35]

The exiles reconstituted their lives in their new communities according to the dictates of Jewish law. They quickly developed a communal structure similar to what they had known in Spain. The new Sephardic communities established schools, courts, and a system of administration and taxation. Rabbinic law dominated in the governing of the communities, and boundaries of jurisdiction were carefully drawn. Rabbi Shemuel de Medina of Salonika articulated the generally accepted policy that each community had responsibility for its own members. Members of one community were not permitted to bring their cases before the rabbinic court of another community. No court had the right to impose its will on Jews who were not under its jurisdiction.

He said:

I call to witness heaven and earth that it is well known here in Salonika concerning each sage of each congregation—be he who he may—no individual of that congregation can cast off his authority or rebel from his rulings. And no sage may enter the boundaries of another sage, even if he be among the greatest sages on the level of Rabban Gamliel while the other is very insignificant.[36]

The study of halakhah reached a very high level during the period following the expulsion from Spain. The classic legal works of Rabbi Yosef Karo, notably the *Beit Yosef* and the *Shulhan Arukh*, were composed during this period, and have become basic halakhic texts for every generation since.

This was also a golden age in the flowering of rabbinic responsa literature, with monumental contributions made by such Sephardic scholars as Rabbis David Ibn Abi Zimra, Shemuel de Medina, Yosef Karo, Yaacov Berav, Moshe Alashkar, Yosef Taitatsak, and Levi Ben Habib. As Professor H. J. Zimmels has commented, it was "amazing that soon after the expulsion in the year 1492 the contributions to the responsa literature by the rabbis who had come from Spain and settled in Turkey reached a height never witnessed before."[37]

Sephardim established presses in the Ottoman Empire to publish books of Jewish interest. In 1504, the first Hebrew printing press was established by David and Samuel Nahmias in Istanbul. Significantly, the first book published was the code of Jewish law known as *Arba Turim*, by Rabbi Yaacov ben Asher. In 1515, a Hebrew publishing house was established in Salonika. Many of the works published during the sixteenth century dealt with matters of Jewish law and ethics.[38]

The emphasis on halakhah was also reflected in the educational method of the talmudic academies. Rabbi Yitzhak Confanton, who had headed a yeshiva in Castile during the period just prior to the expulsion from Spain, developed a method of study that prevailed during his own and subsequent generations. He called for rigorous analysis of talmudic texts, utilizing rules of logic. Mornings were devoted to in-depth study of a particular text; afternoons, to covering extensive portions of the Talmud as quickly as was feasible. In the analysis of the Talmud and its commentaries, the texts had to be studied carefully to see whether they conformed to the rules of logic. Along with the theoretical study of rabbinic texts, Rabbi Confanton stressed the importance of arriving at the practical halakhah. [39]

Kabbalah

While this was a burgeoning period for the study of halakhah, it was also a creative and dynamic era for kabbalah, Jewish mysticism. Even the most rigorous legal minds devoted themselves to mystical study and meditation. Indeed, the Sephardic yeshivot included both the halakhic and the kabbalistic disciplines in their curricula.

Some insight into the nature of educational life among the exiled Sephardim can be gleaned from the example of Rabbi Yosef Garson, a Sephardic rabbi who arrived in Salonika in the year 1500. He had migrated from Spain to Portugal and then made his way to Salonika. After four years there, he went to Damascus. Garson was not one of the outstanding rabbinic scholars of his generation but seems to have been active as a teacher of children. He wrote a book of sermons in which he described his educational philosophy.

Garson insisted that one must learn laws as well as the mysteries of the Torah, both Talmud and kabbalah being basic elements in religious education. This was the general policy in Sephardic yeshivot. Garson, who had been trained in the rabbinic academies of Castile, had extensive knowledge. He believed that students should familiarize themselves with all aspects of biblical and rabbinic tradition. But he opposed secular studies, because they did not improve the soul and sometimes actually undermined proper faith. [40]

Writing later in the sixteenth century, Rabbi Shelomo Turiel, who lived in Safed, strikingly underscored the importance of kabbalah study. In interpreting the Garden of Eden story, Rabbi Turiel stated that the Tree of Life symbolized kabbalah, while the Tree of Knowledge symbolized the basic laws of Torah. Originally, Adam and Eve were allowed to eat from all the trees, including the Tree of Knowledge, as long as they also ate from the Tree of Life. God warned Adam not to eat from the Tree of Knowledge *alone*, meaning that he was not to devote himself exclusively to the study of the basic laws of the Torah. Rather, he had to juxtapose that knowledge with the mysteries of the kabbalah by eating also from the Tree of Life. But since Adam was interested only in the wisdom of the Tree of Knowledge and was not interested in the kabbalah of the Tree of Life, he was punished. One who studies the laws without studying the mysteries that are their soul commits a symbolic murder, separating the body of the Torah from its soul. Therefore, Adam deserved the punishment of death.[41]

Significantly, the leading halakhists of Sephardic Jewry during the period following the expulsion were also leading kabbalists. The classic example was Rabbi Yosef Karo, who authored both the *Shulhan Arukh*, a code of Jewish law, and the *Maggid Mesharim*, a record of the revelations he received from an angel who visited him regularly.

Professor Zwi Werblowsky, in his fascinating biography of Rabbi Karo, has concluded that "his charismatic or mystical life did not spill over into his daylight activities. The Karo of the codes and the responsa remained healthy, realistic, and down to earth."[42] Yet there was no real dichotomy between the mystical and the legal aspects of Karo's personality. Indeed, both aspects taken together shaped his unified spiritual worldview. While Rabbi Karo communed with a special angelic voice, most people did not receive personal revelations. For religious Jews, the voice of God is transmitted through the Torah and the sacred writings. The halakhah is actually a record of the voice of God, so that even if one cannot hear the divine voice directly, it is possible to enter into a living relationship with God through the halakhah. Legalism and mysticism are not two separate entities, but are interrelated and interdependent. At the root, both are listening for the voice of God.[43]

Kabbalah was studied throughout the Sephardic diaspora, but its most dramatic flowering during the sixteenth century occurred in the city of Safed, in the north of the land of Israel. This was the home of Rabbis Yosef Karo, Shelomo Alkabets, Moshe Cordovero, Eliyahu de Vidas, Moshe Alsheikh, and many other mystics. The figure who had the greatest impact in kabbalistic studies was Rabbi Yitzhak Luria, whose teachings were published and popularized by his disciple Rabbi Hayyim Vital and others. Rabbi Luria, popularly known as the holy Ari, developed a kabbalistic system that saw the universe as a battleground between the power of holiness and the power of evil. God chose the people of Israel to redeem the sparks of holiness and overcome evil.

Professor Joseph Dan has concluded that history, according to

Rabbi Luria, "is the story of the repeated attempts of the good divine powers to rescue the sparks and to bring unity to the earthly and divine worlds. Previous attempts had always failed. Luria and his disciples were absolutely certain that they were living in the last moments of the last attempt, which this time could not fail."[44] They thought that the people of Israel were on the verge of messianic redemption, when evil would be overcome once and for all. Luria believed that God, in creating the world, had gone into a sort of self-inflicted exile. He, too, was waiting for the ultimate redemption when the power of holiness would be entirely victorious.

The framework of exile and redemption inherent in Lurianic kabbalah related particularly closely to the spiritual situation of the post-expulsion Sephardic Jewish communities. They could view their own exile as symbolic of God's exile. By fanning the sparks of holiness, by helping to overcome the forces of evil, they could play a role in their own redemption and in the redemption of God Himself.

The kabbalists developed a variety of techniques to enhance their spiritual experience. Among them were the repetition of certain verses or words, as well as the writing of certain Hebrew words and permutations of their letters in various combinations. Through these and similar methods of intense concentration, the mind was made free and open to religious experience. Kabbalists also found value in solitude. Rabbi Eliezer Azikri wrote that "one day a week, a person should distance himself from others and be alone with himself and his Master; he should attach his thoughts to Him as though he were already standing before Him on the day of judgment. He should speak to God, blessed be He, with soft words, as a slave speaks to his master and a son to his father."[45] Azikri also stated that when saintly people were in solitude, their minds transcended the concerns of this world and their thoughts were attached to God.[46]

Rabbi Moshe Cordovero and Rabbi Shelemo Alkabets had the practice of wandering from place to place, almost at random. Cordovero stated that during the course of their wanderings, they received novel insights into the meaning of verses in the Bible. These insights seem to have come suddenly and spontaneously. "The words of the Torah shone within us and were said of themselves."[47]

The kabbalah tended to view events in this world as symbolic of the ultimate world beyond. Human deeds had an effect on the spiritual, mysterious world of holiness. The exile of the Jews was compared to the exile of the Divine Presence. The battle against injustice in this world was symbolic of the battle of holiness against "the other side," the power of evil. The fulfillment of a mitzvah was a cosmic act that influenced the spiritual well-being of the universe, while the commission of a sin shook the foundations of the universe. Rabbi Cordovero taught that "just as a man conducts himself here below, so will he be worthy of opening that higher quality from above. As he behaves, so will be the affluence from above and he will cause that quality to shine upon earth."[48]

Kabbalistic Ethics

The spread of kabbalah led to a more intense desire for piety and saintliness. Professor Joseph Dan has pointed out that the Lurianic demand for *tikkun*, i.e., correcting this world, emphasized the cosmic meaning of each human deed. The performance of a simple mitzvah might bring on the redemption immediately. Committing a sin might plunge the world into chaos. The task of correcting the world, making it holy, was an all-consuming responsibility.

According to Professor Dan, "ethics in Lurianic kabbalah is no longer an attempt to achieve personal perfection. It is a set of instructions directing the individual how to participate in the common struggle of the Jewish people."[49] Indeed, the concept of communal responsibility for one's deeds was current in Safed even prior to the teachings of Rabbi Luria. Rabbi Cordovero had said: "All Israel are related one to the other, for their souls are united, and in each soul there is a portion of all the others. . . . When one Israelite sins, he wrongs not only his own soul but the portion which all the others possess in him."[50]

Mystical pietists emphasized ethical behavior as well as scrupulous observance of the ritual commandments. Circles of pietists met regularly to evaluate their spiritual lives, to criticize each other, to encourage each other. Mystics, including Rabbis Moshe Cordovero, Abraham Galante, and Abraham Halevy, compiled lists of pious practices for their disciples to follow.[51] The students of Rabbi Yitzhak Luria put in writing the various saintly practices of their teacher so that others might emulate his holy ways. Sixteenth-century Safed witnessed a dramatic renaissance in the field of ethical literature that gave rise to such classics as *Reshit Hokhmah* by Eliyahu de Vidas and *Sefer Hareidim* by Eliezer

Azikri. Rabbis Azikri, Luria, and Alkabets were among the leading authors of spiritual poetry and prayer.

Mystical ethics was a fusion of halakhah and kabbalah, legalism and mysticism. The halakhah was deepened by its mystical interpretations and applications. The kabbalah was kept in the practical sphere of everyday life by the halakhah. These two spiritual trends merged not only in the teachings of the greatest rabbis of the generation, but among the masses of Sephardim in their new diaspora. Halakhah provided a pattern for their daily living, kabbalah provided meaning and hope for their lives.

•3•

The Conversos

A feature of medieval Spanish life was the militancy of the church against Judaism and Jews. On the theological level, Christian preachers attempted to discredit Judaism in their sermons and writings. Conversionary efforts were relentless. From time to time, disputations were staged with the purpose of publicly denigrating Judaism. These disputations, whose ground rules vastly favored the Christian participants, were made into public spectacles. The goal was to show the superiority of Christianity over Judaism, and therefore to convince Jews to convert to Christianity.

In 1263, as mentioned earlier, a famous disputation was held in Barcelona. Although from Nahmanides' account of the disputation it is clear that he "won," the effect on the audience is not altogether clear. Certainly, the Christian version of the disputation reflects Christian triumphalism.[1] Regardless of who won, the disputation served to place Judaism in a defensive position. It also demonstrated how passionately the church wanted to undermine Jewish religious life.

Another major disputation was held at Tortosa in 1414–15. Again it was a Jewish apostate, Gerónimo de Santa Fé, who represented the Christian side. The Jewish participants included several of the leading Sephardic rabbis of the time. The disputation was a long-drawn-out event. Anti-Jewish sentiment was fanned by Christian propaganda. Indeed, following the disputation, there was a wave of Jewish conversions to Christianity.

The steady conversionary barrage exacted a heavy toll on Spanish Jewry. For one thing, some Jews did actually abandon their people to accept Christianity. Some of them, such as Pablo Christiani and Gerónimo de Santa Fé, became vicious enemies of their former coreligionists. Even the masses of Jews who remained loyal to Judaism were not unaffected by the hostile religious climate. The Jews of Spain, after all, were a small minority. In spite of their many achievements in Christian Spain, they were vulnerable to societal pressures and actual attacks. It is not easy for a minority group to maintain its dignity and integrity when the majority group constantly denigrates and persecutes it.

Christian propaganda created an intellectual climate hostile to Judaism. But the vilification of Judaism could only result in the vilification of Jews. Thus, in 1391, a wave of anti-Jewish riots broke out throughout Spain. Thousands of Jews were massacred. Jewish property was destroyed or plundered. Many Jews fled Spain for safer haven in North Africa. Others, terrified by the explosion of hatred against them, accepted baptism as a way out. By becoming Christians, they felt, they would no longer be subject to harassment and persecution.

When the riots were over, the Jewish community in Spain had been dramatically shaken. A large number of Jews had left Spain. A large number had accepted Christianity. The remaining Jews lived with the constant fear of renewed Christian oppression.

The conversos, those Jews who had accepted baptism, were not of one mind. To be sure, most of them had been weaker in their loyalty to Judaism than the Jews who had refused to convert. Nonetheless, many of them came to their new religion with great reluctance. They had been forced to convert. Indeed, in Hebrew they were called *anusim*, "forced ones." It is not surprising that most of the conversos felt guilty for abandoning Judaism, and that many of them continued some level of Jewish observance in secret.[2]

The converso group also included Jews who had voluntarily converted to Christianity. As Christian missionary activity intensified, especially during the period of 1412–1415, Jews did accept baptism. Moreover, as the children of the conversos of 1391 grew up, they moved much further away from their Jewish religious past. The generation after the forced conversions was composed of people of Jewish ancestry who had effectively been raised as Christians. Although some continued to maintain Jewish practices in secret, many—perhaps most—were faithful Christians.

Thus, people of Jewish background in fifteenth-century Spain fell into three different groups: (1) Jews, (2) conversos who had unwillingly converted to Christianity and still maintained allegiance to Judaism, and (3) conversos who fully accepted Christianity. One can get a sense of the complexity of Jewish life at the time by considering that many families had members in each of the three groups. Faithful Jews felt a connection to and responsibility for the forced converts, but they also must have felt angry at the conversos for not withstanding the conversionary pressure. The New Christians, to save themselves, had betrayed Judaism. Within the converso communities, one can imagine feelings of guilt, a desire to retain some connection with Jews and Judaism; but also, resignation to the new status, desire to be accepted by Christian society, aversion to being identified as Jews. The conversos, then, were a diverse group, made up of individuals having a wide range of relationships to Judaism and Christianity.

The New Christians found that, as Christians, they were no longer bound by the disabilities which had restricted them as Jews. They could not be prevented from attending Christian schools and universities, from entering any profession they chose, from marrying into well-established, aristocratic Christian families. The New Christians, indeed, did rise spectacularly in many areas of Spanish life, including the church.

The Old Christians, seeing that these one-time Jews were progressing so rapidly, had mixed feelings. Some believed that the converts, as Christians, were entitled to all the benefits of society. Others thought that the conversos were not sincere Christians at all, but were only using Christianity as an external veneer to advance themselves. Subtle and not-so-subtle discrimination was practiced against the conversos, including giving them the appellation of "New Christians" in contradistinction to the authentic "Old Christians." Sentiment against the conversos increased.

This sentiment was fueled by outrage whenever a New Christian was caught in the act of performing Jewish religious observances. Such cases were taken to be typical examples of converso behavior: they were still devout Jews in secret, but pretended to be Christians in public. This behavior was considered scandalous. Spanish Christians became obsessed with the crime of Judaizing among the conversos. This obsession led to the establishment of the Spanish Inquisition, a church body whose responsibility it was to root out heresy among Christians, especially the heresy of Judaizing. Although a papal bull empowering the Spanish sovereigns to institute an Inquisition was issued on November 1, 1478, the actual establishment of the Inquisition took place in the fall of 1480. With the passage of time, its influence, power, and wealth increased. During the following centuries, the Inquisition arrested thousands of people for the crime of Judaizing, confiscating their property, humiliating and torturing them, and in many instances burning them at the stake. The New Christians, along with others who were accused of various heresies, were victims of a diabolical reign of terror in the name of the Christian religion.[3]

With the rise of the Inquisition, there was also increased agitation against the Jews of Spain. To be sure, the Inquisition had no authority over the Jews. It could only prosecute Christian heretics. Yet the argument was made that the Jews of Spain were a bad influence on the New Christians. They maintained contact with their former coreligionists and instructed them in the Jewish religion. Since the New Christians could so easily learn Judaism from the Jews, their complete adoption of Christianity was hindered. This line of reasoning led King Ferdinand and Queen Isabella to issue the decree expelling the Jews from Spain in the spring of 1492. They hoped that if the Jews were driven out, the New Christians would at last be cut off from Judaism.

Thousands of Jewish refugees fled Spain for Portugal. The initial reception was favorable. However, in 1495, King Manoel ascended the Portuguese throne. He wanted to marry Isabella, the daughter of the king and queen of Spain. This marriage would lead to the union of Spain and Portugal under one kingdom. But Isabella would not agree to enter Portugal as long as Jews lived there. On December 5, 1496, a royal decree banished Jews and Moslems from Portugal. They were given ten months to leave. In fact, though, the expulsion never occurred. Instead, the Jews of Portugal were forcibly converted to Christianity or simply were declared to be Christians. In 1497, Judaism ceased to exist legally in Portugal.

The crypto-Judaism which emerged in Portugal was stronger and more vibrant than that which had arisen in Spain. For one thing, it included many pious Spanish Jews who had left Spain rather than convert to Christianity. The Jews in Portugal were declared to be Christians although they had not the slightest desire to be Christians. Portuguese conversos took every opportunity to leave for lands where they could practice Judaism openly. When Portugal forbade the emigration of New Christians, the conversos still found ways of practicing elements of Judaism in private. With the establishment of the Portuguese Inquisition in 1531, crypto-Judaism was driven further underground.

The Judaism of the Conversos

The first generation of conversos, having been raised as Jews, had direct Jewish knowledge and Jewish memories. Those who wished to maintain Jewish observances knew how to do so. But the knowledge and the memories faded with each passing generation. The majority of the descendants of the conversos who remained in the Iberian Peninsula were lost to Judaism. Only a relatively small number were able to maintain any Jewish practices by the end of the seventeenth century.

Understandably, it was difficult to transmit Jewish teachings to the new generation. Parents were reluctant to tell young children about their Jewish heritage. Since the children attended Catholic schools, they might—in a moment of carelessness—reveal their family's Jewish practices. This would bring on an investigation by the Inquisition. It was simply not safe to let children see or observe Jewish practices. It seems, therefore, that children were not told about the family's religious leanings and instructed in the Jewish tradition until they were about thirteen years old—the age of Bar Mitzvah. By then they could usually be trusted with the family secret. These precautions may not always have worked, however, since the Inquisitional files include cases where children accused their parents of Judaizing![4]

Not only was it dangerous to transmit Judaism to children, it was impossible to transmit more than a few basic beliefs and observances. Jewish religious texts were not readily available; owning them was dangerous and could be punished by loss of property and life. In addition, the more observant one was, the greater the possibility of being detected and apprehended by the Inquisition. Conversos had to live the lives of pious Christians in order to defer suspicion from themselves. That crypto-Judaism was able to survive at all under these conditions, let alone for several centuries, is a truly remarkable phenomenon in the history of religion.

The conversos, of course, had access to the Jewish Bible, since Christianity recognized the sanctity of the "Old Testament." They also valued the Apocrypha, which was included in Christian Bibles even though it had never been part of the Jewish holy scriptures. The theory of crypto-Judaism found support in the

Epistle of Jeremy, the last chapter of the Book of Barukh: "When you see a multitude before you and behind bowing down, you shall say in your hearts: You alone are to be praised, O Lord" (Barukh 6:5–6). Conversos applied this lesson to themselves, holding that true worship of the Lord depends on one's heart, not on external actions. Converso theology also found a precedent in the biblical Esther. She kept her Jewish identity secret from her husband, King Ahasuerus, conducting herself outwardly as a Persian queen, but inwardly remaining faithful to Judaism. The story had special appeal to the conversos because, after all, Esther was a heroine. She ultimately saved the Jewish people from destruction. Her crypto-Judaism was, thus, vindicated.

Many of the Jewish observances which survived among the conversos related to the dietary laws, e.g., abstinence from pork; to certain religious festivals, e.g., Yom Kippur, Passover, the Fast of Esther; and to certain Jewish practices, e.g., changing bed linen on Fridays in honor of the advent of the Sabbath.

Inquisitional authorities issued edicts of faith which described the activities engaged in by Judaizers.[5] Intended to instruct would-be informers about Jewish practices, these edicts also provided valuable information to the conversos! Among the Jewish observances mentioned in the edicts are: putting on clean clothes on Saturday in honor of the Sabbath; cleaning the house on Friday afternoon; lighting candles on Friday evening; cooking on Friday such food as is required for the Sabbath; keeping Jewish fasts, especially Yom Kippur and the Fast of Esther; fasting on Mondays and Thursdays; eating unleavened bread on Passover; facing the wall, and moving the head back and forth, while praying; destroying the parings after cutting nails; cleaning meat and cutting away all fat and the sinew of the leg; slaughtering animals in the Jewish fashion; reciting Jewish blessings; reciting a prayer over wine after which everyone takes a sip; not eating pork, hare, rabbit, scaleless fish; mourning the death of a parent by sitting on the floor and eating such things as boiled eggs and olives; pouring water from jars and pitchers in the home of someone who has died; taking out some dough (as *hallah*) when baking bread; not baptizing children; giving Old Testament names to children; blessing children by placing a hand on their head; women not attending church within forty days after childbirth; turning toward the wall when dying; washing a corpse with warm water; reciting Psalms without adding the *Gloria Patri* afterwards; saying that the law of Moses is good and can bring about salvation.

The records of the Inquisitions in Spain and Portugal tell about the heroic deaths of the many conversos who chose to die as Jews, being burnt alive at the stake at public autos-da-fé. Their martyrdom presumably influenced other conversos to strengthen their Jewish commitment and defy the tyranny of the church. But only a relatively small number of the Inquisition's victims were martyrs who died "for the sanctification of God's name." Most of the victims "repented" under torture, and were either subjected to public humiliation or were killed before being burnt at the stake.

A significant feature of the converso religious life was the element of messianism. Crypto-Jews harbored the hope that the Messiah would come and save them from their unfortunate situation. They longed for redemption, for the tables to be turned against their oppressors. According to Professor Yitzhak Baer, "the records of the Inquisition contain file upon file of material on the messianic movement, which attracted all the conversos in Spain." The files reveal the personalities of conversos who considered themselves, or were considered by others to be, prophets or prophetesses. There were a number of people in various places and periods who had messianic pretensions.[6]

Perhaps the most dramatic messianic episode among the conversos concerned Solomon Molho, who was born in Portugal about 1501. He was a cultured, well-educated, and charismatic individual, rising to a position of prominence in the circles of Portuguese officials. He had received secret instruction in Judaism and was deeply affected by spiritual visions and dreams which came to him. His messianic hopes were fueled by the stories told him by David Reubeni, an adventurer who was traveling through Europe claiming to be the ambassador of the ten lost tribes of Israel. Molho, known in Portuguese as Diogo Pires, was circumcised in 1523. He adopted various ascetic practices and believed that he received divine messages in dreams. Leaving Portugal, he lived in Turkey for five or six years and also visited the Holy Land. His mystical and charismatic personality made a strong impression on the Jews he met. At the end of 1529, he was in Ancona, where he preached about the advent of the Messiah. His sermons drew large crowds. He then went to Rome and was received by Pope Clement VII. He let it be known that he was the forerunner of the Messiah. An enemy turned him over to the Inquisition and he was burnt at the stake in Mantua in 1532. Meanwhile, David Reubeni was imprisoned by the Spanish Inquisition, and probably also was put to death.

Because crypto-Jews so wanted the Messiah to arrive, they were prone to follow individuals who made messianic claims for themselves. Inevitably, these episodes had tragic results. The pseudo-messiahs were arrested and murdered by the Inquisition. Hope that the Messiah would soon appear often turned to despair but nonetheless always returned.

Jewish Attitudes Toward the Conversos

Jews who left the Iberian Peninsula without having submitted to baptism could not immediately sever their ties with those Iberian Jews who became conversos. In many cases, the refugees had connections of family and friendship with their former coreligionists who chose to stay in Spain and Portugal. The attitudes of the Jews toward the conversos reflected conflicting feelings.

On the one hand, faithful Jews resented the weakness and betrayal of their less committed coreligionists who became conversos. Rabbi Yitzhak Abravanel argued that those who had converted to Christianity were doubly cursed. They lived in constant fear; their conversions had not made them happy or blessed in this world. Moreover, when Israel was finally redeemed, these "sinners of Israel" would not enjoy the redemption equally with those who had remained faithful to Judaism.[7] It must have been painful for the Jewish exiles, struggling to resettle themselves in new lands, to think about the conversos, who had avoided the trials of exile and were presumably living comfortably in their own homes.

On the other hand, the exiles also recognized the tragedy that had befallen the conversos, so many of whom had been forcibly converted. To be sure, they should have been strong enough to resist conversion; nevertheless, their situation could hardly be considered to be pleasant. The conversos had to live with the guilt and shame of abandoning their own God and their own people; they had to exist in a fanatical Christian society where their lives were endangered by the Inquisition. Rabbi Yosef Garson, preaching in Salonika in 1500, reflected:

It is fitting for me and for all the people of this generation to feel intense anguish, anxiety, and mourning throughout our lives for our parents

and our brothers who now live in the great apostasy in Spain. They want
to come and serve our God, but they are not allowed to leave; they serve
other gods against their will. Who is the God-fearing person who can be
happy in his heart while our brothers and our relatives yet remain in
that apostasy?[8]

The Sephardic diaspora maintained an interest in the fate of the
conversos. Some evidence suggests that Jews occasionally went
to Spain and Portugal in the guise of Christians in order to teach
Torah to the conversos. According to a statement emanating
indirectly from Rabbi Menasseh ben Israel of Amsterdam, "every
year some Jews from Holland went to the capital of Madrid to
circumcise the New Christians."[9] Professor Simhah Assaf noted
the case of a Jew from Salonika who taught Torah to conversos
and was apprehended by the Inquisition, ultimately paying with
his life.[10] Although Professor Cecil Roth questioned the evidence
regarding the case, it is not at all unreasonable to suppose that
Jews living in freedom did risk their lives to teach Judaism to
conversos in the Iberian Peninsula.

When news of a converso's martyrdom at the stake reached
Sephardic communities, a special memorial prayer was recited to
honor the victim who had been "burned for the sanctification of
the Divine Name." The text, included in the prayer books of the
time, called on God to revenge the deaths of His martyrs. It
pleaded:

"May the great, mighty, and terrible God avenge the vengeance of His
holy servant . . . who was burned alive for the sanctified unity of His
name. May He seek his blood from his enemies by His mighty arm and
repay his foes according to their deserts. May the King, in His mercy,
remember unto us His merit, as it is written: "Rejoice, O ye nations,
His people, for He will avenge the blood of His servants, and will render
vengeance to His adversaries, and will absolve the land and His
people."[11]

The rabbinic responsa literature of the fifteenth through the
seventeenth century reflects various attitudes toward the conversos.[12] The fact was that conversos were far from being a monolithic group. While some struggled to retain a Jewish identity,
others became faithful Christians. How could rabbis living in the
Ottoman Empire, North Africa, or Europe know the precise
Jewish status of each converso in Spain and Portugal? Who could

know which converso was a forced convert who secretly longed to observe Judaism, and which was an apostate who had turned against his ancestral religion?

A seventeenth-century Italian rabbi, Shemuel Aboab, argued that as a general rule the conversos should be judged sympathetically. They maintained the public appearance of Christians but retained their attachment to Judaism in secret. They justified their behavior by a verse from the Book of Barukh, which they thought to be part of the Jewish Bible. "How can these blind people be considered to be apostates when the light of our tradition has not shone upon them, when they believe in their hearts those words [of Barukh] as though they were words of a true prophet?"[13]

Rabbi Yaacov Sasportas, a leading rabbinic figure in the European Sephardic communities in the seventeenth century, distinguished between the two categories of conversos. Concerning those who risked their lives to escape the Iberian Peninsula and made great sacrifices in order to return to Judaism, "it is fitting for the congregation of Israel to take pride in them and on their behalf." They should be received with love and respect by the Jewish community. On the other hand, those who abandoned the God of Israel, persisting in their evil ways, will be punished and "will be included among those who have no portion in the God of Israel and for whom atonement is impossible."[14]

When conversos arrived in Jewish communities and returned to Judaism, they were generally accepted as Jews if they claimed to be Jewish.[15] However, many rabbis ruled that marriages contracted in Spain and Portugal, even if performed in a manner the conversos considered to be Jewish, were not valid. Rabbi Shemuel de Medina, writing in Salonika during the sixteenth century, noted that the policy of the sages of Salonika was to invalidate any marriage ceremony performed by conversos in the Iberian Peninsula.[16] This policy was actually for the benefit of the conversos. According to Jewish law, a *get* (bill of divorce) is required when a marriage ends in divorce. If a married woman does not receive a valid *get* and then marries another man, the second relationship is considered adulterous. Children born from it are illegitimate and ineligible to marry legitimate Jews. Since conversos could not possibly have issued proper Jewish divorces while still in Spain or Portugal, converso women who remarried after a divorce were actually entering adulterous relationships and their children were illegitimate. This problem would place a legal cloud over the marriageability of every converso who returned to Judaism. How could he or she prove legitimacy? The rabbinic solution was to invalidate all converso marriages in the first place. Thus, since there were no marriages, there also was no need for divorces to be drawn up according to Jewish law. None of the children were deemed illegitimate. Every converso who returned to Judaism was eligible to marry into the Jewish community without hindrance. This policy was also helpful when one spouse chose to return to Judaism while the other clung to Christianity in Spain or Portugal. The returnee was free to marry a Jew without needing a divorce from the spouse.

Rabbinic leaders demanded that returning conversos be encouraged in every way to rejoin their ancestral faith and people. Jews were warned not to remind the returnees of their former lives as Christians so as not to shame them or make them feel guilty. A letter was written to a community by Rabbis David Ibn Abi Zimra, Yosef Karo, Yisrael ben Meir, and Moshe Mitrani, in which the sages stated:

We have heard that individuals who had been baptized came to you to find shelter under the wings of the Shekhinah [i.e., to return to Judaism]. When they have disagreements with others, the others curse them and call them apostates. This is a horrible sin. They shut the door in the face of those who wish to repent. One who does this commits a sin greater than he can bear, and the sin of the public hangs on him.

The rabbis ruled that anyone who spoke thus to a returning converso was to be excommunicated *(nidui)* for one day and had to agree never to speak similarly again. If the offender refused to admit his sin, then the community was to isolate him until he accepted the law.[17]

A question about a rabbi of converso parentage was addressed to Rabbi Shemuel de Medina. The rabbi's parents had come to Salonika from Portugal. They had two sons, both of whom grew up to be pious rabbinic scholars. One of the sons, the subject of the question, was appointed to a rabbinic post. Someone in the community, though, claimed that his mother was not Jewish and therefore that he too was not Jewish. The question was: Could he serve as a rabbi and judge? Rabbi de Medina responded that the rabbi had an accepted status of being Jewish. He quoted other sages who had ruled that all forced converts who returned to Judaism were to be accepted as Jews. We assume that their parents were Jewish. Even one who claims to be a cohen is accepted as a cohen when he returns to Judaism. Rabbi de Medina said that he rejoiced over this policy, and that in the case under consideration "it is fitting to punish the troublemaker, since one who spreads slander is a fool."[18]

Concern for the feelings of the returning conversos manifested itself also in another question of Jewish law. A person who is called to the Torah, a singular honor and a fulfillment of a commandment, is expected by Jewish law to be able to read his portion. The common practice for centuries has been for an official reader to chant the Torah portion for everyone, but the person called to the Torah is supposed to read along quietly with him. A question arose: may returning conversos be called to the Torah if they have not yet learned enough Hebrew to read along with the Torah reader? Technically, this should not be allowed. Yet it was ruled that calling them to the Torah was permitted even if they could not recognize one Hebrew letter from the other. They simply had to learn the appropriate blessings, and then they were entitled to share in this communal privilege.[19]

Many returning conversos had deep guilt feelings about their past lives. They wanted to live as pious Jews but felt the need to atone somehow for their past sins. Rabbi Levi ben Habib, who lived in Jerusalem during the sixteenth century, had been forcibly baptized as a child in Portugal. This tragic event haunted him. He wrote:

Even though they changed my name at the time of the decree, I did not change. He who examines the heart and searches our intentions knows that I always feared Him. If I did not have the merit of sanctifying His name, my heart trembles from His anger, even though I could not be held culpable in His court (since I was compelled to transgress against my will). I will cry day and night. Woe is me! Woe unto me! I confess my sin.[20]

The guilt feelings of returning conversos are evidenced in the poetry of Daniel Levi de Barrios. In his poem *De un Pecador Arrepentido*, he lamented that tears alone could not erase the stain of his sins, that he longed for the way of true salvation, "for I will flee from myself; and in Your compassion I shall strive so that I will merit praise and be Yours."[21]

Rabbi Yaacov Berav, a contemporary of Rabbi Levi ben Habib, was a leading rabbinic sage in Safed. As has been pointed out, he tried to reestablish formal rabbinic ordination, as it had been practiced in ancient Israel. His goal was to create a qualified and authoritative rabbinic court which would have the power to legislate for the people of Israel. This court would be authorized to punish sinners with corporal punishment. The idea behind this was to sentence returning conversos to some punishment, thus clearing their consciences and assuaging their guilt feelings. By receiving punishment for their past sins as conversos, they could now start their lives as Jews with a clean slate. [22]

Rabbi Yitzhak Aboab de Fonseca, of seventeenth-century Amsterdam, argued that all Jewish souls were assured of salvation in the world-to-come. This included the conversos—even those who had not yet returned to Judaism. Professor Alexander Altmann has suggested that Rabbi Aboab was espousing a teaching of the kabbalistic tradition which exalts the nature of Jewish souls. In so doing, he recognized that conversos were inseparably part of the Jewish people. This benevolent attitude could provide spiritual solace, especially to those conversos who returned to Judaism. They could feel themselves to be organic and permanent members of the Jewish people. Rabbi Aboab's position was rejected by Rabbi Saul Levi Mortera, also of seventeenth-century Amsterdam. Mortera believed that sinners would suffer eternal punishment for their transgressions and that Aboab's attitude was incorrect and misleading. Nevertheless, Aboab stood his ground. [23]

It is perhaps no coincidence that the sixteenth century was rich in ethical literature. Societies of pietists cropped up throughout the Sephardic diaspora, with individuals taking upon themselves rigorous ascetic practices. The ethicists strove for moral perfection, for purification of their souls and the souls of the people of Israel. Books of moral guidance were strongly influenced by kabbalah. They called for a deep inner spirituality. One was obligated to serve God with total devotion, not being disconcerted by the problems and sufferings of this world.

The call for inner piety, asceticism, and moral perfection has a special appeal at times of spiritual turbulence. It provides strength, comfort, and purpose. It makes it possible to turn one's attention from the overwhelming troubles which surround him and focus on his own self-perfection. It provides a transcendent vision of life.

Conversos who returned to Judaism after great personal struggles could find guidance and solace in the teachings of the kabbalists and ethicists. They could learn the ways of Jewish piety, and gain a sense of atonement for their past sins. While the stress on kabbalistic ethics and piety was expounded for all Jews, it had a special resonance for returning conversos.

• 4 •

Return and Reconciliation

Conversos who wished to return to their ancestral faith and to their people found ways to leave the Iberian Peninsula. The possibilities for migration were better during the first quarter of the sixteenth century than in later periods. For one thing, since a large number of conversos had been raised as Jews and had accepted Christianity reluctantly and under pressure, their desire to return to Judaism was relatively strong. Moreover, Portugal allowed conversos the right to migrate during the early part of the sixteenth century, a policy which later was retracted. [1]

As a new generation of crypto-Jews emerged, the possibilities of returning to Judaism diminished. Spain and Portugal made emigration exceedingly difficult for the New Christians. In addition, the new generation had no first-hand experience of Judaism; their connection with their mother religion was tenuous. With the emergence of each new generation, there was less likelihood of strong Jewish religious consciousness.

The return of New Christians to Judaism during the sixteenth and seventeenth centuries is a dramatic chapter in the religious history of the Jewish people. That Jewish identity survived for so long under such difficult conditions is indeed noteworthy. When we consider the spiritual struggles and personal risks which must have accompanied each decision of a New Christian to leave the Iberian Peninsula, we gain a sense of the magnitude and complexity of this phenomenon. The odyssey of the New Christians back to Judaism must be accounted among the most dramatic episodes in Jewish history.

Many of them found safe haven in the domain of the Ottoman Empire, in such cities as Salonika and Istanbul. They generally were integrated into the existing Jewish communities. Many others settled in cities in Western Europe such as Amsterdam,

Hamburg, Venice, Leghorn (Livorno), Paris, Bordeaux, Bayonne. During the seventeenth century, communities of ex-converso background were established in London, Curaçao, Surinam, New York, and other locations in the New World.[2] These "western Sephardic" communities developed unique traditions and patterns which distinguished them from the Sephardic communities in the Ottoman Empire, the Middle East, and North Africa.

Spiritual Struggles

The returning conversos, especially those who had been raised as Christians, faced serious spiritual struggles upon their return to Judaism in freer lands. Many had no direct living experience of Judaism. The sources of their Jewish knowledge were the Bible, family traditions, and descriptions of Jewish practices publicized by the Inquisition. They were almost totally ignorant of the vast rabbinic tradition. They left the Iberian Peninsula expecting, quite naturally, to return to a Judaism that conformed to their understanding of what Judaism was. What they found was considerably different.

Normative Jewish practice and belief have been shaped by the Talmud and ancient traditions passed down by the sages. The returning conversos had never learned anything about this. Thus they would know from the Bible that Jews were not allowed to eat pork, but not that it is forbidden to eat meat and dairy products together. They would know from the Bible that Jews were not allowed to light fires on the Sabbath, but they would not know the numerous observances and prohibitions that characterize the Jewish Sabbath. They would not know the Jewish system of prayers, the laws of family purity, the proper way to observe the festivals, holidays and fast-days not described in the Bible. In short, they would find a Judaism far more comprehensive and all-encompassing than anything they might have imagined. They felt that they had sacrificed much to return to Judaism; but the Judaism to which they returned was largely new to them.

Not all the conversos who intended to return to Judaism ultimately did so. Some were discouraged and overwhelmed; they preferred to return to Spain and Portugal, where, in spite of the Inquisitional dangers, they felt relatively comfortable.[3] Others remained nominal Christians or nominal Jews in their new places of settlement, unable to come to terms with the Jewish teachings and observances which they had found. The returning conversos created spiritual ferment in the Jewish communities where they settled.

The leading rabbinic authorities attempted to make the transition of the conversos to Judaism as pleasant and easy as possible. The goal was to bring them back into the fold, not to alienate or humiliate them.

Rabbi Shemuel de Medina was asked about a practice of Jews who had been conversos in Portugal and had now returned to Judaism. They had adopted Hebrew names when they joined the Jewish community, but they used their Portuguese names when they wished to communicate with family members or business associates in Portugal (or wherever they were known by their Portuguese names). Was this appropriate? Shouldn't they be required to use only their Jewish names rather than the Christian Portuguese names they once had?

Rabbi de Medina responded that the ways of piety certainly should lead one to distance himself from improper things. Those who had been baptized should want to separate themselves from their past, including their past names. Yet, according to the law, there is no prohibition against their using Portuguese names. One is not allowed to deny being Jewish, but signing a document with a non-Jewish name does not constitute a denial. Even Jews in antiquity had non-Jewish-sounding names and were not held culpable for it. [4] Rabbi de Medina's responsum reflects sensitivity to the situation of the former Portuguese conversos.

The Sephardim throughout their diaspora were generally careful in their observance of Jewish law and custom. Religious piety was widespread. Rabbinic scholars and judges were the guiding forces in the spiritual and communal life of Sephardim. The arrival of former conversos, while certainly a welcome phenomenon, generated certain communal tensions. The newcomers needed time to learn and adapt to normative Jewish practice. While many were eager to conform to the usages of Judaism, others were in a spiritual turmoil. They questioned Jewish tenets and practices. Their observance of traditional Judaism was less than complete. How were pious Jews to deal with their nonconforming brethren? How were they to offset the negative influence of those who questioned Jewish beliefs and violated Jewish laws? On the one hand, pious Jews wanted to lead the newly arrived conversos back to full observance of Judaism; they did not want to discourage them or frighten them off. On the other hand, they could not long tolerate violations of Jewish religion in their communities.

Rabbi David Ibn Abi Zimra, one of the leading Sephardic sages of the sixteenth century, dealt with a question which may have been a reflection of the difficulties in dealing with some former conversos.[5] The question concerned the proper approach to individuals who openly transgressed Jewish laws and, when warned to correct their ways, said that they would convert from Judaism if they were not left to do as they pleased. Deviation from Jewish law could not be tolerated, but no one wanted to be responsible for turning people away from Judaism.

Rabbi Ibn Abi Zimra expressed his long-felt anguish over this problem. Initially, he said, he had felt that such people should be left alone when they committed transgressions, so that they would not come to reject all of the Torah. On further reflection, though, he took note of the teaching that all Jews are responsible one for the other. If communal leaders feared to punish transgressors, then communal discipline would be impaired. People would sin as much as they wished without worrying about being chastised. The rabbis and leaders of previous generations had not been intimidated by the threats of sinners; they had maintained the integrity of their communities and punished transgressors.

But then Rabbi Ibn Abi Zimra concluded:

Even though I have written all this as the law, nevertheless the leader of the generation must deliberate on these matters; not every person is the same and not every sin is the same. If a person is accustomed to transgress and is confident in his arguments [against us], then we pay no attention [to his threats], regardless of consequences; we uphold the Torah. But if he is not accustomed to transgress and it is likely that he may listen to us, then we guide him with words so that he will repent little by little; we do not hasten to punish him so as not to generate a harmful reaction. And so is the rule in similar cases. Everything depends on the evaluation of the judge, the leader; but all his deeds should be for the sake of heaven.

In order to ease the transition of conversos to Judaism, an extensive Jewish literature emerged in Spanish and Portuguese. Classic Jewish texts in Hebrew were translated for the benefit of the new arrivals. Also, books were published which explained basic Jewish beliefs and observances.

One who played an important role in providing Jewish literature for the newcomers was Rabbi Menasseh ben Israel of Amsterdam (1604–57). He authored a work in Portuguese, *Thesouro dos Dinim*, under the auspices of the wardens of the Sephardic congregation of Amsterdam. In it, he described the various rules and regulations incumbent on Jews. He also authored other works dealing with the principles of Jewish faith. His *El Conciliador* provided reconciliations of seeming contradictions in biblical narratives. This literary effort was directed at educating the newly returned Jews and refuting criticisms of Jewish beliefs and practices.[6]

The devoted efforts to guide the Spanish and Portuguese returnees to Judaism were often crowned with success. Yet the spiritual turbulence of the times also gave rise to critics and skeptics who were not easily brought back into Judaism. One such person was Uriel da Costa, an older contemporary of Rabbi Menasseh ben Israel in Amsterdam.

Da Costa (1585–1640) was born into a converso family in Portugal. His father was a devout Catholic, and he himself became a minor church official. Through his study of the Bible, da Costa became attached to Judaism. He and his family fled to Amsterdam, where they could practice Judaism freely. However, the Judaism he found was far different from that which he had imagined in Portugal. He was critical of the Jewish attachment to ritual and legalism. He expressed doubt concerning the doctrines of the resurrection of the dead and the immortality of the soul. When da Costa published teachings critical of Judaism, one of his books was burned. In 1624 he was excommunicated for his heretical teachings. After a period away from Amsterdam, he returned in 1633 and sought to be reconciled with the Jewish community. Nonetheless, he moved further away from Judaism, becoming something of a deist and giving up Jewish observances. He was excommunicated a second time. After seven years, in 1640, da Costa asked to be readmitted to the community. He was subjected to humiliating conditions, including the public recanting of his views, receiving a flogging, and prostrating himself so that the congregation could tread on him. This event so traumatized him that he soon thereafter committed suicide.[7]

Uriel da Costa thus became a martyr for the cause of rebellion against religious authority. His defiance of orthodoxy made an impression on sympathizers and detractors alike. He was a dramatic and tragic example of the spiritual and intellectual ferment which existed within the ex-converso communities.

Da Costa's defiance of authority was to be emulated in even stronger form by another Jew of converso background in Amsterdam: Barukh Spinoza (1632–77). Spinoza's father had come to Amsterdam from Portugal. Barukh Spinoza was educated in the schools of the Sephardic community and studied under the community's rabbis and scholars. His inquisitive mind led him to challenge a number of traditional Jewish teachings. He questioned the divine origin of religion; he doubted whether Moses was the true author of the Torah. When he was twenty-four years old, the rabbinic authorities of Amsterdam took him to task for his heretical opinions. He refused to recant and was excommunicated. The rabbis indicated that they had endeavored by various means to turn Spinoza from his evil ways. When these proved, unsuccessful, they had no other choice but to excommunicate him. Thus, the Jewish community of Amsterdam produced another martyr for the rebellion against religious authority. Spinoza, whose converso background cannot be ignored, became a father of modern philosophy and biblical criticism.

The critique of normative Judaism espoused by da Costa and Spinoza was not confined to these two men alone. On the contrary, their opinions reflected a more widespread malaise among the former conversos, as is shown by *Kol Sakhal*, a volume of uncertain authorship published during the seventeenth century, that encapsulated the main attacks against Judaism advanced by skeptical Spanish and Portuguese Jews of converso background.[8]

The *Kol Sakhal* had as its main goal the discrediting of the Oral Torah, the great body of laws and interpretations handed down from generation to generation. According to Jewish tradition, the Bible cannot be taken on its literal level but must be understood only in connection with the Oral Torah, which was essentially the province of the rabbinic sages who were its experts and transmitters. As mentioned earlier, however, the returning conversos had their greatest problems in this very area, for they had been able to study the Bible even while living in the Iberian Peninsula but were ignorant of the Oral Torah. Since the Judaism they found was totally dominated by the Oral Torah, some of them recoiled from it, preferring a more literally biblical religion.

The *Kol Sakhal* presented what its author considered a rational approach to the principles of religion. It also challenged the authenticity of the Oral Torah and the dominance of rabbinic authority. It made specific attacks on certain Jewish laws and observances. The result was a bitter harangue against normative Judaism and rabbinic teachings.

Such critiques could not go unnoticed or unanswered. Indeed, a significant defense of the Oral Torah was presented by several rabbinic leaders. Rabbi Imanuel Aboab wrote his *Nomologia* in Spanish, in which he argued forcefully for the authenticity of the Oral Torah *(la ley mental)*. In part 1 of the *Nomologia*, he presented seven principles which proved the necessity of the Oral Torah.

1. There are seeming contradictions in Scripture which can only be resolved by the teachings of the sages.
2. We cannot know how to observe the commandments properly except through the Oral Torah.
3. Many precepts and obscure biblical passages cannot be understood without the teachings of the sages.
4. We would not know when to give up our lives rather than transgress a Torah precept, and vice versa, without rabbinic tradition.
5. Similarly, we would not know why certain precepts are repeated in Scripture.
6. We depend on rabbinic calendrical calculations to determine the dates of the biblical holy days.
7. The Torah is interpreted by means of thirteen hermeneutic principles handed down by the rabbis.

In part 2, Rabbi Aboab explained the origin and chain of tradition of the Oral Torah. He pointed out that the conversos had erroneously considered the apocryphal Book of Barukh to be sacred and therefore relied on one of its verses to justify the practice of crypto-Judaism. He also demonstrated how non-Jewish biblical translations misconstrued the Hebrew text, leading the conversos to draw incorrect conclusions about the meaning of the Jewish Bible. Aboab explained the origin and organization of the Talmud, and also discussed the works of leading rabbinic authorities through the generations until his own time.[9]

That the question of the authority of the Oral Torah and rabbinic tradition continued to be raised is reflected in the important work of Haham David Nieto, who served as the chief rabbi of the Sephardim in London from 1701 to 1728. Born in 1654, Nieto received an expansive education which included the study of medicine at the University of Padua. He was not only well versed in biblical and rabbinic literature, but was also quite knowledgeable in science, mathematics, classical literature, and contemporary philosophy.

His classic defense of the Oral Torah, published under the title *Mateh Dan*, was billed as the "Second *Kuzari*." The original *Kuzari*, written by Rabbi Yehudah Halevy of eleventh-century Spain, was an exposition of the truths of Judaism. Rabbi Nieto followed its pattern, presenting his material in the form of dialogues between the king of the Khazzars and a rabbinic sage.[10]

Haham Nieto's work consisted of five dialogues. The goal of the first was to prove from Scripture that the Israelites had an Oral Torah during the days of the prophets. The goal of the second was to demonstrate that the rabbis' interpretations of the Torah and commandments were not fabricated. The third dialogue was to show that the controversies of our ancient sages only dealt with details, not with the basic accepted principles of the Oral Torah. The fourth was to prove that the rabbis were experts in all branches of wisdom and were superior to the philosophers. The final dialogue was to demonstrate the veracity of the rabbis through the example of the laws of lunar intercalation. In the last dialogue, Haham Nieto also dealt with several other questions which had been lodged against rabbinic tradition.

In upholding rabbinic authority, Haham Nieto offered a number of ingenious arguments. He asked: is it plausible to argue that a ruler would make laws which are bad for his people and bad for himself? Of course not. No intelligent person could think so. By analogy, it is not plausible to think that the rabbis made up laws on their own which created problems for the people and also for themselves. The rabbinic exposition of the laws of the Sabbath, for example, listed numerous transgressions which carried capital punishment. Would the rabbis have fabricated such serious laws, which were not only applicable to others but to themselves? Why would they make their own lives so difficult? The obvious answer is that they did not make up these laws at all, but only reported the authentic traditions of the Oral Torah. The same logic applied to the other laws which the rabbis taught: they were the transmitters, not originators.

Another proof of the authenticity of rabbinic teachings is that the rabbis made enormous sacrifices in order to maintain them. They often lived in poverty and deprivation. Some were martyred for their devotion to the laws of Judaism. If the rabbis themselves had invented these laws, why would they have been willing to sacrifice so much—even life itself—for them? The only reasonable answer is that they did not invent the laws; they taught the traditions and laws which they themselves had received, generation to generation, going back to Moses.

The veracity of the rabbinic tradition is also evident from the scrupulous division the rabbis made between Torah laws and rabbinic laws. They never claimed that their laws were divinely ordained; they always specified whether the laws they taught were of Torah origin or of rabbinic origin. Moreover, the rabbis of Babylonia willingly ceded authority to the rabbis of Israel in various legal matters. This shows that they were not interested in making laws to enhance their own power and influence. Rather, they were following clearly defined oral traditions which were of great antiquity.

Haham Nieto demonstrated that the rabbis of talmudic times were not only wise in the ways of Torah but were also expert in philosophy, logic, geography, geometry, agriculture, medicine, science, engineering, astronomy, and other branches of knowledge. They were not narrow-minded, narrowly educated people. The broadness and depth of their knowledge should impress us; how could anyone doubt the wisdom of their teachings?

Haham Nieto's book provided refutations of many of the common critiques of rabbinic authority and the Oral Torah. Many other rabbis and teachers also worked diligently in their communities to strengthen traditional Jewish belief and observance. Among the most influential spokesmen for the Jewish religious tradition were individuals who themselves had lived as New Christians in the Iberian Peninsula and had returned to Judaism with complete acceptance. One such figure in seventeenth-century Amsterdam was Yitzhak Orobio de Castro. A towering intellectual leader, de Castro pointed out the danger of maintaining Jewish practices in Spain while living as a secret Jew. Now that divine providence had enabled him to have the privilege of practicing Judaism in freedom, he wanted to observe it in full, as a true Jew. He was a proponent of halakhic Judaism, stressing the essential nature of rabbinic tradition. Indeed, he defended the Talmud against Christian criticisms. [11]

Another influential spokesman for tradition was Isaac Cardoso (1604–81). [12] Cardoso was born in Portugal. He became a prominent physician, was appointed physician at the royal court in Madrid in 1632, and authored a number of medical and scientific works. In 1648, he arrived in Venice, where he openly returned to Judaism. Subsequently, he settled in Verona.

Cardoso plunged himself into Jewish learning and observance. He was able to draw on the Jewish literature in the vernacular, as well as on the teachings of rabbis and others who took an interest in him. He wrote a significant work of Jewish apologetics, *Las excelencias de los Hebreos* (Amsterdam, 1679), in which he strenuously refuted the Christian calumnies against the Jews and detailed Jewish virtues. From this work, non-Jewish readers could learn that their notions about Jews and Judaism were mistaken. Jewish readers, mainly of converso background, could be reinforced in their decision to return to Judaism and find resolutions to any doubts of faith they might have harbored.

Cardoso was eloquent in his preachments on behalf of Jewish religious observance. He wrote that non-observant Jews complained that the 613 commandments of the Torah were too onerous, impossible to fulfill. Cardoso responded that to the observant Jews the Torah is not ponderous at all; rather, it is sweet and gentle. "It is light and smooth to the virtuous, and tough and burdensome to the indolent and the forgetful. To those who fear the Lord, six hundred precepts seem like six, while to the impious and the neglectful, six seem like six hundred."[13]

Professor Yosef H. Yerushalmi notes that Cardoso and others like him were uniquely qualified to refute Christian arguments against the Jews. The ex-conversos had known Christianity first hand, having been raised in that religion. "They are the first body of Jewish writers *contra Christianos* to have known Christianity from *within*, and it is this which endows their tracts with special interest."[14]

Mention should also be made of Abraham Cohen Herrera, who grew up in Florence. His father was born in Cordoba into a converso family. Abraham Herrera received a humanistic education and was much influenced by contemporary Italian Neoplatonism. He studied Lurianic kabbalah under the guidance of Rabbi Israel Sarug, and ultimately wrote a philosophical treatise, *Puerta del Cielo*. In this work, he offered an elaborate discussion of kabbalistic ideas, giving the Spanish-speaking ex-conversos an opportunity to explore another profound facet of Jewish thought.[15]

The Western Sephardic Tradition

Professor Maír José Benardete has characterized the Jews expelled from Spain in 1492 as medieval Sephardim. Those who became conversos and later returned to Judaism in Western Europe, Benardete has termed Renaissance Sephardim. [16]

The medieval Sephardim left Spain, but took with them the culture and character they had acquired over the centuries of their residence there. They continued to speak Spanish in environments where Spanish was not the general language of communication, e.g., in Turkey, Greece, and what was Yugoslavia. To their medieval Spanish vocabulary, they added numerous words from Hebrew and from the languages of the lands in which they settled. The result was a Jewish variant of old Spanish, Judeo-Spanish—called Ladino in the printed form. This was their mother tongue. They created a vast Judeo-Spanish literature published in Hebrew (Rashi) letters.

The Renaissance Sephardim left the Iberian Peninsula during later periods. They had the opportunity to study in the universities of Spain and Portugal and enter deeply into the cultural life of those countries. When they left, they took with them the Spanish and Portuguese languages as they had developed through the sixteenth and seventeenth centuries. Their language did not have significant admixtures of Hebrew or other languages, as did Judeo-Spanish. Moreover, the literature they created was generally printed in Latin letters.

Whereas the medieval Sephardim continued to speak Judeo-Spanish until the twentieth century, the Renaissance Sephardim did not maintain Spanish and Portuguese as their mother tongues nearly as long. They adopted the languages of the lands in which they settled.

The Renaissance Sephardim founded communities in Western Europe and later in the New World. Thus, they had a strongly European character, in contradistinction to the medieval Sephardim, who had mostly settled in Asia and Africa. Whereas the Western Sephardim flourished in Christian lands, the other Sephardim flourished in Moslem lands.

The returning conversos had strong feelings of self-worth and dignity. They were ambitious and industrious. Imanuel Aboab advised the newcomers to be patient in adjusting to their new lives. They should not be overly ambitious nor expect to earn great wealth too soon. He urged them not to carry their hidalgo traditions too far by refusing to work at menial jobs. [17] But this advice was no deterrent to the phenomenal rise of the former conversos in the world of international commerce. According to the historian Fernand Braudel, it is not unrealistic to speak of an "age" of great Jewish merchants "beginning in the decade of the 1590's and lasting until 1621 or possibly even 1650. Their age was one of intellectual brilliance."[18] Many of the chief figures in that "age" of Jewish commercial success were of converso background.

The Western Sephardic communities were characterized by a strong sense of pride, intellectualism, aesthetics, dignity. Success in intellectual pursuits and in commerce was highly valued. Proper social graces were esteemed. Synagogue buildings were expected to be beautiful, dignified, and well maintained. Synagogue services were supposed to be decorous and respectful, rigorously faithful to the traditional customs. Western Sephardim considered themselves to be an elite group.

By the mid-seventeenth century, then, the Sephardic diaspora included communities throughout the Ottoman Empire, the Middle East, North Africa, Western Europe, and the New World. Sephardim had reestablished themselves in their new locales, bringing with them many of the cultural characteristics and traditions which they had developed in Spain and Portugal.

•5•

The Era of Sabbatai Sevi

As has been seen, the century following the expulsion of the Jews from Spain was a period of intellectual and spiritual creativity among the Sephardim. While rationalism and philosophical inquiry were ardently defended by some thinkers, the growing tendency was against philosophy and in favor of kabbalah. While halakhic study and literary output achieved truly remarkable heights, an anti-rabbinic, anti-halakhic tendency was also noticeable, especially in the ex-converso communities. While many argued for the passive acceptance of God's judgments, there were also voices which expressed impatience and activism. These conflicting tendencies continued to develop through the seventeenth century.

Philosophy Versus Kabbalah

Halakhah guides the life of the observant Jew; it provides legal rulings as to what is permitted and what is forbidden. Halakhic literature is vast, encompassing virtually every aspect of life. Halakhah is pragmatic and legalistic. Yet halakhah has always been accompanied by studies related to Jewish religious thought and sentiment. The Talmud is composed both of halakhah and aggadah, the latter of which includes rabbinic homilies, interpretations, and religious teachings.

Like aggadah, both philosophy and kabbalah function alongside halakhah, attempting to provide the spiritual underpinnings of Judaism. While philosophy attempts to make religion intelligible and reasonable, kabbalah stresses the esoteric and mystical. Philosophy presents what can be known by reason; kabbalah focuses on a spirituality that transcends reason. As Professor Jacob Katz puts it, philosophy is somewhat embarrassed by the

68

many details of halakhah and therefore attempts to give them philosophic significance. On the other hand, kabbalah rejoices in the details of halakhah, finding hidden meanings and symbolisms at every turn. [1]

By the seventeenth century, the Sephardic world had more or less moved away from philosophy and had embraced kabbalah. Certainly, there were intellectuals who were not kabbalists or who opposed kabbalah. Rabbi Menasseh ben Israel, for example, was familiar with kabbalah but was not swept up by its religious approach. He tended to maintain a rationalistic worldview. [2] Eliyahu Montalto (b. 1567 in Portugal), who returned to Judaism openly in Venice in 1610, became famous as an anti-Christian polemicist who encouraged ex-conversos to remain faithful to Judaism. He rejected kabbalah, arguing for the efficacy of reason. [3] Leone de Modena, an influential seventeenth-century intellectual, was also quite opposed to kabbalah, considering it a relatively late development in Judaism. He believed that kabbalah had been influenced by Platonic thought. [4]

Nevertheless, kabbalah had great appeal to intellectuals and the masses alike. In particular, the teachings of Rabbi Yitzhak Luria held increasing sway. Professor Gershom Scholem has demonstrated convincingly how the nearly total victory of kabbalah laid the groundwork for the widespread acceptance of the claims of the pseudo-Messiah Sabbatai Sevi. [5] Had people been primarily involved in rationalistic philosophy, it is unlikely that Sabbatai Sevi would have had so much success. He would have been greeted with considerably more skepticism.

Anti-Halakhic Tendencies

In our discussion of intellectual life in the ex-converso communities of Europe, we noted the controversy over the authenticity and authoritativeness of rabbinic tradition. While the communities generally adhered to and defended the Oral Torah transmitted by the sages, some individuals questioned or rejected it. As a response to the criticisms, it was necessary for books to be written in support of the validity of the Oral Torah. In spite of these eloquent defenses of halakhah and rabbinic tradition, anti-rabbinic and antinomian tendencies persisted.

The critique of rabbinic tradition took two different forms. On the one hand, some argued that the rabbis had amplified too much, going far beyond what was required by the Bible. By their interpretations and legal enactments, the rabbis had created a Judaism far removed from the pure biblical teachings. The defenders of rabbinic tradition referred to such critics as "Karaites." Just as the historical Karaites had deviated from Judaism by accepting only the sanctity of the Written Torah, so these critics were breaking with authoritative Jewish tradition, which had always encompassed both the Written and the Oral Torah.

The second type of criticism emanated from a different viewpoint. The argument was not that the rabbis had been too free and creative in their treatment of the Torah, but that they were not creative enough! The rabbis had allowed the legal system to become frozen and had not adapted adequately to the changing times. This approach led to a tendency to belittle contemporary rabbinic authority, to be dissatisfied with the strictures of halakhah as promulgated by the rabbis. In the response to this type of criticism, defenders of tradition stressed the need to trust the sages—past and present. They pointed to the unbroken chain of rabbinic tradition going back to Moses himself. Loyalty to that tradition was considered an essential ingredient for healthy religious life. The seriousness of this issue is reflected in a responsum of Rabbi Yaacov Hagiz, written in answer to the following question: what is the ruling concerning a person who scorns the words of our sages? Rabbi Hagiz ruled that such a person is to be included in the category of heretics (minim) who have forfeited their right to life.[6] Rabbi Hagiz did not mean to say that such people should actually be executed by the Jewish community, but that their crime was so heinous that they deserved to die for it.

In the battle against antinomian trends, many traditionalists found strength in kabbalah. The kabbalah, after all, posited that the ultimate truths of religion transcended human understanding. Critics might offer arguments based on reason; but they did not grasp the real truth of Judaism because they did not understand kabbalah. The critics viewed halakhah incompletely; they did not take into account the kabbalistic meanings and symbols of halakhah. Thus, their critiques were wrong, having been based on incomplete knowledge, sensitivity, and faith.[7]

Acceptance Versus Rebellion

During the sixteenth century, the predominant attitude was that no evil descends from heaven. Rabbi Moshe Cordovero posited that there is no absolute evil; sufferings and persecutions are punishment for sins, or prods to repentance. As we have seen, a number of sixteenth-century thinkers found ways to justify the ways of God to humans without ascribing fault to God. This approach called on people to accept God's judgments with resignation, recognizing that His judgments were for their own good.

By the seventeenth century, though, a "rebellious" spirit had gained popularity, in part due to the increased influence of the kabbalistic teachings of Rabbi Yitzhak Luria. Rabbi Luria had taught that the roots of evil were "as ancient and eternal as the Godhead, *Ein-Sof,* itself."[8] This implied that evil was a constant reality, and that it sometimes prevailed over the forces of good. Instead of blaming themselves for their sufferings, Jews should blame the power of evil which had hold over their oppressors. "When Luria explained the power of the gentiles as derived from the power of Satan, his ideas were much more easily accepted than theories explaining that the tortures inflicted by the gentiles on the Jews sprang from God's eternal love for the people of Israel."[9] The Lurianic approach taught that Jews should engage in the "correction" of the world; they could and should help the forces of good and purity to prevail. Implicit in these teachings of Rabbi Luria was a rejection of spiritual passivity.

The spirit of activism is particularly evidenced in the messianic idea. As we have seen, the belief in messianic redemption was based on a demand which the Jewish people made of God: Since You are just and righteous, You *must* send the Messiah to redeem us. We have suffered so much; the wicked have oppressed us and have prospered. God must redeem us in order to save His own reputation!

We have already noted the messianic tendencies prevalent within the Sephardic world during the first generations after the expulsion from Spain. The messianic drive continued to deepen during the seventeenth century.

The Sephardic world was still nursing the wounds of the trauma of expulsion. Conversos who returned to Judaism were often filled with guilt which they wished to cleanse by spiritual redemption. In 1648–49, horrible persecutions led to the deaths of thousands of Ashkenazic Jews at the hands of vicious Cossacks. All Jews felt the pain of their own vulnerability to oppression and destruction. They felt powerless to avert catastrophe. In this condition, they were particularly sensitive to the messianic idea.

They needed, they demanded, the immediate coming of the Messiah to redeem them from their predicament.

Sabbatai Sevi

As the Jewish world longed for messianic redemption, a charismatic figure arose with messianic pretensions.[10] Sabbatai Sevi was born in Izmir on the fast-day of the Ninth of Ab in the year 5386 (1626). He received a thorough religious education. At around age fifteen he turned to a life of asceticism and solitude and began to immerse himself in kabbalistic lore. By his early twenties, he had experienced states of unusual mental exaltation; but he also suffered periods of dejection and melancholy. His followers referred to these states of mind as illuminations and "hiding of the face."

Although Sabbatai Sevi did not at first actually proclaim himself to be the Messiah, he did strange things which could only be done by someone who thought he was on a spiritual plane far above the rest of the Jewish people. For example, he pronounced God's ineffable name in public. Historically, the name was only pronounced by the high priest on Yom Kippur while officiating in the Holy of Holies of the Temple. Moreover, Sabbatai transgressed a number of laws and traditions, going so far as to recite a blessing over these transgressions. His bizarre behavior led to his excommunication on several occasions.

During his various travels, Sabbatai Sevi attracted adherents who were impressed by his spiritual personality. He arrived in Jerusalem in the summer of 1662, staying there for a year. He fasted from Sabbath to Sabbath. He practiced solitude. Periodically, he would spend several days in the mountains and caves of the Judean hills. He claimed to hear voices from graves. It was said that when he recited Psalms, he was so intense and holy that looking into his face was like looking into fire.

A student in the yeshiva of Jerusalem, Abraham Nathan son of Elisha Hayyim Ashkenazy, married the daughter of a wealthy Damascus family and moved to Gaza, where he began to delve into kabbalah. In February or March 1665, he had a prophetic vision that Sabbatai Sevi was the Messiah. Nathan met with Sabbatai and told him of his prophecy. On May 31, 1665, Sabbatai Sevi announced that he was the Messiah. Nathan of Gaza worked tirelessly to gain adherents for the messianic movement. The majority of the Jews in Gaza and Hebron became believers in

Sabbatai's messianic claim. Many in Safed were also believers. The majority of the leaders in Jerusalem, however, were opposed to the new movement and excommunicated Sabbatai. Some even wanted to have him murdered lest he gain too much influence.

Sabbatai left Jerusalem in the summer of 1665 and went to Aleppo, where he was well received. In September he went to Izmir. The messianic movement spread rapidly. Although there were still some strong opponents, the masses—and even many of the rabbis and scholars—became believers.

Sabbatai abolished the fasts of the Seventeenth of Tammuz and the Ninth of Ab. Instead, he told people to celebrate these days as festivals. In messianic times, these days of fasting and mourning were to be turned into days of joy. The messianic frenzy grew.

The spring of 1666 was set as the time when Sabbatai Sevi would reveal himself as the Messiah and the redemption of the Jews would commence. In anticipation of this event, many Jews were filled with a heightened sense of anticipation. Those who believed that Sabbatai Sevi was of messianic stature devoted themselves to greater piety so that they would be worthy of the expected redemption. They paid little attention to practical matters that required long-term decisions. After all, if the messianic redemption was going to occur so soon, there was no point in making long-term investments or in expanding business or in repairing one's home. The Messiah would bring the Jews to Israel in a miraculous way, and all would be well.

The believers were impatient—even hostile—to those who were skeptical of Sabbatai Sevi's messianic claim. Rabbi Yaacov Sasportas, an opponent of Sabbatai's movement, wrote that only a few people in each community opposed the messianic movement. Even many rabbis feared to speak openly against Sabbatai Sevi; by doing so, they would have aroused the wrath of the masses of believers.[11] Rabbi Sasportas reported that in Hamburg the community greeted Sabbatai Sevi as though he were their king. People undertook fasting and other ascetic practices for the sake of repentance.[12] The faith of the believers was so strong that they did not listen to the voice of reason. Yet there was continued opposition to Sabbatai. Rabbi Sasportas himself thought that Sabbatai was wicked, deserving of execution as a false prophet. In September 1665, twenty-five rabbis in Istanbul issued a writ of excommunication against Sabbatai Sevi, also indicating the opinion of one rabbi that it would be good to bring about Sabbatai's death as soon as possible.

In the winter of 1665, Sabbatai was in Izmir. He pronounced God's ineffable name. He also ate forbidden fat and encouraged his followers to sin. Rabbi Hayyim Benveniste, the outstanding rabbi of Izmir at the time, was opposed to the messianic movement, but was unable to stem its popularity; indeed, he seems actually to have been swept up by the movement.[13]

In February 1666, Sabbatai Sevi went to Istanbul. By this time, the Turkish government was concerned about the messianic frenzy among the Jews. The authorities feared that Sabbatai Sevi's claim to be the king Messiah might lead to a Jewish rebellion. Moreover, they were disturbed by the cessation of normal business life among Jews. As a result, they arrested and imprisoned the would-be Messiah. After two months, he was moved to a prison in Gallipoli.

This seeming setback to Sabbatai's messianic powers did not quell the enthusiasm of his followers. Numerous people traveled to visit him in prison. Moshe Abudiente, a converso who had returned to Judaism in Amsterdam and had become a teacher in Hamburg, preached in favor of Sabbatai Sevi. When he learned that Sabbatai had been imprisoned, he took this as a proof of the authenticity of Sabbatai's claim. He drew parallels from the Bible: Joseph had been imprisoned before rising to greatness in Egypt; Moses had been in exile in Midian before leading the Israelites to redemption from Egypt. Indeed, rabbinic tradition speaks of the suffering of the Messiah before he is able to accomplish his mission.[14] Rabbi Sasportas recorded that "although he [Sabbatai Sevi] was imprisoned in Gallipoli, nevertheless this was not sufficient to weaken the strength of his believers; on the contrary, they bolstered him with false and farfetched attributes, testifying that he performed a number of miracles and wonders."[15] They claimed, for example, that Sabbatai had broken the iron doors and bars of the prison; that a pillar of cloud and a pillar of fire separated him from others.

In September, he was transferred to Adrianople. The believers thought that Sabbatai would take the sultan's crown and initiate the redemption. Instead, he was given the choice of being tortured to death or converting to Islam. Tragically, he chose to become an apostate, changing his name to Mehemed Effendi. This decision, obviously, created serious problems within the Jewish world.

Sabbatai Sevi's wife and leading devotees decided to follow him into apostasy. Believers like Abraham Cardoso offered explanations to justify Sabbatai's conversion to Islam. They argued that halakhah did not apply in messianic times; that the acts of the Messiah to effect redemption were incomprehensible and not subject to normal patterns of reasoning. In order to bring redemption and purification, it was maintained, the Messiah first had to enter into the depths of sin and impurity. This scenario was particularly appealing to ex-conversos who themselves had lived secret lives as Christians before returning to Judaism. Indeed, Abraham Cardoso argued that it was necessary for the Messiah to be a converso; that all Jews were obliged to convert outwardly before attaining redemption.[16]

Believers who had such deep faith in Sabbatai Sevi's messianic claim felt compelled to follow him into apostasy. They believed that he would ultimately return to Judaism and reveal himself as the true Messiah. Meanwhile, they would share his destiny and follow his lead. And they would wait faithfully for him to save the Jewish people.

On the other hand, many believers and sympathizers were stunned by Sabbatai's apostasy. For a Messiah to abandon Judaism for another religion was impossible. There was only one possible conclusion: Sabbatai was emphatically not the Messiah! But how difficult it was to give up the messianic hope. They had been misled, betrayed. One can imagine the severe spiritual depression which set in among the disillusioned former believers.

Those who had opposed Sabbatai Sevi were now vindicated. The abuse they had taken from the believers had been unwarranted; and they were not reluctant to remind everyone that they had been right in the first place. The former believers were embarrassed and confounded. Moslems and Christians mocked the Jews; they were not to be redeemed after all. Their hopes were empty. In Europe, a number of Jews converted to Christianity in disillusionment.[17]

After Sabbatai's apostasy, Nathan of Gaza wandered from place to place trying to persuade believers that he would ultimately return as Messiah. A faith which had been so strongly held was not easily dislodged. The rabbis of Istanbul proclaimed an excommunication on all who continued to believe in the messianic claim of Sabbatai and observed any practices associated with the pseudo-Messiah. In the summer of 1667, the rabbis of Istanbul and Izmir stated that anyone who did not fast on the Ninth of Ab was to be excommunicated. Rabbi Hayyim Benveniste, who had been sympathic to Sabbatai's claims prior to the apostasy, now made very strict rulings concerning the observance of the fast of Ab, which Sabbatai had declared null and void.[18] In Amsterdam, the anti-Sabbatean backlash led to the removal of kabbalistic passages from the synagogue liturgy. The Amsterdam community, under Sabbatai's influence, had instituted the recital of the priestly blessing by the cohanim each Shabbat. Previously, this blessing had only been recited by the cohanim on festivals and holidays. Now that Sabbatai was known to be an imposter, the question was whether the community should continue a practice that had been instituted through his influence. Rabbi Yaacov Sasportas ruled that the practice—though in itself justifiable—should be dropped so as not to give any credibility to Sabbatai Sevi.[19] In this case, however, the community did maintain the custom in spite of the role Sabbatai had played in establishing it.

Isaac Cardoso, the brother of the Sabbatean Abraham Cardoso, had consistently opposed the messianic pretensions of Sabbatai Sevi. Indeed, his differences with his brother on this matter ultimately led to their separation from each other. Isaac had grown to maturity in the Iberian Peninsula as a converso and had returned to Judaism with intense fervor. He had already rejected the messianic claim of Christianity. Thus, when confronted with Sabbateanism, he clung faithfully to his newly acquired Judaism, rejecting Sabbatai Sevi's claim. Isaac could not accept the notion that a messianic figure would transgress the laws of Judaism. Sabbatai's apostasy only confirmed the fact that he was an imposter.[20]

Writing in Venice, Rabbi Shemuel Aboab stated that many Jewish communities—Sephardic and Ashkenazic—had given credence to Sabbatai Sevi's messianic pretensions. Now they sought to destroy any memory of him; they burnt all records and papers which contained his name; they refused to mention him. Rabbi Aboab, together with other rabbis and leaders, interrogated Nathan of Gaza when he was in Venice. They received his confession that he had made an error of judgment in following Sabbatai Sevi but had not meant to be rebellious. He publicly admitted that he had been wrong and that his so-called prophetic visions had been false.[21] Nathan's influence declined, and after 1668 he was mostly ignored by the rabbinic community. He died in 1680.

But Sabbatai Sevi himself was still a puzzle. In 1667 his wife bore him a son, whom he circumcised according to Jewish practice. During the following years, he did a number of Jewish religious acts. These actions provided fuel to a small body of faithful followers who still believed that he would reveal himself as the Jewish Messiah. When he died on Yom Kippur in 1676, his followers at first tried to keep this news a secret. Nathan himself was despondent. A belief arose that Sabbatai Sevi had not really died at all, but had been removed to Paradise, where he would remain until the day of redemption. A group of believers, known as Donmeh, continued to maintain this faith for centuries.

Amazingly, Sabbateanism survived long after Sabbatai's death. The basic ingredients which had provided impetus for the movement's success were still in place. The masses of Jews still put great emphasis on kabbalah; rationalistic philosophy was not widely popular. Antinomian tendencies were still evident in some circles, as were arguments against rabbinic authority. Moreover, the Jewish people had grown impatient for redemption. Many were tired of accepting their exile passively; they wanted a radical improvement in their condition. The messianic idea offered a hope, and the people were anxious to have that hope fulfilled.

The continued existence of Sabbateanism sometimes led to serious controversies. Those who still accepted Sabbatai's messianic claim were forced into a spiritual underground. Being accused of adhering to the Sabbatean heresy could ruin one's reputation. On the other hand, several works by authors of known Sabbatean leanings were well accepted by rabbis and laymen alike. An example of this is the ethical tract *Hemdat Yamim*, attributed to a Sabbatean author, yet widely accepted and read. Eighteenth-century mainstream authors, such as Rabbi Yaacov Huli and Rabbi Hayyim Yosef David Azulai, quoted from works whose authors were known to have had Sabbatean tendencies. Apparently, they believed that the merits of the works justified their being quoted, in spite of the theological error of the authors.[22]

Rabbi Moshe Hagiz

The spiritual aftermath of the Sabbatai Sevi episode is well illustrated in the life and work of Rabbi Moshe Hagiz (ca. 1672–1751). Born in Jerusalem, Moshe was the son of Rabbi Yaacov Hagiz, a strong opponent of the Sabbatean movement. Moshe received a thorough rabbinic education in the Yeshiva of Jerusalem, studying both with his father and his grandfather, Rabbi Moshe Galante. He was a strong-willed person who often found himself in conflict with others. In 1694, he left the land of Israel to seek funds to establish a yeshiva in Jerusalem—a project which he never fulfilled. He traveled through the Jewish communities of Europe, became embroiled in a number of controversies, and ultimately returned to Safed in 1738. A prolific author and polemicist, he devoted much of his talent to the battle against the continued influence of Sabbateanism.

As has been mentioned, messianic frenzy did not disappear with the death of Sabbatai Sevi. Some of his followers expected him to return as the Messiah forty years after his apostasy, i.e., in 1706. During this waiting period, active messianism continued. Abraham Cardoso called on believers to go to Jerusalem to await the coming of the Messiah. Even great rabbis called for immediate migration to the land of Israel as a prelude to the redemption. Rabbi Abraham Rovigo, a sage known for his piety and righteousness, settled in the holy land, hoping that he would be designated as viceroy to the Messiah.[23]

When 1706 passed without the appearance of Sabbatai Sevi, new calculations and speculations were made and expectations were turned to the year 1740. Meanwhile, the mainstream Jewish leadership was attempting to calm the people in the aftermath of the Sabbatai Sevi debacle. Those who continued to stir up hopes for Sabbatai's return were not allowing the communities to recover from their serious spiritual shock at Sabbatai's failure. Sabbateanism was seen not merely as mistaken but as dangerous. It kept people suspended in an unrealistic messianic bubble that was destined to burst, leaving their lives in a shambles.

Moshe Hagiz fought energetically against the Sabbatean heresy, zealously attacking individuals and works that fostered it. His first battle was against Nehemiah Hiya Hayon, an itinerant kabbalist who published works of a Sabbatean nature. In 1713, Hagiz drew many leaders from various communities into this controversy. A similar controversy broke out in 1725. During the 1730s, Hagiz turned his efforts against Rabbi Moshe Hayyim Luzzatto (born in Padua, 1707). Luzzatto was a gifted writer, a man of deep spirituality. His ethical writings were very significant and were destined to become classics in Jewish ethical literature. Yet Luzzatto was given to kabbalistic study, and claimed to have visitations from an angel. Moreover, he was suspected of Sabbatean leanings. As a result of Hagiz' campaign against Luzzatto, Italian rabbinic authorities compelled him to refrain from publishing kabbalistic works and excommunicated him for a period of time.

A dilemma in the opposition to Sabbateanism concerned the status of kabbalah. On the one hand, kabbalah was widely held to be an essential ingredient in Jewish religious life. Rabbi Hagiz himself published a number of kabbalistic works and was deeply committed to the truth of kabbalah.[24] For him, kabbalah and halakhah enjoyed a harmonious relationship, each performing a specific function. Halakhah, of course, was the final authority in the realm of action; but kabbalah provided the spiritual basis of halakhah and the emotional context of one's relationship with God.

On the other hand, though, kabbalah was more volatile than halakhah. Since it dealt in mysteries and symbolism, it was subject to manipulation by teachers who claimed special expertise. Indeed, the spread of kabbalah served as a backdrop to Sabbateanism; it created receptivity to metarational and nonrational ideas. It provided a seemingly authoritative and traditional interpretation of Sabbatai's antinomian behavior, of his apostasy, even of his death. Thus, though kabbalah was basic to Jewish religious life, it also contained elements which could destabilize that life.

Both Rabbi Hagiz and Rabbi Yosef Ergas of Leghorn had been proponents of kabbalah for the masses. Following the controversy surrounding the works of Hayon in 1713, Rabbi Hagiz reconsidered his position. Realizing the dangers that would result if the kabbalah was popularized, he came to argue that kabbalistic study should be confined only to a select few. He published no more kabbalistic works. On the other hand, Rabbi Ergas felt that it was necessary to strengthen the foundations of kabbalah among the masses and devoted his literary efforts toward that goal.[25]

The transmission of kabbalah is dependent on the authority of the teacher and the authenticity of the kabbalistic texts. One may only study this wisdom directly from one who is truly imbued with it. Printed texts contain errors and may not be trusted in full. Since kabbalah deals with esoteric and delicate topics, a student might easily go astray, not fully understanding the concepts and lessons. Only a proper teacher is able to convey the real meaning of kabbalistic texts, and therefore a trustworthy teacher is an absolute necessity. Rabbi Hagiz was troubled by the fact that unfit teachers were expounding kabbalistic topics openly and misleading the public. Kabbalistic teachers of Sabbatean leanings were corrupting the masses with their erroneous and dangerous interpretations. They had weakened some individuals' commitment to the observance of halakhah.[26]

Rabbi Hagiz believed in the importance of kabbalah, but came to argue that kabbalistic study should be confined to qualified teachers and students. His desire to circumscribe the influence of kabbalah did not lead him to promote the virtues of rational philosophy, however. On the contrary, he believed that religious faith is based ultimately on deep emotion and mystical understanding rather than on philosophic conviction.

Rabbi Hagiz respected the intellect and argued that Jews were obligated to understand Jewish tradition well, not merely relying on the guidance of others. Yet he deemed philosophy an inadequate basis for faith. Some philosophers, for example, had come to conclusions that rejected basic principles of Judaism. Obviously, their reason had misled them. Moreover, arguments which seem logical and foolproof to one philosopher are rejected and refuted by another. Philosophic truth is simply not reliable. We do not need philosophy to establish our faith; we know religious truth from the Torah and our rabbinic tradition.

Rabbi Hagiz felt that the study of general wisdom could help Jews to appreciate the greatness of God. But secular study should not include topics which go against the faith. Moreover, no one should engage deeply in secular study who was not already well versed in Torah wisdom.[27]

A major area of concern for Rabbi Hagiz was the challenge to rabbinic authority in general and halakhic observance in particular. In the ex-converso communities of Europe, an antirabbinic, antihalakhic undercurrent continued to flourish. The legacy of Spinoza was still evident. The antinomian tendencies of Sabbateanism also challenged the hegemony of traditional rabbinic halakhic authority. Rabbi Hagiz found the Sabbateans to be even more dangerous than the "Karaites" in that they were more audacious and disrespectful to rabbinic sages.[28]

Moshe Hagiz devoted considerable effort to bolstering rabbinic authority. He emphasized that the Jewish tradition rested entirely on the authority of the sages. They had received the traditions from their predecessors in an unbroken chain going back to Moses; and had transmitted the traditions to their students.[29]

In his book *Mishnat Hakhamim*, Rabbi Hagiz elaborated on the concept of *emunat hakhamim*, "trust in the sages." He was perhaps the first author to deal specifically with this phrase in so dramatic a fashion. While the other topics considered in *Mishnat Hakhamim* are treated properly, it is *emunat hakhamim* which received by far the most thorough and lengthy discussion.

His premise was that Judaism rests on the authority of the rabbis; to attack the rabbis is to attack the foundation of Judaism. Someone who does not trust the truth of the words of the rabbis is to be considered the same as one who denies the entire Torah. Such people begin by rejecting the sages but proceed to reject the Torah itself. Rabbi Hagiz expressed his distress concerning those who had challenged this premise, noting that it was the task of the sages of each generation to refute such cynics. He pointed to notorious offenders—Sabbatai Sevi, Abraham Cardoso, Nehemiah Hayon—as examples of people who must be strenuously and vigorously opposed. Their teachings undermined rabbinic authority, and, therefore, Judaism itself.[30] Halakhah could not be abrogated. God's law was eternal. No mitzvah could be altered or negated. Not understanding the reason for a mitzvah was not an excuse for treating it lightly. We are responsible for fulfilling God's commandments regardless of whether we understand them or not. This also applies to rabbinic teachings; we are not allowed to reject or ignore them simply because we do not understand the reason for them. On the contrary, it is our duty to respect the words of our sages.

Rabbi Hagiz called on the rabbis of his generation to preach on the basic topic of *emunat hakhamim*. All other teachings were ultimately dependent on this fundamental principle.[31] He expressed his gratification that works on this topic had been composed in the vernacular so as to reach the largest possible audience. In particular, he recommended the *Nomologia* of Rabbi Imanuel Aboab and the *Excellencies of the Hebrews* of Dr. Yitzhak Cardoso.

Moshe Hagiz was realistic enough to know that contemporary rabbis were contributing to the public mistrust of rabbinic authority. Some rabbis, wrote Hagiz, preached on topics which they did not fully understand. They puzzled the uninitiated by presenting rabbinic homilies and interpretations without proper explanations. It would be better for such preachers to remain silent.[32] He had no patience with unqualified people who passed themselves off as rabbis and scholars. He pleaded with preachers not to speak on topics which they did not properly understand, and not to quote rabbinic aggadot that would seem strange to their audiences.[33]

Moshe Hagiz was also realistic enough to know that even competent rabbis can make mistakes. *Emunat hakhamim* did not mean that the sages were infallible. Everyone errs; it is to the credit of the great sages that their errors can be counted. Most people, even the wisest, are guilty of innumerable errors.[34] Yet, although rabbis could err individually, the consensus of rabbinic tradition is true and is binding on the faithful.

In insisting that rabbinic authority had to be accepted, Rabbi Hagiz was really calling for a stabilization of the religious turmoil which had ensued in the wake of Sabbatai Sevi. People were confused, frustrated, disillusioned. Different approaches were being promulgated on the role of kabbalah, the authority of halakhah, the imminence of the coming of the Messiah. By playing down kabbalah and stressing halakhah, Rabbi Hagiz hoped to restore a more normal, stable kind of life. He also thought that when Jews governed their lives according to hala-khah as taught by the sages, they would be less prone to be influenced by Sabbatean teachings.

Rabbi Hagiz realized that people were restless; they wanted immediate salvation by the Messiah. They wanted an end to their exile and suffering. To counter this restlessness and activism, he stressed the importance of accepting one's destiny with happiness and faith. He emphasized the virtue of relying on God, of accepting God's will without rebellion or complaint.

For example, wealth and poverty are in God's power. It is He who decides how to distribute material goods. One who is rich should be grateful for his portion and use his wealth to serve God and humanity. On the other hand, one who is poor ought not to be upset by this. God knows that poverty is actually a benefit, inducing humility and a tendency to turn one's eyes to heaven.[35] Therefore, regardless of our economic condition, we must accept God's decrees and make the best of them. Wealth and poverty are neither good nor bad in and of themselves; they are distributed by God as a test, in the hope that we will use them well.

A classic question has long bothered the Jews: Why do the Jewish people suffer so much? Why are Jews persecuted, and why do their enemies succeed? Rabbi Hagiz offered an answer. The nations of the world commit much evil and only a little good; but the people of Israel do much good and only a little evil. God uses chastisements and punishments as a way of purifying people. Through suffering, they are cleansed of their sins and are left in a state of purity and holiness. Since the nations of the world are so filled with evil, there would be almost nothing left of them if God were to punish them to purify them from their evil. On the other hand, God can purify the Jewish people, since their sins are few and their good deeds are so many.

Going further on this topic, Rabbi Hagiz argued that the non-Jewish nations would complain and rebel if God chastised them. They would commit even more sins, thus losing the entire lesson of their suffering. But the Jews receive their sufferings patiently and are led to repentance. Therefore, they are the only ones to merit this form of divine purification. Moreover, the day will certainly come when the Jews will be well rewarded for their patience and their piety. Their oppressors will surely be punished.[36] Jews should recognize God's many kindnesses to them even while they are suffering in exile. God has not abandoned them and helps them in many ways. In His compassion, God knows what is best for the Jews and how to guide them through their history.[37]

The level of acceptance and passivity advocated by Rabbi Hagiz may be illustrated by the following case. He wrote: if a non-Jew should come up to a Jew and spit in his face and humiliate him, how should the Jew react? One might think that the Jew would believe this non-Jew to be an uncouth person who deserved to be rebuked and put in his place. Yet, stated Rabbi Hagiz, the Jew should not rise against the non-Jew. He should suffer the humiliation patiently, assuming that it had come to him as a result of his sins, and should confess and repent, realizing that this incident had occurred because God wanted it to occur.[38] In general, a person should accustom himself not to react against anyone who scorns or humiliates him. Rather, he should interpret such events as signals from God, calling upon him to repent. One should accept chastisements and sufferings calmly, with a cheerful countenance.

Rabbi Hagiz stressed the classic Jewish virtue of humility. It was a sign of royalty and greatness to be humble, to speak softly. People should conduct themselves humbly, keeping their eyes trained to the ground.[39] It might be added that humble people are less likely to be aggressive and rebellious. They are better able to accept the status quo than those who lack humility.

In addressing the dimensions of the spiritual turmoil in his time, Rabbi Hagiz clearly was trying to move the Jewish people to a calmer, more accepting frame of mind. It has been argued that his approach came to typify rabbinic efforts to suppress all forms of religious renewal.[40] While there is truth in this assertion, it seems to be an overstatement. Rabbi Hagiz' role was to quell a spiritual storm. To do so, he used a variety of arguments and techniques. However, we need not assume that he would have made the same arguments in the same way had he lived in a period of spiritual tranquility. If subsequently, some of his teachings were utilized in such a manner as to stifle religious creativity, he can hardly be blamed for that development.

The era of Sabbatai Sevi was to have a long-lasting impact on the various Sephardic communities throughout the world. To the extent that it aroused messianic hopes and anticipation but failed to produce a real Messiah, it led to deep despair and disillusionment. The various controversies surrounding Sabbateanism left spiritual scars. Rabbi Hagiz, and others who shared his opinions, worked to heal the Jewish people at a time of distress.

·6·

The Promised Land: Maintaining a Dream

During their many centuries of exile, the Jewish people maintained the dream of returning to the land of Israel, the land which God had promised to their ancestors—Abraham, Isaac, and Jacob. Following the destruction of Jerusalem and the razing of the Holy Temple by the Romans in the year 70 C.E., a small number of Jews continued to live there, generally under very difficult conditions. Over the centuries, the Jews of the diaspora sent funds to support the communities in Israel; they made pilgrimages; they faced in the direction of Jerusalem while praying. Indeed, so important a part did the land of Israel play in the Jewish religious outlook that Jewish religion and peoplehood cannot be understood without reference to it. The awaited messianic redemption, it was taught, would see the restoration of Jewish sovereignty in Israel. Jews from throughout the diaspora would be returned miraculously to the promised land, where they would enjoy peace and tranquility, free to serve God according to Jewish law and custom in their own land.

Following the expulsion from Spain, a number of exiles made their way back to Israel. Messianic anticipation was palpable. A major center of Jewish spiritual life developed in Safed. The scholars, pietists, and kabbalists of Safed left a lasting legacy to Jewish religious thought. A central concern of theirs was the messianic vision of Judaism, a yearning for the spiritual and material fulfillment which would ensue in the days of the Messiah.

The Jews of the diaspora felt a special responsibility for the Jews living in Israel. By supporting them, the Jews of the exile could feel that they were vicariously participating in the mitzvah

85

of living in the Holy Land. Their support was a reflection of their genuine concern and commitment to Jewish life in Israel.

On the other hand, the Jews in the Holy Land felt a responsibility for their coreligionists in the exile. Rabbi Shelomo Mainstral wrote a letter in 1607 in which he described his visit to Safed.[1] He said that he found a community there with about three hundred great and pious rabbis; there were eighteen yeshivot and twenty-one synagogues. Nearly four hundred children attended a large study hall which was staffed with one hundred teachers. There was no tuition charge. The teachers were supported by wealthy Jews from Istanbul.

Following morning prayer services in all the synagogues, everyone remained to sudy in various groups, each group studying a different text, e.g., Maimonides, Talmud, Zohar, *Ein Yaacov*. They had this practice also following the evening prayer services.

After services on Thursday mornings, all the Jews gathered in one of the large synagogues and recited a special prayer for the Jews of the diaspora and for the exile of the Shekhinah (Divine Presence), mourning the destruction of the Holy Temple in Jerusalem. Then they offered a blessing for those who sent funds to help support the poor Jews of the Holy Land, praying that God would grant them long life, success, and protection from suffering and pain. This special prayer was chanted with great emotion and tears. Before the congregation began this prayer, Rabbi Moshe Galante ascended the pulpit and preached a moving sermon, arousing them to fear and love the Lord. He spoke with eloquence, sweetness, and profound erudition. Then, two of the leading sages led the community in the prayer.

This description reflects the symbiotic relationship which characterized the Jews of Israel and those of the diaspora. All Jews recognized the land of Israel as the Holy Land, and Jerusalem as the Holy City. Those who dwelled in the land depended on their coreligionists in the exile for support; those in the exile depended on their coreligionists in the land for spiritual sustenance. Israel was considered the spiritual center of the Jewish people, "for the Torah will go out from Zion, and the word of God from Jerusalem."

Sabbatai Sevi was himself quite aware of the role the land of Israel played in Jewish religious consciousness. He spent many months in Jerusalem and strove to win adherents throughout Israel. Nathan of Gaza, Sabbatai's "prophet," was raised and educated in the Holy Land. Sabbatai's success among Jews who dwelled in Israel gave him greater credibility among those in the diaspora.[2]

As we have seen, the apostasy of Sabbatai Sevi did not end the messianic movement. Sabbateanism was still a potent force in Jewish life, and continued to manifest itself in the Holy Land. Rabbi Moshe Galante, son-in-law of Rabbi Yaacov Hagiz, left Israel following Sabbatai's apostasy and served as an emissary of Jerusalem on an extended tour in the diaspora. His ostensible goal was to raise funds for the community in Jerusalem. But his trip may also be seen as an attempt by the Jerusalem rabbinate to provide leadership to the Jewish world and strengthen the battered morale of their disillusioned brethren.[3] Galante visited important communities in Istanbul, Salonika, Belgrade, and elsewhere. His travels kept him away from Jerusalem until 1673. He considered the years of his service as an emissary as a period of exile. Galante, and the many emissaries from Israel through the eighteenth century, worked to maintain the historic link binding Jewish spirituality to the Holy Land. They not only raised funds among their diaspora coreligionists; they also kept the dream and the reality of Jewish life in Israel alive. This task became considerably more difficult with the failure of Sabbatai Sevi. A large percentage of diaspora Jewry had vested their hopes in Sabbatai. They truly believed he would redeem them, return them to the land of Israel. With the destruction of that hope, many began to wonder if they would ever be redeemed. The messianic idea of a return to Israel now began to seem hopelessly utopian. Even in the midst of this period of despair, hope was rekindled by messianic eruptions in 1706 and 1740. But with the failure of the Messiah to appear and to bring the Jews back to Israel, the hope for an imminent return faded.

While most Sephardic communities continued to harbor a deep longing for the promised land—even if that longing seemed unlikely to have a practical realization—the Sephardic communities of Western Europe were experiencing a change in worldview. The Jews of Holland and England, for example, were beginning to enjoy the climate of religious toleration which was growing in those countries. While they still suffered from various legal disabilities, the Jews of Western Europe were now able to practice their religion freely and were given a degree of human consideration that had not generally been accorded to diaspora Jews. Absorbing the rationalistic philosophy which dominated the non-Jewish societies in which they lived, they began to feel at home in the diaspora; the idea that they were in exile from their own land of Israel became dulled.

As Professor Yitzhak Baer has written: "In Sephardic circles of this period we find for the first time an optimistic consciousness of progress. . . . From the Sephardim of England and Holland, rationalism spread to the Jewish skeptics in France and even to the Jews of Germany."[4] Baer has argued that this tendency among the Western Sephardim was the beginning of a long process of disintegration of the concept of Jewish nationhood. It ultimately "led to a complete or partial abandonment of the nation. Loss of faith in the national future and in the folk strength of the religion led to a denationalization of the religion."[5] Jews of this new perspective wanted to adapt to their host countries; they were content to see themselves as part of a religious group rather than as a nation. Yet Judaism has always entailed a specifically Jewish nationalism tied inextricably to the land of Israel. Though the "modernized" Jews did not want to face this fact directly, and may even have been embarrassed by it, Jewish nationhood is intrinsic to Jewish religion.

Rabbi Moshe Hagiz was perhaps the first emissary from the Holy Land to confront the incipient alienation between religion and nationhood among the Western Sephardim. In his *Sefat Emet,* he emphasized the centrality of Israel for the Jewish people. He explained that the Jews of the diaspora had not settled in Israel because they did not fully understand the religious significance and obligation of living there, perhaps because they were unable to undertake such a big move. All Jews, however, really did want to settle in Israel, and were only prevented from doing so by extraneous and extenuating circumstances.

Rabbi Hagiz found that this theory was inadequate when it came to some of the Jews he met in Amsterdam. They were affluent, comfortable in Dutch society. They said mockingly: "if the Messiah is going to come to equalize the poor and the rich, let him not come; what do we need him for?"[6] Others said that they would be glad if the Messiah came, because he could take care of the poor and they would no longer have to spend any of their own money for such purposes. Rabbi Hagiz scorned these arguments. He called on the Jews of the diaspora to support the communities in Israel generously and to seek ways of tying themsleves closer to the destiny of the people and the land of Israel. Rabbi Hagiz well understood the latent danger of divorcing Jewish religion from Jewish nationhood.

The problem addressed by Rabbi Hagiz was still an issue in the following generation. Rabbi Hayyim Yosef David Azulai (1724–1806) echoed the arguments of Rabbi Hagiz. He stated that the Jewish people would not achieve redemption unless the Jews of the diaspora realized that they were in exile, and mourned the desolation of Israel and the destruction of Jerusalem. Although the Jews of Europe felt that their social condition had improved, they should not be deceived by their newfound success. Rabbi Azulai, following in the footsteps of Rabbi Hagiz, expressed the fear that the Jews of the Western European diaspora would become like the non-Jewish citizens of their countries, adopting non-Jewish modes of life and ceasing to mourn for the destruction of Israel. The redemption of the Jews, he warned, was tied to the Jewish yearning for redemption, to the longing for a return to the land of Israel.[7]

Rabbi Hagiz, and Rabbi Azulai after him, argued that diaspora Jews were obligated to support the Jews in Israel not merely as an act of charity but because doing so benefitted themselves. By contributing to the well-being of Jews in the Holy Land, the Jews of the exile were fulfilling a great mitzvah for which they would be rewarded by the Almighty. Moreover, the more they bound themselves to the land of Israel, the more they fulfilled the teachings of Judaism. They needed to be helpful and considerate to the Jews of Israel; the latter, after all, were sacrificing much in order to maintain the Jewish dream of resettling Israel. The least the diaspora Jews could do was to give priority to assisting them.

Preparing for Redemption in Israel

Meanwhile, attempts were made in Israel to prepare for the coming of the Messiah. A dramatic effort involved Rabbi Hayyim Abulafia (ca. 1660–1744).[8] Born in Hebron, he moved with his parents to Jerusalem while still a young man. There he studied at the yeshiva of Jerusalem, under the tutelage of Rabbi Yaacov Hagiz, Rabbi Moshe Galante, Rabbi Shelomo Algazi, Rabbi Abraham Amigo, and others. One of his fellow students was Hizkiah de Silva, who became the author of a remarkable halakhic work, *Peri Hadash.*

Hayyim Abulafia was known for his erudition and saintliness. In 1710, he took a position as rabbi in Izmir. Continuing to yearn for the land of Israel, Rabbi Abulafia was among those who believed that the Messiah would come in the year 1740. As this year neared, his restlessness increased. He wanted to do something great as a preparation for the Messiah.

It occurred to him that the holy city of Teveria (Tiberias) was in ruins. During the latter half of the sixteenth century, Don Yosef Nasi and his aunt Dona Gracia had attempted to restore Jewish life in that historic city in the north of Israel. The community had taken hold and had attracted highly regarded rabbis and scholars. Rabbi Yitzhak Luria is said to have traveled to Teveria to pray in the synagogue there. Other great sages also visited the city, which became an important center for Torah study. Rabbi Abulafia's own great-grandfather had served in a rabbinical position there. However, with the passage of time, life in the city became impossible. Warring Arab sheiks fought for control of Teveria, and their battles left the city in ruins; by 1670 its Jewish community had disappeared.

Rabbi Hayyim Abulafia decided to reestablish the Jewish community of Teveria. He hoped to attract Jewish pietists to the sacred city to build synagogues and study halls. In this way, he would be paving the way for the messianic redemption, because a statement in the Talmud indicated that the future redemption of the people of Israel would take place in Teveria (Rosh Hashanah 31).

When Rabbi Abulafia wrote to the Arab sheik who controlled Teveria, he received warm letters of encouragement in response. The sheik said that he and the Jewish community would be welcomed in Teveria. They would play an important role in the rebuilding and revitalization of the city.

In 1738, Rabbi Abulafia—then well advanced in years—made the voyage to Teveria. He was received with honor by the sheik. The process of rebuilding and beautifying the city commenced. Rabbi Abulafia sent emissaries to the communities in the diaspora to raise money for the enterprise, and was pleased with their generous response. He sent a letter detailing the progress that had been made—a synagogue, study hall, and school had been built. He rejoiced that this holy city which had been desolate for seventy years was now in the midst of a rebirth.

A legend reports how determined Rabbi Abulafia was to maintain the Jewish community in Teveria. An enemy of the sheik of Teveria assembled a large army to attack the rebuilt city. The sheik was outnumbered, but he and his troops fought valiantly. Many Jews wanted to flee the city during the war, fearing injury and death. Rabbi Abulafia told his community to remain there. God would not have let them restore Jewish life in Teveria if He only wanted to have the Jews flee so soon. No one left. In the end, the sheik of Teveria defeated his enemy. Not one Jew was injured; not one Jewish home was damaged. This was taken as a sign of God's pleasure with the Jews of the city for having demonstrated their faith in Him and their trust in the ultimate restoration of Israel.

Rabbi Abulafia attracted pious individuals to settle in or to visit Teveria. A memorable visit took place on the twenty-third day of Adar II in the year 5502 (in the spring of 1742). The venerable Rabbi Hayyim Benattar came to Teveria to meet Rabbi Hayyim Abulafia.

Rabbi Benattar (1696–1743), born in Salé, Morocco, was a leading talmudic scholar, kabbalist, and pietist. When he learned of Rabbi Abulafia's interest in reestablishing Jewish life in Teveria, Rabbi Benattar was stimulated to migrate to the Holy Land. He hoped to establish a yeshiva in Israel which would attract students from the diaspora. This effort, he believed, would help hasten the redemption.

Rabbi Benattar left for Israel together with several of his leading disciples, including David Hasan and Shemtov Gabbai. In 1739, they arrived in Leghorn, where they hoped to gain support for the proposed yeshiva in Israel. Rabbi Benattar immediately attracted an enthusiastic following; his public sermons were attended by large audiences. From Leghorn he traveled extensively throughout Italy, urging the Jews to migrate to Israel. During this period, though, reports arrived of epidemics in the Holy Land. Some of Rabbi Benattar's disciples became apprehensive at the prospect of going to settle there. Rabbi Benattar responded: "It is immaterial to me who comes and who remains; he who has ideals will immigrate and inherit the land."

In 1741, Rabbi Benattar and his entourage set sail from Leghorn for the Holy Land. Because of the epidemics in Jerusalem and Jaffa, he decided to establish a temporary yeshiva in Akko and then moved it to Peki'in.

In 1742, he visited Rabbi Abulafia. The latter tried to persuade Rabbi Benattar to establish his yeshiva in Teveria; but shortly afterwards Rabbi Benattar set out for Jerusalem and established his yeshiva there.

The meeting of these two great sages in Teveria was viewed with metaphysical symbolism. Here were two of the saintly men of the generation meeting together in the city which was destined to be the scene of the redemption of Israel. The meeting of two such holy souls in a holy city during a period of messianic expectation could not go unnoticed. Indeed, the symbolism of this confluence of personalities, time, and place was not lost on the two sages themselves.

The story handed down of the meeting of Rabbis Abulafia and Benattar describes the events as follows. Upon arriving in Teveria, Rabbi Benattar went to the study hall of Rabbi Abulafia. The edlerly rabbi of Teveria was surrounded by students. When he realized that Rabbi Benattar had entered the room, he rose to his feet as a sign of honor to his distinguished guest. The two of them engaged in a talmudic discussion. Rabbi Benattar then asked Rabbi Abulafia to accompany him to visit the grave of Rabbi Akiba. As they entered the cave where Rabbi Akiba was buried, Rabbi Benattar began to cry. He lamented the fact that Rabbi Akiba and Bar Kokhba had tried to lead the Jewish people to redemption from the hands of the Romans. Rabbi Akiba had believed that Bar Kokhba was the Messiah. And yet, though two such great souls had joined forces for the salvation of Israel, the moment of redemption was lost. The Jewish rebellion was crushed, and both Rabbi Akiba and Bar Kokhba lost their lives in the process. Rabbi Benattar and Rabbi Abulafia wept together. They told each other that both of them would die within a year. And so it was. Rabbi Benattar died in the summer of 1743 and Rabbi Abulafia in the spring of 1744. [9]

While Rabbi Abulafia pinned his messianic hopes on the rebuilding of Teveria, Rabbi Benattar saw the establishment of a yeshiva in Jerusalem as his mission. After his meeting with Rabbi Abulafia, Rabbi Benattar went to Jerusalem and opened his yeshiva. One division of the school was for young scholars, and one was for very advanced scholars. The yeshiva was characterized not only by serious intellectual study, but by devotion to piety. The students of the advanced division of the yeshiva studied the mysteries of the kabbalah. Rabbi Benattar and his students (one of whom was Rabbi Hayyim Yosef David Azulai) prayed each night for the redemption of Israel and for the well-being of the Jews of the diaspora. In short, Rabbi Benattar headed an enclave of pietists who eagerly awaited messianic redemption.

Rabbi Benattar's fame spread throughout the Jewish world. His Torah commentary, Or ha-Hayyim, became an instant classic. It was popular not only among Sephardim but among Ashkenazim—especially among the Hassidim. Rabbi Israel Baal Shem Tov, the founder of Hassidism, is said to have stated that Rabbi Benattar had the soul of King David.[10] A popular legend has it that Rabbi Israel Baal Shem Tov and Rabbi Benattar dreamed about each other on the same night and both received the same message: if they were to meet in the land of Israel, the Messiah would come. The two of them were of such a high spiritual level that their meeting in the Holy Land would bring on the redemption of Israel. It was after this dream that Rabbi Benattar set out for Israel from Morocco. The Baal Shem Tov also set out from Russia—but was unable to complete his trip to Israel. The two, therefore, never met—except in the dream.

A story was told that the brother-in-law of the Baal Shem Tov was planning to travel to the land of Israel. The Hassidic master told him to go to Jerusalem and to study in both of Rabbi Benattar's yeshivot—the regualr one, and the advanced one which studied kabbalah. When the brother-in-law arrived in Jerusalem, he asked Rabbi Benattar for permission to study in the yeshiva. After a week of attending classes in the regular yeshiva, he inquired about the advanced academy. The students were amazed that he knew anything about it, since its existence had been kept secret. Even many of the students in the regular yeshiva did not know about the school's advanced division. Unable to elicit a response from the students, the visitor asked Rabbi Benattar himself if he could study in the advanced program. Surprised that he knew about it, Rabbi Benattar told him that he would be picked up after midnight and brought to the yeshiva. The Baal Shem Tov's brother-in-law studied there for three sessions but was not admitted for a fourth. The reason he was told was that he had failed to serve Rabbi Benattar actively. He was readmitted when he found a way to help Rabbi Benattar, again studied there for three days, and again was not admitted on the fourth. When he asked Rabbi Benattar for an explanation, the sage replied that he had not been aware of his connection with Rabbi Israel Baal Shem Tov. Rabbi Benattar said he had only learned of this fact because he knew the Baal Shem Tov through "the upper worlds." The visitor, he stated, would no longer be admitted to the yeshiva, since one who could study with the Baal Shem Tov needed no other teacher.[11]

The saintliness of Rabbi Benattar, and his profound wisdom in halakhah and kabbalah, won him a wide following. He deeply hoped that by settling in Israel and establishing a yeshiva he would attract many to the Holy Land. More than this, he hoped that his actions would help make the Jewish people worthy of receiving the Messiah. A strong anti-Sabbatean, Rabbi Benattar nevertheless fostered an active expectation of the imminent arrival of the messianic salvation.

The Shadarim

During the eighteenth century, many of the rabbis of the Holy Land devoted part of their lives to serving as emissaries to the communities in the diaspora. They were known as "shadarim," a word created from the initials of the Hebrew term *sheluhei de-rabbanan*, "emissaries of the rabbis." Indeed, the list of sages who served as shadarim is long and impressive, and includes men who were the leading figures of their generations.[12]

As was indicated earlier, the emissaries strove to maintain the link between diaspora Jewry and the Holy Land. They visited the diaspora communities to collect money, but also to teach and preach love for the land of Israel and its centrality in Jewish religious life. They provided halakhic guidance; they preached to the public; they gave encouragement to the local rabbinic leadership.

Shadarim served as transmitters of Torah knowledge, bringing the insights of the scholars of Israel to the diaspora; and collecting the teachings of diaspora scholars and disseminating them in Israel as well as in the various communities they visited. For example, Rabbi Hayyim Yosef David Azulai became a world-renowned rabbinic resource. On his travels as an emissary for the Holy Land, he consulted whatever rare books and manuscripts were to be found in the communities he visited. He copied important material. In his many published works, he incorporated textual and conceptual information derived from these generally inaccessable sources, thereby expanding the world of Torah knowledge to a broader audience of scholars.[13]

Shadarim also served as models of selflessness and faithfulness. For example, Rabbi Amram Ben Diouan traveled as an emissary to Jewish communities in North Africa. He won great respect for his learning and piety. While in Morocco, his son—who was accompanying him—fell seriously ill. The situation seemed hopeless, with the young man apparently destined to die. Rabbi Ben Diouan offered a prayer, asking God to restore his son to health and volunteering to contribute to the youth whatever years were still left to him for his own life. And so it was. Rabbi Amram Ben Diouan died in exile; and his son was blessed with a complete recovery. Word of this happening spread quickly. The rabbi was buried in Asjen, Morocco, and his grave became the object of veneration. Each year, a *hiloula*—a special prayer event—was held at his tomb. Numerous pilgrims traveled to the grave of Rabbi Ben Diouan in recognition of his holiness, his self-sacrifice, and his power of prayer. [14]

The shadarim strove to strengthen traditional religious life among the Jews of the exile, since a diminution in religious observance and commitment would lead to assimilation and delay the coming of the Messiah. We have discussed previously the attempts of Rabbis Hagiz and Azulai to stem the tendency among some Western Sephardim to deemphasize the national aspects of Judaism. Shadarim also found themselves battling against reforms and innovations in religious practice among diaspora Jews. On one occasion, for instance, a French newspaper published a report to the effect that rabbinic leaders in Italy had agreed to annul certain religious prohibitions and institute various reforms. Rabbis Azulai, Ephraim Navon, Hayyim Barukh Saporta, Yehudah Leon, and other eminent shadarim threw their authority into a forceful campaign against the reforms. When it turned out that the newspaper story had been based on an unfounded rumor, they expressed their support for the Italian rabbis who had rejected the possibility of innovating reforms in Judaism. [15]

Aside from the practical concerns which motivated the shadarim to spend many years wandering in the lands of the exile, we must also try to understand the less obvious psychological and spiritual motivations. In a sense, these messengers who worked for the redemption of Israel imposed upon themselves a period (or periods) of exile. Their lives were caught between the two themes of exile and redemption. While in Israel, they recognized painfully that the redemption had not yet come. They wanted the Jews of the diaspora to participate with them in the restoration of Israel. They grew restless. They needed to go into the exile to bring the message of Israel to their coreligionists. But once in the diaspora, the shadarim longed for the Holy Land. They sensed the deracination of the Jews in exile. Wandering in the lands of the diaspora created within them a desire to return to Israel. Their wanderings were an expression of their abiding love for the Holy Land; and also a reflection of their desire for self-inflicted exile and penitence. The shadarim were torn by the dissonance between their messianic vision and the nonmessianic reality in which they lived.

An example in point was Rabbi Moshe Israel (ca. 1670–1740). Born in Israel, probably in Jerusalem, he studied with the great scholars of the Holy Land. One of his main teachers was Rabbi Abraham Yitzhaki, author of a book of responsa entitled *Zera Abraham,* and an opponent of the Sabbatean movement. Rabbi Israel's wife, Hannah, was the daughter of Rabbi Moshe Habib head of the rabbinical court in Jerusalem.

Rabbi Israel served as an emissary in North Africa, the Middle East, and Europe. His vast erudition and genuine piety made favorable impressions on the communities he visited. As was the practice of other shadarim, Rabbi Israel taught and lectured, and also responded to questions on Jewish law. In 1710, a student in Morocco compiled notes on Israel's lectures and circulated them in manuscript form. Israel authored three volumes of responsa under the title *Masat Moshe,* and was considered an important rabbinic authority of his generation.[16]

On one of his missions, Rabbi Israel visited the Jewish community on the island of Rhodes. Although the community there was relatively small, it was a significant landmark in the Sephardic diaspora. It boasted learned scholars and successful merchants, and was an important stopover for pilgrims traveling from Europe and Turkey to Israel. The members of the community were very taken with Rabbi Israel and offered him the position of chief rabbi. Indeed, they persuaded him to take a vow that he would accept the post and never again leave Rhodes. Rabbi Israel decided to take the vow, with the proviso that he could first return to the land of Israel and settle his affairs there. This was granted. He returned to Rhodes and assumed the post of chief rabbi in 1715.

Rabbi Israel had many advantages in Rhodes. He was generally well regarded and respected by the community. He apparently made a good living. He was able to devote time to rabbinic scholarship—teaching, preaching, writing. His international reputation enabled him to conduct correspondence with important scholars and laymen in many communities outside Rhodes. In short, he had what seemed to be an ideal rabbinic position.

But love of the Holy Land burned within him. The yearning to wander from place to place for the benefit of the communities in Israel could not be suppressed. After twelve years as chief rabbi, Rabbi Israel felt the need to leave Rhodes. But he had taken a vow never to leave the island. He wrote to the leading rabbis in Istanbul, asking them to annul it. His basic premise was that he had taken the vow under false pretenses. He had based it on the assumption that all the members of the community would respectfully follow his decisions as chief rabbi. But he reported to the rabbis of Istanbul that in several instances his authority had not been properly respected. He claimed that he had not envisioned such distressing circumstances when he had vowed not to leave Rhodes. Moreover, it was unrealistic for the community to have bound him to the island; after all, they should have assumed that he would have the right to leave for the sake of performing a mitzvah, or simply for a brief vacation. The rabbis agreed to annul the vow. Shortly thereafter, Rabbi Moshe Israel left Rhodes to resume his work as an emissary for the Holy Land.

Rabbi Israel's ostensible reasons for justifying the annulment of his vow are problematic. In fact, he must surely have been aware of the vow's consequences from the outset. Moreover, the fact that the community did not want to free him of the vow is itself an indication that they wanted him to remain as their chief rabbi.

The real explanation of his desire to leave probably related to tensions within his own soul. As his lifetime of traveling indicates, he was a wanderer. His deep-seated desire to be an emissary for the Holy Land drove him on. It must have been painful for him to have remained tied to the community of Rhodes for twelve years. Indeed, one might say that his departure from the island was inevitable.[17]

The wanderings of the shadarim reflected the spiritual restlessness of religiously sensitive people. Realistic hopes of redemption and return to the land of Israel diminished, but the dream of redemption and return had to be maintained. One might say that the shadarim represented a profound but sad messianism, blending faith in the possibility of miraculous redemption with despair at the long delay in the arrival of the Messiah.

Faith and Despair

As people gradually recovered from their disillusionment with the Sabbatean messianic promises, they felt as though they had been robbed of hope. Western Sephardim tried to see their growing acceptance in European society as an alternative to miraculous redemption. If the Messiah was not coming right away, they might as well make the best of their situation in the diaspora. They strove to adapt to the societies in which they lived, and looked forward to attaining growing political, economic, religious, and social freedom.

The Sephardim in Moslem lands, on the other hand, had no expectation of becoming equal citizens in their countries of residence. Moslem society had sharp lines dividing the status of Moslems and non-Moslems. Jews lived in those lands but could not realistically hope to be considered indigenous to them. Jewish communities were relatively autonomous islands in the vast sea of the Moslem world.

During the late sixteenth and early seventeenth centuries, the Sephardim of the Ottoman Empire saw their situation deteriorate. The Sabbatai Sevi debacle had scarred them spiritually. It had also hurt them economically, since in their messianic frenzy they had neglected to attend to their long-range business interests. Beyond these problems, the Ottoman Empire itself was undergoing severe struggles. It had suffered serious military defeats. Its economy was plagued by periods of high inflation and currency devaluations. The Ottoman Empire steadily lost ground economically to the increasingly industrialized centers in Christian Europe. And, of course, it was the European nations which were establishing trade routes and colonies in the New World, bringing to themselves considerable wealth. The Mediterranean Sea, dominated by the Ottoman Empire, now became secondary to the Atlantic Ocean, controlled by the countries of Europe. As the Ottoman Empire declined, its inhabitants—including the Jews— were dramatically affected. Many of the former merchant princes were reduced to poverty. Indeed, poverty was to become a basic feature of the Sephardic communities of the Ottoman Empire throughout the eighteenth and nineteenth centuries. Certainly, some Jews continued to engage quite successfully in large-scale business activity; there was also a middle class of shopkeepers and merchants. But large numbers of Jews lived under very difficult economic conditions; poverty was widespread.[18]

The Jews of the Ottoman Empire, then, were in a situation which naturally bred despair. They were practically powerless politically. Their economic status had declined. Their messianic hopes had been dashed. The future seemed bleak.

The motif of acceptance of God's decrees gained predominance. If Jews were unable to change their condition, they could at least accept it as being God's will. Their sufferings were an atonement for their sins; their exile provided them with an opportunity to refine themselves spiritually. A willing acceptance of *yisurin*, God's chastisements, was a sign of religious greatness. Rabbi Moshe Hagiz taught, for example, that Jews should accept humiliation and oppression with a calm spirit, not even considering the possibility of taking revenge or fighting back. Rather, one should repent for his own sins, asking God to grant him and the Jewish people atonement.[19] This attitude planted within the Jews a deep passivity. It reflected a feeling of powerlessness in this world, of total dependence on the absolute dictates of God. Nothing could be done to alter the Jewish situation except to pray and seek atonement for sins. This viewpoint manifested itself a century later when Rabbi Michael Yaacov Israel—descendant of Rabbi Moshe Israel and also a chief rabbi of Rhodes—attempted to explain to his community the reason for the malicious blood libel that took place there in 1840. The blood libel involved some non-Jews who had fabricated a lie that Jews had murdered a Christian child in order to drink his blood for Passover. Leaders of the Jewish community in Rhodes, including Rabbi Israel, were actually imprisoned and tortured. Happily, the libel was proven to be false and the Jews were released. In his sermon on the Shabbat prior to Passover, Rabbi Israel explained that this terrible suffering had befallen the Jews of Rhodes because of their own sins! The tragedy was a signal from God that they needed to repent. It was actually intended to benefit the Jews, by prodding them to turn to the Lord. Rabbi Israel pointed out that the Jews were powerless and oppressed: their only hope was to turn to Heaven for assistance.[20]

The tone of powerlessness reflected itself in the rabbinic writings of the time. It was common for rabbis to lament the degradation of the Jews and to pray for the speedy arrival of the Messiah. Rabbi Eliyahu Israel, a son of Rabbi Moshe Israel, for example, generally concluded his sermons with a prayer for redemption, for the restoration of the Jewish people in the land of Israel under the rule of a king from the house of David.[21] Rabbi Abraham Israel, another son of Rabbi Moshe Israel, who also served as an emissary for the Holy Land, mourned the desperate condition of the Jews. He asked God how long He would wait before bringing salvation to His chosen people.[22]

The hope of return to Israel, of messianic redemption, was the flickering hope which sustained the Jews during these difficult

·7·

The Folk Mind and Spirit

The deterioration in the conditions of life in the Ottoman Empire had a variety of consequences. For one thing, wealth and prosperity were now the blessings of a privileged few; the masses of people were compelled to work long and hard just to eke out a living. It was difficult for laborers to earn enough to support their wives and children. It became a luxury for children to remain in school once they were old enough to find some kind of employment. Their education was therefore limited both in Jewish and general subjects. They learned how to read their prayers in Hebrew; they studied some Torah and Jewish law, rabbinic homilies, Psalms. They also learned the rudiments of math and other subjects that would be necessary for them to earn a living. Most students never mastered the Hebrew language, nor did they study formally the language of the land in which they lived. Their native language in Turkey, the Balkans, Israel, and parts of North Africa was Judeo-Spanish. Many of the Jews in Arab countries spoke Judeo-Arabic. Some communities in Greece spoke Judeo-Greek.

With the decline in the comprehension of the Hebrew language, the masses were cut off from direct access to the classic sources of Jewish religious and intellectual life. With the limited elementary education available to them, their knowledge of science, world history, literature, and other general subjects was constricted. Their intellectual horizons diminished.

To be sure, there still existed an active and creative intellectual elite. Yet, to a large extent, even this elite group underwent a constriction of intellectual endeavor. The study of science and philosophy—at one time characteristic of Sephardic intellectuals—declined. Rather, Sephardic scholars now devoted themselves almost exclusively to rabbinic scholarship—halakhah, kabbalah, homiletics, biblical commentary. In a sense, rabbinic

101

study became more abstract, more convoluted, more removed from universal human concerns. Intellectual life was turning in on itself, digging ever deeper into a more limited range of subjects.

A reflection of this tendency may be found in the homiletic literature created by Sephardic rabbis during the eighteenth century. For example, books of *derashot* (sermons) were published by the rabbis of Rhodes throughout the century, including works by Rabbis Moshe Israel, Eliyahu Israel, Moshe Israel II, Yedidiah Shemuel Tarica, and Ezra Malki.[1] The sermons collected in these works were characterized by vast erudition, amazing mastery of the entire range of rabbinic scholarship; but at the same time they were generally tedious and uninspiring. The authors went to great lengths to exposit on complicated passages, to reconcile seeming contradictions within rabbinic texts; they offered ingenious solutions and reconciliations, drawing on a wide array of biblical and rabbinic sources.

Sermons were generally given only on special occasions and on specific Sabbaths, not each week. This may explain why they were lengthy. However, many of them were so long and so complicated that it is difficult to imagine an audience that could have sat through them with profit. Only the most highly educated and trained Talmud students could even have hoped to follow the discussion. The purpose of a sermon, though, is to inspire the congregation to greater knowledge and observance of Torah. If the audience could not understand the sermon, obviously the preacher had failed in his primary goal.

It seems, therefore, that the authors of these sermons were aiming their words not at the masses, but at the intellectual elite. It is unlikely that most of the Jewish population would have been interested in purchasing or reading the books of sermons. Only scholars would find them of interest and benefit.

A similar observation might be made concerning the style of rabbinic responsa. Rabbis of the eighteenth century often responded to questions of Jewish law with responsa written in a relatively complicated style. Rabbi Moshe Israel, for example, wrote lengthy responsa in which he brought in many sources and side issues. In contrast, the great responsa writers of the sixteenth century, such as Rabbi David Ibn Abi Zimra and Rabbi Shemuel de Medina, wrote with much greater lucidity and brevity.[2]

Just at the time when the masses needed clear and simple instruction in the truths of Judaism, many rabbis became more introspective. They turned their talents to deep and comprehensive erudition, as though trying to escape from the growing ignorance that was spreading among the Jewish population.

On the other hand, there were serious attempts to reach the populace with works they could understand and appreciate. The most important and lasting contribution in this field was initiated by Rabbi Yaacov Huli in his *Me'am Lo'ez*.[3]

Rabbi Yaacov Huli

Rabbi Yaacov Huli (1689–1732) was born and raised in Jerusalem, where he received an excellent rabbinic education. When he went to Istanbul in 1714, his profound and expansive rabbinic knowledge won him the respect of the great scholars of that city. Rabbi Yehudah Rosanes, chief rabbi of the community and a world-renowned scholar, appointed the young Rabbi Huli to his rabbinical court. When Rabbi Rosanes died some years later, it was Yaacov Huli who compiled and edited his master's classic commentary on Maimonides' *Mishneh Torah*, known as *Mishneh le-Melekh*.

Rabbi Huli was disturbed by the low level of Jewish instruction available to the working class and the poor. If they had no access to the Hebrew Bible and rabbinic texts, how were they to be fully observant Jews? How were they to know what the Torah required of them? The proliferation of scholarly rabbinic texts in Hebrew did nothing to imporve the spiritual conditon of those whose academic training was deficient.

Rabbi Huli conceived the idea of producing a comprehensive work in Judeo-Spanish for the benefit of the Sephardic public. Entitled *Me'am Lo'ez*, it was framed as a commentary on the Torah. The first volume, published in 1730, dealt with the Book of Genesis. In this work, Rabbi Huli provided classic rabbinic interpretations and commentaries on the biblical verses. Laws and customs, rabbinic homilies, and ethical lessons were interspersed throughout the work. The book was written in a popular, engaging style. Indeed, Rabbi Huli worried that it would be used merely for entertainment rather than for serious Torah study. As a work in the vernacular, it was available to a wide audience. It was written in a language and style which they could understand, appreciate, and enjoy. The *Me'am Lo'ez* was something of an encyclopedia of biblical and rabbinic learning, so that those who studied it derived a wide array of information and inspiration.

Rabbi Huli intended to publish similar volumes for all the books of the Torah. He did complete Genesis and much of Exodus. After his untimely death at the age of forty-three, other rabbis continued the work in the spirit of Rabbi Huli, completing the Five Books of Moses and other biblical books as well.

The *Me'am Lo'ez* was an immediate success. It went into numerous editions and was read enthusiastically by a large audience. Rabbi Huli had constructed the work so that people would be able to study the weekly Torah portion from it. The book was used in this manner by families and study groups, and in synagogues. By studying one portion of the *Me'am Lo'ez* each week, readers could hope to gain a comprehensive view of the Torah and its teachings within one year. They would then have the basis of knowledge by which they could conduct themselves as religiously informed Jews. As they studied the material year after year, the knowledge would become deeply ingrained within them, helping them to lead proper, pious lives according to the Jewish tradition.

Rabbi Huli did not think of the *Me'am Lo'ez* as an original work. Rather, he viewed himself as a compiler of many and diverse classic Jewish sources. He was pleased to be a popularizer, bringing comprehensive knowledge to the public in a lucid and pleasant style. But his approach was indeed original. It was he who decided what material to include and what to exclude; how to present it in a lively manner; how to capture the interest of his readers and speak to their everyday needs. In many ways, the *Me'am Lo'ez* mirrored the spiritual life of the Judeo-Spanish-speaking world of the time.

Rabbi Huli introduced his work with a presentation of four fundamental principles of Judaism: (1) that God created the world, guides it, rewards righteousness, and punishes wickedness; (2) that God gave the people of Israel both the Written Torah and the Oral Torah, which together teach Jews their responsibilities; (3) that God commanded us to love our neighbors as ourselves; (4) that each person must regularly contemplate his own mortality, realizing that it is foolish to follow the ways of sinfulness. Rabbi Huli urged his readers to contemplate these four principles; in this way they would attain righteousness and avoid sin.

The *Me'am Lo'ez* spoke to the common person. It was undergirded with themes to which the reader could readily relate. It is constructive to consider some of the main themes which Rabbi Huli wove through his work.

Obviously, Rabbi Huli stressed the importance of Torah study, the foundation of Jewish life. God created the world on condition that the people of Israel would study Torah and fulfill its commandments. If they fail to do so, the world will return to chaos and void (Genesis 1:31). Jews must find sufficient time each day to study Torah and not devote themselves entirely to their business (Exodus 20:1). The Sabbath is an ideal time for Torah study; since one may not engage in business, there is absolutely no excuse for not engaging in Torah study. Those who are unable to study by themselves can go to the synagogue and listen to the teachings of the rabbi (Exodus 20:1). Studying should be exciting and creative. The commandment to be fruitful and multiply also applies to Torah study. After learning and mastering the text, then one "gives birth" to novel ideas and interpretations; one who does not do so is like a barren tree that produces no fruit (Genesis 1:28). The Torah is very profound, having many levels of meaning. Although great mystics have penetrated deeply into the mysteries of the Torah, the average person cannot attain such knowledge. Yet, it is important to realize that such knowledge exists, and that one's own accomplishments are imperfect (Genesis 36:39). Rabbi Huli noted that one should devote time not only to the study of Halakhah, but also to aggadah and midrash, the nonlegal portions of the Talmud, rabbinic homilies and interpretations. Such study deepens one's spirituality and attachment to the Jewish way of life (Genesis 12:4).

Rabbi Huli's work reflected the attitude of resignation toward the non-Jewish rulers who had power over the Jews. Being in exile, the Jews were obligated to accept humbly their servile position, recognizing that this was God's will. A reed is flexible and therefore can withstand strong winds. By bending its head it is able to survive. Likewise, the Jews in exile must bend their heads before the power of the nations. They should be as quiet and inconspicuous as possible (Genesis 15:11).

Rabbinic literature contains considerable discussion concerning the opening verses of chapter 32 of Genesis. Jacob was bringing his family and flocks back to the land of Canaan. He feared that his brother Esau would attack him and murder his family. To preclude this eventuality, he sent messengers to Esau with lavish gifts. He humbled himself by referring to Esau as his master *(adoni)* eight times. Some rabbinic sources took Jacob to task for his servility, saying that he was later punished by God for it. He should rather have shown greater strength of character and self-respect. He should not have humbled himself to his godless brother. On the other hand, some rabbinic sources praised Jacob, arguing that someone who was in a position of weakness had to use diplomatic skills—including humbling himself in the presence of those with power. According to this view, Jacob was entirely correct in being submissive to Esau and in showing him honor. It was simply a diplomatic strategy utilized for the sake of avoiding confrontation. Significantly, Rabbi Huli only cited the latter opinion. He did not mention the sources which condemned Jacob's deferential behavior. Obviously, he felt that when Jews were subject to the power of others, subservience was their best defense.

Rabbi Huli was writing for a popular audience. Many of his readers were poor and intellectually unsophisticated. He wanted the Me'am Lo'ez to instill within them feelings of self-worth, a belief that they could serve God admirably in spite of their difficult condition. He often stressed the values of sincerity and righteousness, since even simple people could attain them. Indeed, Rabbi Huli suggested that these values were more important than intellectual achievements. The Bible did not praise the prophets for their wisdom or scholarship but for their moral qualities. Noah was righteous and upright; Moses was humble. God commanded people to be righteous (Exodus 18:24–25).

God wants Jews to serve Him with a pure heart. One who has a good heart will be forgiven whatever occasional sins he may commit. But if one has an evil heart, even the good deeds he performs will be blemished (Genesis 14:13).

The Me'am Lo'ez appealed to the masses because it was sympathetic to the poor and downtrodden. Rabbi Huli drew on traditional Jewish sources which extolled humility and honest labor. He reminded his readers that life was full of surprises. He who is rich today may be impoverished tomorrow. On the other hand, he who is poor may suddenly become wealthy. Our level of material prosperity is ultimately dependent on God's will. Although we are all under the obligation of working to try to earn a living, yet it is God who actually determines how much income we will have. We should accept our economic status as God-given; regardless of our financial level, we should devote ourselves to being righteous and therefore worthy of God's blessings.

Rabbi Huli explained that there was no shame in working for

an honest living. One should not think it beneath his dignity to work at a craft or any other honest occupation, and should not attempt to live in a style beyond his means (Genesis 12:4). When our forefather Jacob prayed, he asked only for bread and clothing, not for any luxuries. Truly pious people did not seek superfluous things, but were happy with the basic necessities which God provided them (Genesis 28:22).

The wealthy are not more important than the poor in God's eyes. An earthly king favors the rich and powerful, not allowing the poor to enter his royal palace. But God, the King of kings, treats rich and poor equally. In many cases, He is even more responsive to the prayers of the poor because they are recited with tears and sincere emotion (Genesis 19:27).

Those who have received the blessing of wealth are required to share it with the poor. Just as the sun shares its light with the moon, so the rich must share their blessings with the poor (Genesis 1:19). A wealthy person should not reject or ignore his impoverished relatives (Genesis 13:14). Rabbi Huli reminded his readers that it was particularly important to support the poor who were living in the land of Israel. The poor of the Holy Land had precedence even over the poor of one's own town (Genesis 14:22). By giving charity, one thereby showed himself worthy to have been blessed by God (Genesis 14:20).

The wealthy needed to realize that moral virtue was far more significant than material possessions. To be considered truly wealthy, one must be compassionate, humble, upright, and merciful. Those who lack these qualities are not wealthy in the true sense of the term (Genesis 18:1).

Rabbi Huli discussed the virtue of humility in various contexts. He noted that God Himself was the role model of humility; He began the Torah with the word *bereishit* rather than with His own name. According to a traditional interpretation, the word *bereishit* referred to the people of Israel. Thus, God gave precedence to His people over His own name. If God was humble enough to mention Israel even before mentioning Himself, so humans should certainly learn to give precedence to others, even those who are thought to be less important (Genesis 1:1).

God created Adam from dust, not from gold (Genesis 2:7). He created a vast universe. One who looks at the sky at night and contemplates the countless stars cannot help but be overwhelmed by the grandeur and power of God. He is humbled by his own smallness in the universe. This feeling of humility leads one to serve God with devotion and purity (Genesis 2:7).

Humility is the foundation from which we can attain every other good moral quality. It is the first step in the proper service of the Almighty (Genesis 13:14). The heroes of the Bible were characterized by humility. Abraham said: "I am dust and ashes." Moses and Aaron said: "What are we?" King David said: "I am a worm and not a man." In contrast, the heathens were arrogant, thinking themselves great and powerful. The Torah teaches that humility is virtuous and will ultimately be rewarded (Genesis 14:14).

Those in positions of power are especially obligated to remind themselves to remain humble. They should not allow their position to generate pride or vanity within them. According to rabbinic tradition, King David had a coin struck. On one side was a depiction of a tower, representing a fortress he had built. On the other side was a depiction of a shepherd's crook and pouch. Even as king, David did not forget or hide his humble beginnings as a shepherd (Genesis 12:4). Even when a person has great status and is like the "stars of the sky," he must stay humble as the "sand on the seashore" (Genesis 22:18).

A person should not consider himself too lofty or dignified to serve others. For example, Moses served his people with outstanding devotion, ignoring the fact that he was their leader. He even served as a waiter at a feast in honor of his father-in-law, Jethro (Exodus 18:12). In this, he followed the example set by Abraham, who served the three guests who visited him. Indeed, Abraham's humility won him the respect of the people of Heth. They said to Abraham: "You are a prince of God among us." That is, they felt that although Abraham was a prince, he was nevertheless "among" them; he did not act as though he were greater than they (Genesis 23:4). The ultimate lesson is that one who is small in this world will be great in the world-to-come; and one who considers himself great in this world will be small in the world-to-come (Genesis 23:1).

A facet of humility is that one should not try to show off his piety and righteousness. On the contrary, one should walk humbly with God, keeping his piety as private as possible. Rabbi Huli reminded his readers that one is allowed to bow only in designated places during the silent devotion, the Amidah. To bow more frequently would be a sign of presumptuousness and false piety. One should not do things which will make him appear to be more pious than other worshippers (Genesis 12:4). In a similar vein, if one is attending a kasher meal, he should eat the food served to him along with everyone else. This is especially true if Torah scholars are present and are eating the food. By not eating, one would appear to make himself more scrupulous and more pious than the scholars. This is not appropriate behavior (Genesis 21:33).

In this connection, an interesting story is told about Rabbi Huli himself. He once undertook a three-day fast as an act of piety and repentance. On the afternoon of the third day, when he had just about completed this strenuous period of fasting, he was obliged to visit the home of a friend. The host offered Rabbi Huli a cup of coffee. Not wanting to offend his host and not wanting to reveal that he was fasting, Rabbi Huli took the coffee and drank it. He later had to fast another three days to make up for having broken his fast with the coffee. Obviously, he felt it was better to break the fast than to let anyone know of his own private act of piety.[4]

A word should also be said about the messianic longings of Rabbi Huli. There is no conclusive evidence that he adhered to Sabbateanism, although he did quote authors who were followers of Sabbatai Sevi.[5] He lamented the pitiful condition in which the Jews lived in exile. In his introduction to Rabbi Rosanes' *Mishneh le-Melekh,* Rabbi Huli wrote a passage beseeching God to redeem the captive people of Israel by sending the Messiah. Like many of the Jews of his time and place, he was stirred by messianic hopes.

The work of Rabbi Huli reflected the midrashic/kabbalistic view of life which then predominated among the Sephardim in Moslem lands. Philosophic inquiry was no longer a vital part of the intellectual life of the community. The emphasis was on an absolute commitment to observing the halakhah in all its details. Kabbalah was recognized to have inestimable value and was a necessary ingredient in religious life. The willing acceptance of God's decrees with equanimity was encouraged, engendering a relative passivity. The predominant worldview emphasized loyalty to rabbis and the rabbinic tradition. The messianic hope was expressed longingly, wishfully.

It should be noted that Rabbi Huli, while the most significant author who wrote in the Judeo-Spanish vernacular for the benefit of the masses, was not the only one who tried to meet their spiritual needs. The eighteenth century witnessed a striking increase in the number of publications in Judeo-Spanish, including texts for children, translations of Hebrew classics, and even a history of the Ottoman rulers. In 1739, the first volume of a Bible with a Judeo-Spanish translation appeared in Istanbul; subsequent volumes appeared in later years. The publication of Judeo-Spanish works continued through the early twentieth century.[6]

Folk Wisdom and Intellectual Wisdom

In considering the intellectual and spiritual life of any human society, one must not ignore the people's folk culture. While individual thinkers and authors may create cultural monuments that are identifiable generations later, the masses of people live and die without leaving such monuments. The names of most of them are forgotten within a generation after their deaths. They write no immortal books, achieve no lasting fame. Nevertheless, the anonymous mass of people form the overwhelming bulk of any society. The few outstanding figures who manage to create lasting cultural monuments are only able to do so in context of the society in which they live. Their works should be seen in relationship to the values permeating their people.

The attitudes and thoughts of the Sephardic masses may be gleaned from folk literature, customs, popular sayings, and songs. To an important extent, the folk wisdom of the Sephardim was transmitted and preserved by women.

During the sixteenth century, several women distinguished themselves for their cultural contributions. Among them were Dona Gracia Nasi and Bienvenida Abravanel. However, these women did not gain fame for their own creativity, but because they made it possible for men to discuss ideas and publish books. They were patronesses rather than creators of cultural works. The role of women in public intellectual life was small, and during the seventeenth and eighteenth centuries it almost vanished. The fact was that the desired role of women in society was to be good wives and mothers, not to be scholars or intellectuals. Girls received education more rudimentary than that received by most boys. Few, if any, had the opportunity to pursue advanced study in a formal setting.

The absence of women from the formal intellectual life of their societies does not mean that they played no role. On the contrary, they often had a profound influence on what their husbands and sons thought and did.

Women played the dominant role in the preservation of Sephardic folk culture. It was they who sang and transmitted the Judeo-Spanish ballads, who told Judeo-Spanish folktales to their children, who peppered their conversations with witty and humorous Judeo-Spanish proverbs. The folk culture which they maintained and reflected was a vital part of the intellectual and cultural life of their people. Though the women—like most of the men—were content to fulfill their role without gaining public recognition or lasting fame, Sephardic intellectual and spiritual life cannot be understood without taking their anonymous contributions into consideration.

Folk wisdom and more formal intellectual wisdom are related; indeed, they are often intertwined. The following examples illustrate this idea.

Sephardic folk culture valued the quality of respect for the common person, the worth of the individual. A popular Judeo-Spanish proverb states: *el rey es con la gente,* "the king is with the people." That is, true royalty is not characterized by haughtiness and aloofness; rather, a real king will associate with and be part of the people he rules. Another proverb teaches: *el diamente briya, pero al fin y al cavo es una piedra,* "a diamond glitters, but in the final analysis it is only a rock." In other words, a wealthy person and a poor person are essentially the same; we should not be deceived by external glitter.

These popular sentiments found expression in the literary creations of the time. The *Me'am Lo'ez,* for example, cited the rabbinic teaching describing Moses receiving the Ten Commandments. Originally, God gave the Ten Commandments to Moses in a dramatic episode. Moses ascended Mount Sinai alone. The people of Israel surrounded the mountain with great anticipation. There was thunder and lightning and the sound of rams horns. The voice of God was heard. Yet when Moses found the children of Israel dancing around the golden calf, he threw the tablets of the law from his hands and they were crushed. Later, Moses ascended the mountain a second time. This time there was no public fanfare, no miraculous sounds and lights. God told Moses that he himself would have to carve out the stone on which the Ten Commandments would be inscribed. The second set of the tablets of the law—received by Moses alone and through his own hard labor—was preserved. The first tablets were given with much ado, and yet they were destroyed. The second tablets were given privately and quietly, and yet they survived. This teaches that the really lasting things in life are often done by individuals in privacy, through their own exertions. Things done with much publicity are not as permanent.[7] This interpretation conveys the folk respect for the individual who works quietly, without public fame or glory.

This concept was also manifested in the teachings of Rabbi Yitzhak Luria, whose ideas gained a wide following in the Sephardic world. A central theme in Rabbi Luria's system of Kabbalah was *tikkun*, "correction." That is, each Jew participates in the correction of the world by redeeming sparks of holiness and lessening the forces of impurity. By performing mitzvot, Jews are thus playing a major role in preserving the cosmos. Each Jew, regardless of his degree of wealth or wisdom or social status, is able to help in the correction of the universe.[8]

This attitude fostered compassion and sympathy for others. Each person deserved respect—or at least deserved to be judged charitably. After all, who but God knew the true spiritual worth of a person?

The Sephardic folk spirit maintained a sense of pride in the individual. A proverb says: *basta mi nombre que es Abravanel,* "my name is enough; it is Abravanel." That is, even though the individual Sephardic Jew may have been reduced economically, socially, and educationally, he still had pride in his illustrious ancestry. Some Sephardim had a notion that they were descended from the aristocracy of ancient Judea. Though their actual living conditions were bad, they considered themselves to be aristocrats who had temporarily fallen on hard times. Sephardic culture fostered respect and good manners.

Judaism had always taught the virtue of respecting the elderly. Sephardic culture was infused with this value, and it led to the development of a number of customs. For example, when an older relative was called to the Torah during synagogue services, all of his younger relatives would stand in his honor. It was common to kiss the hands of parents and grandparents in order to receive their blessings. Children would be named after their grandparents, who were generally alive to enjoy this custom. The first-born son and daughter would be named after the father's parents; the second-born son and daughter would be named after the mother's parents. Subsequent children would be named for other older family members, alternating between the father's and the mother's sides of the family.

Respect for rabbis and rabbinical scholars was also fostered. When the rabbi was called to read from the Torah, the congregants arose in his honor. They kissed his hand, after which he would give his blessing to them. Sephardic communities were normally organized with a chief rabbi as their spiritual head. They generally sought his decisions in matters of Jewish law and turned to him for religious and personal instruction. Rabbis were respected especially for their saintliness and piety rather than purely for their intellectual attainments. Among the Jews of North Africa, reverence for the holiness of rabbis transcended their actual deaths. Annual pilgrimages were made to the graves of saintly sages. People would pray, asking God to be merciful to them for the merit of the pious rabbi whose grave was being venerated. The popular custom reflected the intellectual concept that saintliness is the ultimate virtue in life, bringing one closer to God.[9] Respect for rabbis was extended to include the sages of previous generations. Rabbi Hayyim Yosef David Azulai, for example, stressed the importance of having reverence for the rabbinical scholars of previous generations. "We have heard with our own ears from rabbis that individuals were punished for the disrespect they showed to books and their authors [of the past]. One who fears for his soul will measure his words when he engages in Torah debates; he should be careful in his writing."[10] He pointed out that many times those who criticized their predecessors were later shown to be wrong: the earlier authors had been correct. Therefore, one should not dispute earlier authorities unless very sure of himself; and should always show them respect, even when disagreeing with them.

Sephardic folk culture included Judeo-Spanish folk songs and love ballads. The songs dealt with heroes of royal pedigree, with romantic, even erotic, themes, and with life-cycle events, such as birth, marriage, and death. They drew on imagery from the beauties of nature. That such songs could be sung easily and naturally among very religious and traditional Jews reflects the broadness of attitude toward religion and life. The Sephardic folk mind did not separate religion from the beauties and pleasures of life. It accepted natural aspects of human concern in an easy going, non-introspective way. It was not afraid of seeming somewhat inconsistent.

An Ashkenazic rabbi, Simhah ben Joshua of Zalozhtsy (1711–1768), made a pilgrimage to the Holy Land with a group of ascetic Hassidim in 1764. On the same ship were many Sephardic Jews. It was the month of Ellul, the month prior to Rosh Hashanah, the Jewish New Year. Customarily, Jews devote this month to thought, prayers, and deeds of repentance. The rabbi noted, evidently with some surprise, that the pious Sephardim awoke each morning before daybreak in order to recite the *Selihot*, the penitential prayers. Yet, "during the day they eat and rejoice and are happy of heart."[11]

It should also be noted that Sephardic prayer services were chanted in a lively, optimistic tone. The congregation participated actively in the worship service, singing along with the leader of the prayers. Even on such solemn occasions as Rosh Hashanah and Yom Kippur, the High Holy Days, the general mood of the services was happy and confident.

Sephardic folk culture respected the value of humor in life. Judeo-Spanish proverbs were often humorous and witty. People who appeared glum were described as having *cara de Tisha b'Ab*, "a face like the Ninth of Ab," the mournful fast-day commemorating terrible tragedies that had befallen the Jewish people. This folk quality found expression in *Midrash Talpiot*, a noteworthy volume by an eighteenth-century sage, Rabbi Eliyahu ha-Cohen of Izmir. Citing a talmudic story about two jokesters who were said to have been granted eternal reward in the world-to-come, Rabbi ha-Cohen explained its message:

Anyone who is happy all his days thereby indicates the greatness of his trust in God. This is why they [the jokesters] were always happy. Even the evils which befell them they knew were brought on by their own sins. They were also happy that these *yisurin* [chastisements] cleansed them of their sins. This quality [of accepting life with happiness] is enough to give a person merit to have a place in the world-to-come; for great is trust [in the Lord], even if a person is not perfect in all other moral perfections.[12]

Sephardic culture also fostered an appreciation of aesthetics and gracefulness. Even family members and friends conducted their relationships with a certain decorum and respect. Foods served to guests on Sabbaths, festivals, and other special occasions were elaborate and delicious. The women took pride in their cooking skills and prepared meals that were not only tasty to the palate but pleasant in appearance and fragrance. Even the poorest women could make remarkable meals from simple and inexpensive ingredients. Sephardic homes were well acquainted with the fragrances of rose water, rutha (rue), jasmin, mint, and a variety of other herbs and spices. They were blessed with the colorful and multi-shaped fruits and vegetables characteristic of the sunny climate of the Mediterranean littoral.

Popular Sephardic folk culture was inherently tradition-minded and did not approve of nonconformity to existing social and religious patterns. Nevertheless, communities were not altogether monolithic. For the most part, however, the Sephardic communities maintained a spirit of tolerance. Extremism was rare and was not widely approved. A responsum of Rabbi Moshe Israel illustrates this point. A controversy arose concerning a popular Sephardic food, *yaprakes* (stuffed grape leaves). Some pietists protested that eating *yaprakes* should be forbidden according to Jewish law, since the grape leaves were infested with tiny bugs; and eating bugs is prohibited by the Torah. They argued that it was impossible to clean the leaves thoroughly enough to remove all the insects. One rabbinic authority, Mahari Zin, wrote a responsum that permitted the eating of *yaprakes*, believing that people would continue to eat them and would not be swayed by the argument of the zealots. He pointed out that the Jews were accustomed to this food, and that their parents before them had also eaten *yaprakes* regularly. Rabbi Moshe Israel rejected some of Rabbi Zin's legal proofs but nevertheless agreed with his approach. He wrote: "It is incumbent upon us to seek the benefit of the public." He went on to write a lengthy responsum describing the halakhic basis for eating *yaprakes* and the care which must be taken in cleaning the grape leaves.[13] Both Rabbi Zin and Rabbi Israel rejected the position of those who sought to introduce new legal stringencies that would have caused distress and inconvenience to the Jewish public.

The opposition to pietistic innovations is further evidenced in a responsum written by Rabbi Eliyahu Israel, who served the community in Alexandria, and maintained close ties with the community in Rhodes, where his father, Rabbi Moshe Israel, had been the chief rabbi. A controversy arose concerning the general Sephardic custom of remaining seated when the Torah reading included the portion with the Ten Commandments. Some pietists felt that this custom was incorrect. Since the Ten Commandments were so important, and had been received by the people of Israel while standing, they felt that the congregation should arise during the reading of the Ten Commandments. (It was indeed customary for Ashkenazim and some Sephardic communities to stand for this portion of the Torah reading.) Faithful to their principles, the pietists rose for the Ten Commandments, while the rest of the congregation remained seated, as was their custom. The congregants resented the innovation of those who stood up, and an argument ensued. Rabbi Eliyahu Israel ruled emphatically that the pietists were entirely in the wrong. They had no right to stand while the congregation remained seated. They were guilty of presumptuousness and arrogance. Even though they thought they were acting from pious motives, they were forbidden to deviate from the accepted practice of the community. Rabbi Israel stated that such disregard for communal norms and standards was worthy of the punishment of excommunication.[14]

Rabbi Hayyim Yosef David Azulai believed that Jews should follow the rules of halakhah with great care. But he opposed the introduction of new stringencies and regulations which did not have the stamp of authority of the great rabbinic decisors of previous generations.[15] He quoted the opinion of Rabbi Yosef Shemuel Cazes of Mantua who had said that Sephardim tended to the quality of *hesed* (compassion) and therefore were lenient in halakhah, Ashkenazim tended to the quality of *gevurah* (heroism), and therefore were strict in halakhah, whereas Italians tended to the quality of *tiferet* (grandeur) and therefore were akin to the Sephardim.[16]

The Sephardic folk spirit was characterized by an easy going, benevolent attitude. André Chouraqui, describing the outlook of the Jews of North Africa, commented that "the Judaism of the most conservative of the Maghreb's Jews was marked by a flexibility, a hospitality, a tolerance." The Jews of North Africa had a "touching generosity of spirit and a profound respect for meditation."[17] Rabbi Michael Molho, in his study of the customs and practices of the Jews of Salonika, noted that Salonika's Jews generally eschewed extremism; they were optimistic, tolerant, hospitable, gracious.[18] While these characterizations may reflect a certain amount of romanticization and wishful thinking, yet for the most part they accurately conveyed the Sephardic self-image.

Formal intellectual wisdom and popular folk culture enjoyed a symbiotic relationship. Both were manifestations of the thought and attitudes of the Sephardim.

•8•

Musar: Ethics and Moral Guidance

Professor Joseph Dan has delineated three types of Jewish musar (ethical) literature.[1] Works of philosophic ethics were created by individuals who sought to present ethical teachings based on rational philosophic principles. They adduced biblical and rabbinic texts in order to bolster or enhance their points, and in order to relate to the Jewishness of their readers. But their basic frame of reference was philosophy. Works of this type include the *Hovot ha-Levavot* of Bahia Ibn Pakuda and the *Shemonah Perakim* of Maimonides.

The second category may be called rabbinic ethics. Authors of such works rooted their teachings in biblical and rabbinic sources, and drew their conclusions from the texts they studied. They believed that Jewish traditional literature contained all the truths necessary to conduct one's life properly; there was no need to resort to philosophy or any other intellectual discipline. They saw it as their task to present the classic wisdom of Judaism in a systematic way. Writers in this category included Rabbi Moshe ben Nahman (Ramban) and Rabbi Yonah Gerondi.

Professor Dan referred to the third category of musar literature as kabbalistic ethics. Authors of this genre were committed to the centrality of kabbalah in Jewish life; they understood halakhah and ethical behavior through the prism of kabbalistic ideas. They had little regard for general philosophy. They, of course, drew heavily on the same sources as the authors of rabbinic ethics; but their works were permeated with kabbalistic ideas and symbols. Authors of works of kabbalistic ethics included Rabbi Moshe Cordovero and Rabbi Eliyahu de Vidas.

Philosophic ethics reached its zenith among the intellectuals of medieval Spain who were versed in the teachings of Greek philosophy. Since so many Jews were receptive to philosophy, it was

117

necessary to present Jewish ethical principles to them in a philosophically respectable fashion. Rabbinic ethics was a reaction against philosophic ethics. Its proponents felt that the Bible and rabbinic literature were the sources of truth; philosophy was unnecessary, even harmful.

Kabbablistic ethics flowered in the sixteenth century among the mystics of Safed. Drawing on kabbalistic ideas and symbolism, this genre emphasized the need not only to be righteous, but to be pious and saintly. Kabbalistic ethics came to dominate the musar literature of the Sephardim.

One of the features of the union of kabbalah and ethics was the emergence of individuals and groups who sought ways to deepen their spiritual relationship with God. Sixteenth-century Safed witnessed the emergence of groups of pietists who met regularly to review their spiritual progress and their religious failings. Kabbalists like Rabbi Moshe Cordovero and Rabbi Abraham Galante composed lists of rules by which pious people should govern their lives.[2]

The patterns established in the sixteenth century continued to influence musar thought and behavior during the subsequent centuries. Another luminous period in Sephardic musar creativity occurred during the eighteenth and early nineteenth centuries. Major figures in this phenomenon were Rabbis Moshe Hagiz, Yaacov Huli, Hayyim Benattar, Hayyim Yosef David Azulai, Moshe Hayyim Luzzatto, Eliyahu ha-Cohen, Raphael Berdugo, and Eliezer Papo. An important musar work, *Hemdat Yamim*, was composed in the eighteenth century by an author (or authors) of Sabbatean tendencies, but was issued without naming the author(s) specifically. All of these authors produced works deeply imbued with musar teachings; all were steeped in kabbalah; all attempted to live their lives at an elevated level of spirituality and piety. They, as well as other authors and teachers, stressed the importance of musar study. A number of them offered specific practices to enhance religious sensitivity. Taken together, these rabbis created a significant epoch in the history of Jewish musar literature.

The efflorescence of musar works during this period may reflect various motifs in the intellectual climate of the time. For example, messianic salvation was widely thought to be contingent on the Jews being worthy of receiving the Messiah. According to this way of thinking, the Messiah might be ready to come at any moment, but was prevented from doing so because of the sins of the people of Israel. If all the Jews would observe the laws of the Torah and perfect themselves religiously, then the Messiah would surely arrive to redeem them. Musar literature was an impressive effort to lead the Jews to lives of religious devotion and repentance. Ultimately, the goal was not merely to make individuals more spiritually elevated, but to make the entire Jewish people worthy of receiving the Messiah.

Musar teachings also rested on the premise of *tikkun*, "correction," as promulgated by Rabbi Yitzhak Luria. Since sparks of holiness were hidden within impure "shells," they had to be released for the sake of the correction of the universe. The forces of holiness needed to gain power over the forces of impurity. By performing mitzvot, Jews removed holy sparks from their impure shells. On the other hand, sinful behavior generated more unholiness in the world. It followed that Jews must do as many mitzvot as possible, and avoid sin. Musar literature provided the prodding and the emotional framework that would make Jews want to fulfill the laws of the Torah. It focused on why they should be religiously observant, on how to develop a proper religious attitude. While halakhic literature provided the specific actions to do and to refrain from doing, musar literature provided reasons for wanting to observe the halakhah.

In the worldview of Rabbi Yitzhak Luria, each Jew was responsible for all Jews. Therefore, striving for individual spiritual perfection was not the main focus; rather, each Jew needed to achieve spiritual perfection for the sake of the collectivity of Israel. Professor Dan has stated: "Ethics in Lurianic Kabbalah is no longer an attempt to achieve personal perfection. It is a set of instructions directing the individual how to participate in the common struggle of the Jewish people. . . . The individual's deeds are not his own private affair, because they profoundly influence the fate of the people as a whole."[3] This pattern of thought led to the conclusion that each Jew should guide every other Jew along the proper path. Musar literature is a logical outgrowth of Lurianic thought. Musar authors felt a responsibility for the collective spiritual health of the Jewish people.

As has been pointed out, Jews were filled with despair following the Sabbatai Sevi episode. As economic and political conditions in the Ottoman Empire eroded through the eighteenth century, the feeling of helplessness became painfully evident. Jews did not know how long the exile would continue; they had no power to control their physical destiny. They were in the hands of non-

Jewish rulers and governments, and there was nothing they could do but pray that the Messiah would come to redeem them. Musar literature, however, offered an avenue of hope. If in fact Jews could not control the physical world in which they lived, they could control their own inner spiritual world. Instead of seeing themselves in relation to the non-Jewish rulers and oppressors, they could view their lives in relation to God, their true King and the Ruler of the universe. In a world which to a large extent was hostile (or neutral, at best), the Jews could find solace in deepening their relationship with God. Musar literature generally stressed the quality of acceptance, receiving whatever good or bad came one's way. Piety demanded equanimity concerning matters of this world. Those who were faithful to God would be rewarded in the world-to-come. Those who mistreated the Jews in this world would ultimately be punished in the next world.

The receptivity to musar works was evidenced by the fact that books of this sort became popular among mainstream traditionalist Jews even when the authors were believed or known to hold Sabbatean views. The *Hemdat Yamim* is a prime example of this phenomenon. Rabbi Eliyahu ha-Cohen of Izmir was known to have Sabbatean leanings, yet his musar work, *Shevet Musar*, was widely read and highly regarded. Similarly, Rabbi Moshe Hayyim Luzzatto was a very controversial personality, accused of Sabbateanism by Rabbi Moshe Hagiz. Indeed, Rabbi Luzzatto was chastised by the rabbis of Venice and was even excommunicated for a period. Nevertheless, his musar works were popular and respected. His *Mesilat Yesharim* became arguably the most influential musar work ever published.

Musar Study and Musar Practices

Rabbi Hayyim Yosef David Azulai wrote:

Anyone who has acquired knowledge of laws [halakhot] but not of midrash has not tasted the taste of fear of sin. This means that the aggadot and midrashim are filled with musar chastisements and parables which lead a person to the fear of sin. . . . Sometimes rabbinic scholars become haughty, thinking that they are wise, and—heaven forbid—they come into the category of arrogance. The evil inclination pursues them more. . . . Therefore, they must study musar in order to awaken themselves to the fear of God and to humility. Then their Torah attainments will be acceptable.[4]

Musar study, thus, was imperative not only for the masses of people, but also for the scholars and sages. It provided moral guidance and inspiration, helping everyone to live with a heightened religious sensitivity.

Rabbi Azulai noted that musar study made it possible to overcome the evil inclination. Those who did not regularly study Torah and musar would not realize when they were sinning or would not sense the gravity of their sins. In consequence, they would justify their behavior and not be motivated to repent. On the other hand, studying philosophy in the hope of improving ethical conduct was a waste of time. Philosophy would not lead to proper ethics; on the contrary, it led away from moral behavior. Those who studied philosophy would end up becoming philosophers, challenging the words of the sages and walking in spiritual darkness! Philosophy was powerless to give control over the evil inclination. Rabbi Raphael Berdugo agreed that the study of philosophy was problematic for a Jew who wanted to be pious. Time spent reading philosophy or other sciences would be better spent studying Torah. Those who studied other subjects ended up forgetting some of the Torah they had learned.[5]

On the other hand, those who studied Torah and musar would truly be inspired to righteous conduct. Musar spoke not only to the mind, as did philosophy; it spoke to the heart. It was interested not merely in truth, but in piety, saintliness, holiness. Rabbi Azulai emphasized the importance of setting aside time on a regular basis in order to read works of religious inspiration and guidance. In particular, he suggested the Zohar, parts of the *Sefer ha-Rokeah, Sefer Hassidim, Hovot ha-Levavot,* and other classic musar works. Upon completing one book, a person should go on to another. In this way, the material would always seem fresh and interesting. One who regularly devoted himself to musar study would experience spiritual renewal.

It should not be thought that the study of musar alone would lead to the suppression of the evil inclination. Torah study was also necessary. The combination of Torah and musar study would strengthen the good inclination. Moreover, Rabbi Azulai stressed the value of reading the Zohar even if one did not understand the words or could not read them with the proper pronunciation. Reading the Zohar was loftier than any other endeavor and was of profound assistance to one's soul. The Zohar contained the ultimate mysteries of the Torah; just realizing that one was reading such a holy text would help to enhance one's relationship with God.[6] This idea was also conveyed by Rabbi Moshe Hayyim Luzzatto: "The true means of acquiring [spiritual] cleanliness is perpetual study of both the halakhic and ethical pronouncements of our Sages of blessed memory."[7]

Although Rabbi Azulai did not hold philosophy in high esteem, he engaged in philosophical discussions and debates while traveling among the Sephardim of Western Europe. The Jews of Amsterdam, Bordeaux, Bayonne, and other communities were versed in modern philosophy. In order to win them to his point of view, it was necessary for him to have at least some knowledge of philosophy and to speak to them in terms they could understand and appreciate.[8] Perhaps his statements stressing the value of musar and the inefficacy of philosophy reflected his concern for the spiritual well-being of the Western Sephardim.

Rabbi Eliezer Papo pointed out that musar study was intended to lead to proper action. It was not simply an intellectual pursuit for its own sake. The more books of musar one read, the more he would be led to increased Torah study and observance. A teacher of Torah was responsible not only for teaching the text but for inculcating good manners and proper attitudes in his students. Musar was thus an integral part of the educational process.[9]

Musar teachers were known for their personal piety. Striving to reflect musar teachings in their lives, they adopted various practices to enhance their spirituality. Rabbi Hayyim Benattar, for example, would wear his prayer shawl and *tefillin* while studying Torah. He conducted himself with extreme humility and piety, imagining himself to be in the presence of God, especially when he was engaged in creative Torah study.[10]

Rabbi Azulai, who studied briefly under Rabbi Benattar in Jerusalem, belonged to a group of pious individuals who made a spiritual contract among themselves. They agreed to help each other in the quest for religious perfection, to chastise one another and to be deeply involved in each other's emotional lives. Obliging themselves to follow any pious practice or custom which the majority of the group approved, they agreed not to show each other excessive honor, but to treat each other as equals. This fellowship was to be a private matter among the members, not to be revealed to anyone else. Each member agreed not to take offense at comments or suggestions made by the others, and to forgive the others for any sins committed against him. Eleven men signed the contract; subsequently, several additional people were added to the group.[11]

There were several groups in sixteenth-century Safed similar to the one described above. Rabbi Eliezer Azikri described the group of which he was a member in the introduction to his musar book, *Sefer Hareidim*. The concept behind these fellowships was that religious perfection could not be achieved alone. The assistance of others was needed, because human beings are too likely to forgive or overlook their own shortcomings. With the aid of a sympathetic yet objective group of people, however, one is enabled to recognize his sins and thereby aided in the process of repentance. Since such groups were often "secret," it is impossible to know how widespread they were or how many people they involved. However, it may be assumed that groups of this kind flourished throughout the Sephardic world. Since Rabbi Azulai, a well-known figure, published information about his group, it is likely that other pious individuals would have followed his example. It is also likely that other groups of pietists would have formed quite independent of his influence.

Another musar practice utilized by Rabbi Azulai was the recording of his resolutions in his diary. For example, in the year 5536 (1776) he wrote that he had taken it upon himself to be very careful to avoid haughtiness and anger. He also resolved not to speak against others, not to lie, flatter, or overeat. He prodded himself to concentrate more intensely while reciting his prayers, to contribute to charity, and to be among the oppressed rather than among the oppressors. He also noted that he must devote himself conscientiously to the study of Torah and musar. Rabbi Azulai advised that his readers write down any good ideas they had that would help them lead more pious lives. They were to review their lists each week to see whether they had been successful in implementing their own suggestions. If possible, they were to discuss their spiritual progress and shortcomings with a friend. [12]

Rabbi Moshe Hayyim Luzzatto taught the necessity of constantly reflecting upon the Torah path of life and of setting aside fixed times for reflection in solitude. Separating oneself from others enhanced the ability to be introspective and thoughtful, making it possible to evaluate one's life without being distracted. Too much social interaction hindered spiritual perfection. But Rabbi Luzzatto also warned that Judaism did not want people to be hermits. Solitude was valued, but not in extreme forms. Associating with upright people and participating in society were desirable, but one must still find time to be alone. [13]

Rabbi Eliezer Papo, who very much followed in the tradition of Rabbi Azulai, also recommended musar practices that would enhance religious life. In his classic work of moral guidance, *Pele Yoets*, Rabbi Papo wrote: "It is proper to learn all the books of musar one by one, and to repeat them regularly without fail, day by day and night by night. And even when rereading the books, they should seem new to him. He should find new inspiration according to the time and to the state of his soul, for not all times are the same."[14]

Rabbi Papo urged scholars to write books of musar in the vernacular. In this way, they would give guidance to a large audience and help people to improve themselves.[15]

Rabbi Papo recommended a number of practices that would be helpful in the quest for spiritual progress. Writing down one's resolutions and reviewing them regularly would ensure that one did not lose sight of his goals. Special efforts were to be made to observe mitzvot that others generally ignored. Pious customs beyond what the law required should be adopted, but inconspicuously, so that others would not know of one's extra piety.

A common thread running through the teachings of the musar writers was their insistence that true righteousness could only be attained through musar study and pious behavior. Ethics was not seen as an abstract philosophical topic, but as a practical requirement for those who wanted to follow God's law. It was inculcated by study, the observance of Jewish laws and customs, and the adoption of special musar practices that heightened one's commitment to religious perfection.

Musar Teachings

One of the important musar themes was the relationship between this world and the world-to-come. By fulfilling God's commandments in this world, one would gain merit for the world-to-come. Ultimate reward was not given in this world; the righteous could expect their reward in the eternal world-to-come, the world of souls.[16]

This world, it was taught, was like an entrance hall to the world-to-come. Only those who were righteous here would enter the real, eternal life of the world-to-come. Rabbi Eliyahu ha-Cohen wrote that it was important to compose new and creative interpretations of Torah and to learn as much Torah as possible, because one's new insights would be like a royal crown when he finally left this life to enter the world-to-come. How shameful it would be to be asked in the world-to-come to recite one's Torah insights and be unable to respond.[17]

This world was transient; it did not exist as an end in itself, but only as a brief prelude to the eternal life of the world-to-come. Therefore, it made little sense to place much value on the material things of this world. The goal had to be to fulfill God's word in this world, so as to ultimately enjoy the spiritual blessings reserved for the righteous in the world-to-come. Rabbi Eliyahu ha-Cohen warned that this-worldly matters should not be cause for rejoicing.[18] Rabbi Moshe Hayyim Luzzatto taught that "a person should make himself rootless in the world and rooted in service to God. He should accept willingly and be satisfied with all matters of the world as they occur to him. . . . He should not fear the future and its harms."[19]

Although the musar teachers emphasized the superiority of the world-to-come over this world, they did not negate the value of this world. On the contrary, this world was created by God and therefore must have great significance. Rabbi Benattar said that two qualities were needed if one was to give moral chastisement to others: (1) a sensitivity to the ultimate spiritual good of the world-to-come; (2) a sensitivity to the good of this world and of worldly possessions. People would not heed the words of someone who preached humility, charity, and cooperation but was himself poor and without worldly property. They would say: "What does he know about these matters? If he faced the same problems and conflicts as we face, he would not say what he says now. And what does he know of the blessings of the world-to-come? Has he seen them himself?" Therefore, the musar teacher was more effective if he had worldly possessions and if he understood the conflicts and pressures of this world.[20]

All the musar teachers taught that the way to obtain blessings in the world-to-come was to observe the ways of the Torah in this world. They stressed scrupulous devotion to the halakhah. Ethics divorced from halakhic observance was inadequate; rather, ethics had to be viewed as a necessary result of properly fulfilling the halakhah.

The universe depended on the Jews' observance of halakhah. Rabbi Hayyim Benattar recorded the tradition that God had created the world conditionally. If the Jews observed the Sabbath according to the rules of Jewish law, then God would continue to sustain the world until the following Sabbath. But if it ever happened that no Jew observed the Sabbath, God would return the universe to void and chaos.[21] He also taught that the well-being of the nations was dependent on the Jews observing the mitzvot. "If Israel walks in the way of Torah and mitzvot, God gives His beneficence to the world, and all the nations are sustained and satisfied together."[22]

It was important not only to keep the well-known and popularly observed mitzvot, but also to observe those commandments which were generally ignored or forgotten. Rabbi Benattar warned against being devoted to certain mitzvot but careless about the others. He drew an analogy. If a person had a pain in one of his organs and cried out in anguish, would he be consoled if he were told that he had 248 organs and only one of them was in pain? Obviously not. He would want all his organs to function properly, because his total health depended on the well-being of all his organs. Similarly, the total health of the organism of mitzvot requires the well-being of each mitzvah. If one mitzvah was in "pain," was not observed, then the spiritual health of the system of mitzvot was harmed.[23]

This idea was also conveyed by Rabbi Eliezer Papo. He lauded a report about a certain rabbi who used to sleep through the night on the eve of Yom Kippur but stayed awake on Purim. Rabbi Papo explained that many pious Jews remained awake on the night of Yom Kippur studying Torah; but on the night of Purim, which the rabbi in question spent in Torah study, everyone was busy eating, drinking, and rejoicing. God had no one who was devoting himself to the study of His Torah. Therefore, this sage had taken upon himself a responsibility which everyone else was ignoring.[24]

Kabbalists took care to emphasize the observance of mitzvot which people tended to treat lightly. The mystics of Safed, for example, stressed the importance of the third meal on the Sabbath, the festive meal at the conclusion of the Sabbath (melaveh malkah), the observance of Rosh Hodesh with special clothing and meals, etc. Since the spiritual well-being of the universe depended upon the observance of all the mitzvot, the kabbalists sought to highlight the religious significance of mitzvot that were relatively "unpopular" or unappreciated. The musar writers, themselves steeped in kabbalah, reflected this kabbalistic concern.

Rabbi Eliyahu ha-Cohen, in stressing the great value of the performance of mitzvot, considered the plight of a poor and desperate person who wished he were dead. Life was such a burden to him that he preferred to be freed from its toils and sufferings. Rabbi ha-Cohen advised such a person to remember that death would prevent him from doing mitzvot and serving God. The commandments were only possible in this world. Thus, it was better to withstand any pain and suffering with joy than to lose a moment of life, since each moment can be used for the fulfillment of a mitzvah. Each mitzvah was of inestimable value, well worth any sacrifice a person may have to make. [25]

The musar teachers were themselves accomplished halakhists. They recognized the need to study halakhah in depth. Indeed, Rabbi Azulai was a world-renowned decisor, whose halakhic writings were very influential among Sephardim and Ashkenazim alike. He not only wrote responsa and erudite halakhic commentaries aimed at a learned audience, but he also compiled a number of works of a halakhic nature that were aimed at the general public. [26] He believed that the role of a rabbi was not to impress the public with profound scholarship, but to present the laws clearly and concisely so that people could understand and obseve them. [27] Rabbi Eliezer Papo also recommended that scholars devote their major intellectual efforts to the field of halakhah. They should study the law with great care and devotion so as to understand it with perfect clarity. Then they should write books presenting the halakhah in a lucid way—without extraneous discussion and argumentation—to benefit the public. [28]

Adherence to halakhah, though, should not be merely technical and formal. Rather, the law should be studied and observed in a spirit of religious devotion. Musar provided the emotional underpinning for the proper observance of halakhah.

Following halakhah was the way to serve God properly and to merit the rewards of the world-to-come. Yet one who truly loved God with enthusiasm would not be satisfied merely to fulfill the letter of the law. He would naturally want to do more. Rabbi Moshe Hayyim Luzzatto compared love of God to the love of a child for his parent. The child wants to fulfill his parent's desires; he is so eager that even a slight hint is enough to set him into action. If he knows what his parent wants—even if the parent has not actually expressed it—the son will want to satisfy these wishes. He will be glad to bring pleasure to his parent without waiting to receive explicit instructions. Likewise, one who serves God with love will not only want to fulfill the halakhah—God's explicit instructions. He will also want to live in the spirit of the halakhah, to bring pleasure to God by doing even those things which He has not specifically commanded. This trait was called piety, *hassidut*, and was a basic characteristic of a truly religious person.[29]

Rabbi Luzzatto stated that the ultimate human goal was to achieve the state of holiness. This goal could be attained by perfecting oneself in the qualities of watchfulness, zeal, cleanliness, separation, purity, saintliness, humility, and fear of sin. Holiness entailed the constant clinging to God. No deed or thought should remove a person from his closeness to God. Even mundane activities necessary for life—such as eating, drinking, and engaging in business—should be performed in such a way as to keep one in the category of holiness. These activities should be seen as part of one's service to God.[30]

Rabbi Hayyim Benattar compared human spiritual development to the productivity of land. In order to produce its abundance, land must be cultivated. It needs rain. It must be protected from destructive forces. Likewise the human soul must be cultivated, nurtured, protected from destructive forces. It is the fulfillment of commandments that allows the soul to yield its fruits.[31] In striving for human perfection, one must fulfill the mitzvot with devotion, happiness, and humility.

Rabbi Azulai, drawing on the teachings of Rabbi Eliezer Azikri, listed the main qualities needed for the proper observance of mitzvot, arranging them in alphabetical order. Among the qualities listed were: imbuing mitzvah observance with love of God; preferring to do mitzvot oneself rather than delegating them to others; performing mitzvot with happiness, precision, beauty, generosity, and eagerness; doing mitzvot together with others in a group; trying to understand the reasons and the moral lessons of the mitzvot; doing mitzvot with the fear of God; doing them completely, with a full heart, promptly, in cleanliness, in privacy; considering oneself a servant of God; performing mitzvot while properly dressed, not for personal benefit; preferring to pay to fulfill mitzvot; pursuing opportunities to do mitzvot; waiting alertly for occasions to perform mitzvot; doing mitzvot with purity as best as one can.[32]

Kabbalistic ethics taught that it is necessary to be in a perpetual state of repentance. Repentance is a continuous process even for the most righteous people. One may sin without realizing it. Moreover, repentance is not just for oneself but for the entire people of Israel.[33]

Rabbi Eliyahu ha-Cohen devoted considerable attention to the

topic of repentance in his *Shevet Musar*. He cited rabbinic statements relating to repentance; he also offered specific methods of
repenting for various sins. Comparing a human being to a micro-
cosm, he stated that to sin was to create a blemish in the harmony
of God's universe. Fortunately, God was compassionate and receptive to repentance. Therefore, we must take advantage of the
privilege of repentance by sincerely improving our ways.[34] Repentance entails correcting one's behavior. Someone who sins by
eating or drinking that which is forbidden by the Torah must
repent by fasting, melting away that part of his body which has
been fattened by the forbidden foods. Someone who sins by
turning his eyes to forbidden things must repent by looking at the
holy letters of the Torah. Someone whose ears listened to improper sounds should constantly listen to words of Torah. Someone who spoke unkindly to others must now speak kindly to
them, bringing peace among his fellow human beings. And a
person who gained money through improper means not only had
to return the money but also had to disburse funds to the poor.[35]
The ability to repent was enhanced by staying in the company of
poor people, as well as by attending synagogue regularly and
participating in Torah study sessions in the study hall. These
taught humility and fear of God.[36]

Those who have repented, however, should not become proud
of their achievement, for pride will unravel the purity of the
repentance. Rabbi Azulai warned that a penitent should keep his
repentance to himself, and not try to gain public recognition or
approval. Humility and privacy were at the root of real piety and
repentance.[37] Rabbi Luzzatto remarked that "many great pietists
refrained from some of their pious practices when among the
public so as not to appear presumptuous."[38]

Rabbi Papo, in his various writings, strongly emphasized that
piety should not be advertised. Calling attention to one's religious
practices entailed the risk of growing haughty and self-content.
One must always evaluate the effect his acts of piety will have on
others. If they will cause resentment and gossip, it is better to
avoid unrequired pious deeds than to generate these negative
consequences. Rabbi Papo stressed the value of the inwardness
and privacy of religion. One should see himself in relationship to
God, not in competition with human beings. A person who was
not carefully observant of halakhah should especially avoid doing
acts of extra piety in public. People will regard him as hypocritical,
and will thus be guilty of speaking badly against another person.

Even a person who is well known for his piety should avoid public shows of excessive religiosity in the presence of his father, his rabbi, and other sages—unless they too perform these pious practices.[39]

Rabbi Papo cited several examples of the need for humility and privacy in performing acts of extra piety not required by halakhah. For example, a person should pour out his heart and cry when praying. "But he should let his soul cry out in secret between himself and his Creator, so that others will not come to mock him, and so that he does not appear to be presumptuous."[40] Yet Rabbi Papo also recognized that under certain unusual conditions, it was justified for a pious individual to raise his voice with tears, in order to awaken the congregation to more intense prayer.

Rabbi Papo told a story about a pious man who once visited a certain synagogue. The reader of the prayers, who had a wonderful voice, sang the prayers beautifully. The congregants later asked the visitor if he had been pleased by the service. He answered: no, he had not been at all pleased. The reader "sings in order to impress me, and not for the sake of Heaven."[41]

Rabbi Papo considered the case of those who followed the custom of Rabbi Yitzhak Luria and wore white clothing on the Sabbath. When such individuals found themselves in communities where the majority of people wore dark clothing on the Sabbath, they should not wear the white clothing in public. Rather, they may wear the white clothing under dark garments so that no one would know that they were following that custom. A great principle of piety was: to walk humbly with God.[42] Rabbi Papo wrote:

Our sages have said: a person should always keep his spirit in harmony with others. He should not rejoice among the mourners, not cry among those who are rejoicing. He should not sit among those who are standing, nor stand among those who are sitting. The general point is: whatever others are doing, one should also do, as long as there is no element of prohibition involved.[43]

Rabbi Raphael Berdugo was critical of those who exhibited excessive piety in some matters but were quite careless in their observance of other mitzvot. He cited the example of a certain individual who was notoriously lax in his observance of mitzvot, and yet on Passover was careful to eat only non-baked goods in the fear that he might thereby eat a minuscule amount of *hametz*.[44]

As has been pointed out, kabbalistic ethics viewed the perfection of the individual as a means toward the perfection of all the people of Israel. Each Jew was responsible for every other Jew. A religiously elevated person was obligated to share his knowledge and inspiration with others, to lead them to a higher religious level.

Rabbi Hayyim Benattar, drawing on kabbalistic thought, stated that all the souls of the people of Israel stemmed from the highest spiritual level. They were attached by their root to God's love and compassion.[45] Jews nourished their spirituality by observance of mitzvot and study of Torah.

The Torah was given to the totality of the Jewish people. Every Jew was obligated to fulfill the Torah to the best of his ability, and to help others to do likewise. No individual Jew can perform all of the 613 commandments: some are only for priests, some for Levites, some for men, some for women, some only for certain circumstances that will not befall each person. For the entire Torah to be fulfilled, therefore, all the people of Israel have to cooperate. All are responsible for the success of the entire enterprise, and each shares in the fulfillment of mitzvot accomplished by others.[46] When a Jew sins, he causes harm to the totality of the Jewish people.[47]

Rabbi Berdugo commented that the fulfillment of the Torah includes devotion to both the Written and the Oral Torah. It also involves adherence to rabbinic rulings and ordinances. He expressed displeasure with those who treated rabbinic traditions with disdain or negligence. Proper Torah observance, he said, depended on faithfulness to rabbinic authority.[48]

The musar writers taught that one should speak in praise of the people of Israel, not finding fault with them, but judging them charitably. It was said that Rabbi Hayyim Yosef David Azulai was a reincarnation of the author of *Hemdat Yamim;* since the earlier author had spoken harshly against sinners, his soul had been given to Rabbi Azulai for "correction." Rabbi Azulai's works are characterized by an absence of harshness and fault-finding against Jews.[49] Rabbi Azulai advised that anyone who was giving musar instruction should present his ideas as though he were speaking to himself. He should always include himself in any fault he described. "The one who comes to chastise must measure his words so that he not make a case against the people of

Israel, and certainly he must not treat them lightly. Our rabbis themselves taught explicitly that God does not want anyone to speak against the Jews nor to say that they have sins.[50] The musar teacher had to point out sins so that people would know how to correct their ways, but this must be done with love, gentleness, and sensitivity.

The same idea was conveyed by Rabbi Eliezer Papo. He warned preachers not to awaken judgment against Israel by speaking badly of the Jews in their sermons. Instead of mentioning the sins of the public, the preachers should simply state what was the proper thing to be done and what were the things to be avoided. "And everyone who judges favorably will be judged favorably by God."[51]

Rabbi Papo elaborated on the need for all Jews to speak well of each other and to try to get along nicely with each other. He stated that Jews—whether Sephardim or Ashkenazim—should receive each other with compassion and friendship. One group of Jews should not discriminate against any other group of Jews. It was very painful to learn of

those who speak in disparagement of a family or the people of a city or a tribe of Israel, such as Sephardim against Ashkenazim and Ashkenazim against Sephardim. And it is known from the words of our sages that God is very strict with those who cast aspersions on Israel. There is no city or family or tribe or person who does not have chaff and wheat . . . and people should not disparage anyone for a fault.[52]

Rabbi Eliyahu ha-Cohen dealt with the popular notion that the present generation was on a much lower spiritual level than previous generations. Frustrated by the long duration of their exile and their many sufferings, Jews felt that they were not spiritually fit to win God's mercy. They no longer had prophets and sages of the same quality as the early generations of their people. Responding to these feelings, Rabbi ha-Cohen wrote that the Jews had been sent into exile by God in order to do His service. God had not abandoned them; on the contrary, He wanted them to teach the truths of the Torah to the world and to gather proselytes. Since the exile entailed so much suffering, the Jews could expect all the more reward. Even if they were on a lower spiritual level than the great Jews of earlier times, yet God appreciated even the small things they did. "One who studies the Bible and aggadah in our times is equal to one who studied

Mishnah or halakhah in former times. The reward of one is equal to the reward of others."[53] In this way, Rabbi ha-Cohen spoke on behalf of his people, finding merit in their pious efforts.

His comments echo the same message attributed to Rabbi Yitzhak Luria. Tradition has it that Rabbi Hayyim Vital worried that the spiritual level of his generation was much lower than that of earlier generations. When he told this to Rabbi Luria, the latter responded with a parable: Once there was a great and powerful queen. All the dignitaries of the kingdom brought her precious gifts and lavished much attention on her. But one day she was sent into exile. Now she was no longer recognized as queen and was not given valuable gifts. Indeed, she was grateful if anyone even remembered her. And if someone brought her a piece of bread she would rejoice even more than when she had been on the throne and received gifts of jewels. Likewise, when God was on His throne and all the great prophets and sages served Him, He certainly appreciated their service. And yet, after having gone into exile, so to speak, He is exceedingly happy to receive any gifts, however simple. We are not on the same level as the prophets and sages; yet since we are in exile, our little acts of service amount to a great deal in God's eyes.[54]

Relationship with Hassidism

Just as the eighteenth century witnessed a flowering of musar literature among the Sephardim, it also witnessed a dramatic spiritual revival among the Ashkenazim with the emergence and spread of Hassidism. Founded by Rabbi Israel Baal Shem Tov, the Hassidic movement stressed many of the same themes emphasized by the Sephardic musar writers: the centrality of kabbalah, the need for spiritual self-improvement, the responsibility of each Jew for all others. Early Hassidic literature was devoted to musar and homiletic writings. It inspired Jews, giving spiritual dignity to all—regardless of their level of intellectual learning. Hassidism taught the value of serving God with joy, song, and dance; of involving oneself emotionally in the observance of halakhah.

Hassidism addressed the frustrations of the Ashkenazim who were living under oppression in Russia and Eastern Europe. It provided hope for people who otherwise sensed their own helplessness and powerlessness. It spoke to the needs of the common Jew, the poor and downtrodden. Indeed, Hassidism was a response to conditions quite similar to the ones that engendered the musar movement among Sephardim.

It should be noted that Hassidism was influenced considerably by Sephardic spiritual contributions. Hassidic masters chose a form of prayers which differed from the classic Ashkenazic text. Known as *nusah sefard*, it reflected a conscious effort to model religious life on Sephardic norms. To be sure, *nusah sefard* is not identical with the Sephardic prayer book; yet it contains many similarities, and represented a daring break from standard Ashkenazic practice. Hassidic customs were strongly influenced by the teachings of Rabbi Yitzhak Luria and his circle of students. (Although Rabbi Luria himself was of Ashkenazic origin, his religious milieu was Sephardic.) The Hassidim adopted the Sephardic method of putting on tefillin. They began to venerate their saintly teachers by making pilgrimages and praying at their graves, a practice akin to that common among the Jews of North Africa. Even the characteristic Hassidic practice of letting the earlocks grow long was originally a custom taught by Rabbi Luria, and was practiced first by Sephardim.

We have already noted the high esteem in which Rabbi Hayyim Benattar and his classic Torah commentary *Or ha-Hayyim* were held by the Baal Shem Tov. Indeed, Rabbi Benattar's personality and work were venerated by the Hassidim. Likewise, Rabbi Hayyim Yosef David Azulai was well respected by the Hassidim. In the early stages of Hassidism, this movement was almost entirely unknown in the Sephardic world. When Rabbi Azulai's books began to spread in the Hassidic community, this led to the establishment of contacts between Hassidic leaders and Rabbi Azulai. He in turn read the works of the Hassidic masters and spread their teachings among Sephardim.[55] The Hassidim regarded Rabbi Azulai as a holy and righteous kabbalist, and his books were studied with respect.

Many works by the Sephardic musar writers enjoyed popularity among Hassidim and other elements of Ashkenazic Jewry. Rabbi Eliyahu ha-Cohen's *Shevet Musar*, Rabbi Moshe Hayyim Luzzatto's *Mesillat Yesharim*, Rabbi Eliezer Papo's *Pele Yoets*, all found enthusiastic Ashkenazic audiences.

The Sephardic musar teachers provided important spiritual guidance to the Sephardic world at a time when it was generally engulfed in a mood of despair. They provided an emotionally powerful framework for religious life. Their works went beyond the Sephardic communities so that they really influenced all of world Jewry.

•9•

Acceptance and Rebellion: Prelude to Modernity

Rabbi Eliezer Papo was a major exponent of the musar tradition, especially as taught by Rabbi Hayyim Yosef David Azulai. Born in Sarajevo in 1785, Rabbi Papo became an outstanding rabbinic scholar, deeply devoted to piety and spirituality. He authored books of halakhah, homiletics, and musar, and was profoundly committed to kabbalah as well. His wife was well known for her own personal piety; their two sons, Yehudah and Menahem, became rabbinic scholars, and their two daughters married husbands committed to rabbinic tradition. Rabbi Papo served as rabbi of the community of Selestria (Bulgaria). He died in 1826 at the age of forty-one.

In spite of the brevity of his life, Rabbi Papo achieved remarkable depth and breadth in his rabbinic scholarship, and left to posterity a significant literary legacy. His musar works reflected the deep influence of Rabbi Azulai, both in content and style. In one of his works, *Orot Elim,* Rabbi Papo included a section of selected passages from the writings of Rabbi Azulai. Likewise, in his commentary on *Sefer Hassidim,* a classic Ashkenazic musar work, Rabbi Papo added comments from the teachings of Rabbi Azulai. Rabbi Papo's most influential work, *Pele Yoets,* was much in the spirit of Rabbi Azulai's musar writings, both in content and in literary style. It may be said that Rabbi Papo, in the early nineteenth century, was the exemplary spokesman of the Sephardic musar tradition of the eighteenth century. It was he who advocated this tradition most poignantly to his contemporaries and to succeeding generations.

Rabbi Papo stressed the need for sincere piety and saintliness. He generally felt that Jews should devote themselves to fulfilling

God's commandments, without worrying too much about the problems of this world. It was the world-to-come which had ultimate value; it was that goal to which Jews should direct their lives. "This is a great principle of Judaism: that a person should not seek extraneous things. He should not be fussy about food or clothing or a beautiful home. . . . His entire aim should be toward the world-to-come, because his [real] home is there."[1] Elsewhere, Rabbi Papo wrote: "It is not proper to worry about any matter of this world, but only about the worries of Heaven. There is no point to worrying about the vanities of this world, since all is vanity."[2]

His attitude was one of acceptance: whatever happened was for the best since it was God's will. Suffering and adversity were to be received with equanimity; they provided opportunities to demonstrate true faith in God and to repent.

A striking example of this outlook may be found in Rabbi Papo's discussion of marriage.[3] He stated that if a man had married a woman who turned out to be querulous and unpleasant, he should not therefore separate from her. On the contrary, he should treat her as nicely as possible and accept whatever abuse she gave him. By suffering in this world, the man would receive increased blessings in the world-to-come. Rabbi Papo even said that a man should prefer to have a bad wife if he felt he could manage the situation without being led to anger or other sins. Likewise, a woman married to a boorish husband should suffer in silence, not complaining to her parents or to anyone else. She should pray for him to improve his ways but should accept her situation as having been destined by Heaven.

Similarly, Rabbi Papo taught that it was wrong to be overly concerned with earning a livelihood. To be sure, one had to work for a living, not relying on a miracle to sustain him and his family. But income is determined by God. If God wants someone to be poor, he will be poor no matter how hard he works. And if God wants him to be rich, he will be rich even if he does not work hard. We are all obliged to devote some time to making our living, but we must realize that our level of success is determined by God. Therefore, we should dedicate as much time and effort as possible to the study of Torah and observance of mitzvot. Spending excessive time on attaining income is neither useful nor wise.[4]

Rabbi Papo stressed the attitude, already expressed in the writings of earlier rabbis such as David Nieto and Moshe Hagiz, that one must have faith in the words of the sages, submitting to their authority, and indeed, practicing intellectual subservience to anyone greater than oneself. It is proper not to speak with definitive certainty, but to be open to the possibility that others may have more understanding of truth.[5] We must assume that the words of our sages were filled with profound wisdom; and therefore we must not rely on our own intelligence in rejecting rabbinic statements that seem to be unreasonable. The sages often spoke enigmatically, hiding mysteries and truths in their words.[6] We have no right to set their teachings aside but are obliged to accept with perfect faith that the rabbis spoke with wisdom. Someone who finds any of their words problematic should ascribe the deficiency to his own intellect—not to the rabbis.[7] Obviously, this bent of mind emphasized the authority of tradition, and discouraged the development of new ideas that conflicted with long-held rabbinic teachings.

Rabbi Papo's devotion to fixed tradition was also manifested in his comments about life in Moslem and Christian lands. He argued that Jews were much better off living among Moslems than in Christian Europe. Moslem societies were more traditional. People dressed more modestly. It was easier for a Jew to adhere to his own traditions among Moslems than among Christians. In Christian countries, Jews were given certain freedoms and tended to assimilate into the non-Jewish society. They adopted non-Jewish fashions; they shaved their beards. Rabbinic authority diminshed considerably.

This is not the case in the kingdoms of Ishmael [Moslem countries], where the flag of Torah raises its horn. The Jews camp according to the Torah and travel according to the Torah. There is power in the hands of the sages and the communal leaders to chastise the wicked and to strengthen the faith. And they are modest in conduct between the sexes. Growing a beard is important among them.

While Jews suffered disabilities in Moslem lands as well as in Christian lands, Rabbi Papo thought that this was fine, since they were thereby reminded that they were in exile. They needed to remember constantly that they were entirely dependent on God for their salvation. Rabbi Papo suggested that Jews in Christian countries should move to the domains of Turkey, or at least send their children there. In this way, they would be spared from the breakdown of tradition characteristic of Christian lands. They could avoid the pernicious influences of modern philosophy—which led to heresy.[8]

Rabbi Papo noted that the Jews in Moslem lands were all careful to observe the mitzvah of getting married and having children. "But in Christian countries there are many who do not get married, and grow old and die as a thorn in the wilderness."[9] Moreover, women in Moslem lands were more modest in conduct and dress than women in Christian lands.[10]

In sum, Rabbi Papo advocated a tradition-bound, static view of Judaism. He called for a life of piety and acceptance of God's will. He demanded total allegiance to rabbinic tradition, stressing the need to live according to traditional patterns and preferring the traditionalism of Moslem lands to the modernity of Europe. His ultimate focus was not on life in this world, but on the world-to-come.

A New Approach

Yehudah Alkalai (1798–1879), like Eliezer Papo, was born in Sarajevo. Indeed, Alkalai studied under Rabbi Papo. While a young man, he had the opportunity to study in Jerusalem. He was a fine rabbinic scholar, having received an excellent grounding in all areas of rabbinic literature, including kabbalah.

At age twenty-five, Rabbi Alkalai was appointed chief rabbi of the community of Semelin, in Serbia. His intellectual concern, though, transcended his own community; he was troubled by the general powerlessness of the Jewish people in their exile. He lived during a period of rising nationalistic aspirations among the peoples of the Balkan countries. Early in his career, Rabbi Alkalai focused his concern on the national needs of the Jewish people.

Whereas Rabbi Eliezer Papo may be taken as a symbol of the policy of accepting one's destiny, Rabbi Alkalai may be taken as a symbol of a policy of activism and rebellion. These two figures, born in the same community and only thirteen years apart in age, represented very different worldviews. Rabbi Papo emphasized acceptance of the status quo; Rabbi Alkalai emphasized changing it. Rabbi Papo stressed the ultimate importance of the world-to-come; Rabbi Alkalai stressed the need for justice and security in this world. Rabbi Papo believed that Jews should devote themselves to piety and religious devotion, leaving their redemption entirely to God; Rabbi Alkalai believed that Jewish piety necessitated that Jews work for their own redemption. God would bless their labors. Rabbi Alkalai sharply rejected the attitude of passivity which characterized the outlook of his teacher, Rabbi Papo.

In 1834, Rabbi Alkalai published his first work, *Shema Yisrael*. In it, he called upon rabbis to inspire their communities to migrate to the land of Israel. This was to become a central theme in all his subsequent publications.

Several of his earliest writings were published in Judeo-Spanish and were clearly aimed at the Sephardic masses. He argued for a practical approach to solving the "Jewish problem"—the problem of being a disliked minority in Christian and Moslem lands. For him, the solution was a return of the Jewish people to their ancestral homeland and the restoration of Jewish self-government.

Drawing on calculations based on mystical texts, Rabbi Alkalai had originally thought—along with others—that 1840 was the year for the destined messianic salvation of the Jews. Although this hope proved false, he continued to work for practical implementation of his plan for Jewish hegemony in the Holy Land. He called for the revitalization of the Hebrew language as the medium of communication among Jews. He proposed the establishment of Jewish national funds to support settlement in Israel. In 1852, he traveled to Berlin, London, Amsterdam, Vienna, Breslau, Leipzig, and Paris in order to advocate his message among the Western European Jewish communities. In 1871, he went to Jerusalem, where he tried to establish a practical framework for supporting and developing Jewish settlements in Israel. In 1874, he settled in Jerusalem. Among Rabbi Alkalai's friends and disciples was the grandfather of Theodor Herzl.[11]

Seen in the light of the musar tradition which preceded him, the thought and work of Rabbi Alkalai represented a revolutionary change of perspective. He was certainly committed to halakhah and traditional Jewish religious practice; yet he was daring enough to challenge the policy of acceptance. His advocacy of active Jewish participation in their own redemption in their own land was a historic innovation of the first magnitude. Though in previous periods there had always been some who worked actively for the messianic restoration of Jewish sovereignty in Israel—such as Rabbi Yaacov Berav and Don Yosef Nasi in the sixteenth century—none had developed such a practical and comprehensive plan as Rabbi Alkalai, and none had argued their case so openly and passionately. Rabbi Alkalai tried to couch this revolutionary new approach within the framework of rabbinic tradition so that it would be more acceptable to the people he was attempting to convince.

Rabbi Alkalai firmly believed that the spirit of the time called for the freedom of the Jewish people and their return to their own homeland.[12] Yet he recognized that he was obliged to demonstrate the truth of this proposition by relying on the classical sources of the rabbinic tradition.

He argued that Jewish tradition recognized two phases in the redemption of the Jews. The first was a natural, gradual return to the land of Israel; the second was a miraculous redemption led by the Messiah. The first phase was characterized by the Messiah from the house of Joseph, a Messiah who would struggle for the redemption of Israel but would fail and die. The second phase would be headed by the Messiah from the house of David, the saving Messiah prophesied by our prophets. The first stage of redemption involved the migration of Jews from all over the world to Israel. After this had occurred, the Messiah from the house of David would come to completely redeem the Jews and would establish their eternal hegemony in Israel. The era of the Messiah from the house of Joseph was not characterized by overt miracles; rather, it witnessed the beginnings of Jewish return to Israel and the establishment of Jewish involvement in all aspects of the land's governance and development. All of the miraculous events associated with messianic times in biblical and rabbinic literature referred not to this period, but to the era of the Messiah from the house of David. Rabbi Alkalai believed that his generation was living during the period of the Messiah from the house of Joseph. Therefore, Jews had the right and responsibility to pursue the active settlement of the land of Israel.[13]

Rabbi Alkalai called on Jewish leaders, especially those in Europe, to seek permission from the rulers of the various countries for Jews to settle in Israel. He felt that the support of world leaders was critical to the success of the enterprise. He also urged philanthropists to contribute generously to enable Jews to migrate and settle in Israel.[14]

Some pietists objected that when God wanted the Messiah to redeem Israel, He would send him. Jews should not take the initiative to reestablish Jewish government in Israel, but should await a miraculous, messianic redemption. To this objection, Rabbi Alkalai retorted: "The way of the Torah is to command a person to do all he can according to natural means; whatever natural means leave incomplete, a miracle will complete."[15] Those who relied upon miraculous salvation outside the laws of nature, those who used mystical and magical techniques to hasten the coming of the Messiah—they actually were violating God's will because they were contravening the Torah. Human beings were obliged to do all in their power and to rely on God to help them. They were not allowed to sit back waiting for miracles.

Rabbi Alkalai was remarkably pragmatic in his analysis. He was not a starry-eyed visionary unconcerned with the practical means of accomplishing his dream. On the contrary, he provided specific suggestions. He believed that Jews should not flock to Israel all at once but should go there gradually. Those who went first would lay the groundwork to enable others to come later. In this way, the Jews would return to Israel in honor and dignity, not as migrants forced to live in tents.[16] He called on Jews to work in agriculture in Israel, as well as to establish commercial ventures there. This would lead to employment possibilities and to the ability to feed the population of the country.[17]

Rabbi Alkalai recognized the difficulties inherent in implementing his plans. The Jewish people was not a unified group living in one place. Rather, the Jews were scattered throughout the world. Each community had its own leaders. It was an enormous task to reach all these communities and win their support for the cause. In some countries, the Jews had chosen to forsake their own historical nationalism in order to blend into the nations in which they lived. How could the Jewish people be rallied to undertake the remarkable challenge of reestablishing Jewish sovereignty in Israel?[18]

Rabbi Alkalai believed that the Jewish religious tradition contained within it the necessary power to lead the Jews to return to Israel. He viewed a Jewish state as a religious ideal, not as an expression of nationalism like the states established by all other nations. A Jewish kingdom in Israel rested on the premise that the Jews would first accept the kingdom of God and the authority of His Torah.[19]

The land of Israel was the best place for the fulfillment of the Torah's commandments. Certain laws, especially those related to agriculture, could *only* be observed in Israel. Redemption was contingent on three things: Torah, charity, and prayer. All three were best accomplished in Israel.[20]

The Hebrew word for "repentance" is *teshuvah,* which also means "return." Rabbi Alkalai argued that true repentance entailed returning to the land of Israel. He cited rabbinic passages highlighting the spiritual superiority of the Holy Land over any other land. Among them was the statement that one who lived outside the land of Israel was compared to one who had no God; one who left Israel was as one who had worshipped idols; the air of Israel made one wise. Rabbi Alkalai countered the critics who said that they would not be able to make a living in Israel: if all the Jews went there, they would make the land provide for them. He cited the example of Moses Montefiore, a leading Sephardic philanthropist in England, who had started a cotton factory in Jerusalem. He called on others to follow this example. If the Jewish people were serious about returning to the land, they would find practical ways to earn their livelihoods there. [21]

In spite of the fact that Rabbi Alkalai presented his proposal within the context of religious tradition, many rabbinic leaders rejected it. This was to be expected. For well over a century—in the aftermath of the Sabbatai Sevi episode—the dominant trend of thought had favored passivity, acceptance, total reliance on God's miraculous intervention for redemption. It was not surprising that Rabbi Alkalai met with strong resistance; it was surprising that he was able to formulate an activist, pragmatic program for Jewish redemption—and that he did manage to find adherents for his ideas.

Nevertheless, Rabbi Alkalai's writings reflect his painful frustration that so many rabbis were not receptive to his point of view. He lamented that some pious rabbis actually discouraged Jews from returning to the land of Israel, mocking Montefiore's factory in Jerusalem. They felt that Jews should wait until the Messiah came before trying to establish a Jewish national home in Israel. Rabbi Alkalai stated that these rabbis were in fact hindering the redemption process. In the name of piety, they were guilty of misleading the Jewish people. "And now, our holy rabbis, give due honor to God and do not hinder the redemption of Israel."[22]

In reviewing Jewish history, Rabbi Alkalai was quite critical of those rabbis and leaders of the past who had not directed Jews to settle in Israel. Their lack of foresight had caused much suffering to the Jewish people through the generations. The many expulsions which Jewish communities had undergone in the past were all reminders to the Jews to return to their own land. But this message had been missed, the result being that the exile had continued for so many centuries. [23]

Rabbi Alkalai criticized his contemporary rabbis and leaders for not working energetically to bring about the rebirth of Jewish nationhood in Israel. He responded to those who attacked his viewpoint; he expressed impatience with those who remained silent, not courageous enough to take a public stand in favor of active work to establish a Jewish homeland in Israel.[24]

Rabbi Alkalai took the offensive, presenting his position as though it were the only reasonable and appropriate one. While recognizing the intellectual framework of his religious opponents, he did not present his ideas apologetically or diplomatically. Rather, he was forceful and confident. He felt that his critics needed to justify their viewpoint and could not do so; religious tradition was with him and against them. He rebuked those pietists who opposed the economic and social development of Jerusalem, those "who say with full mouth that Jerusalem was only created for the sake of Torah study. While their intention is acceptable, their deeds are unacceptable. It is impossible to conduct life in this world as though it were the world-to-come, where there is no need to eat or drink."[25] He had no patience for impractical pietists who were unwilling to face the difficult realities of pragmatic living.

Jewish tradition includes the notion that repentance leads to redemption. As was noted above, Rabbi Alkalai believed that repentance, *teshuvah*, entailed returning to Israel. He made emotional pleas, calling on Jews to repent—and return to their ancient homeland. By remaining in the exile, they caused great sadness to God, as it were. They caused pain to Jerusalem, the holy city, where non-Jews were now in control. They caused pain to their ancestors buried in Hebron, with whom God had made a covenant that their descendants would inhabit the land of Israel.[26]

A certain messianic expectation was associated with the year 5600 (1840). Rabbi Alkalai himself thought it possible that the Messiah would come during that year.[27] When the year passed without the arrival of the Messiah, a number of faithful Jews became dejected. Rabbi Alkalai described their despair, saying that many Jews had given up hope of redemption. They scorned the rabbinic teachings in regard to the Messiah, arguing for a universalist concept of messianism which would bring knowledge of God to all the world. Such people had lost hope in the specific messianic ideals of Judaism, speaking instead of universal peace and knowledge of God. Apparently alluding to the incipient Reform movement, Rabbi Alkalai deeply regretted their emendations of the prayer book, deleting passages relating to the return of the Jewish people to their land. They had forsaken the national aspiration of the Jewish people, an aspiration intrinsic to Judaism.[28]

For Rabbi Alkalai, redemption was not merely the physical ingathering of Jews to Israel so that they might be freed from exile and oppression. It was also the spiritual redemption of Israel, the realization of the religious ideals of the Torah and the rabbinic tradition. In order to achieve Jewish sovereignty in Israel, Jews first had to accept the authority of the Torah.[29] He looked forward to the time when the Jewish people living in Israel would be led by a group of appointed elders whose goal would be to unify all Jews religiously. "They will make us the same in our writing and speaking, in our Torah observances and customs. Our Torah and our prayers to God will not be divided into the custom of Sephardim, Ashkenazim, Polish, Italian. There will only be the custom of Israel."[30]

Rabbi Alkalai was strongly opposed to those who argued that Israel should be like every other country, that the Jews were no different from any other national group. Such opinions inevitably led to a dissolution of Jewish nationhood, to assimilation of Jews among the non-Jewish majority.[31] A century earlier, Rabbi Moshe Hagiz had warned of the deterioration in religious life that would accompany the loss of Jewish national identity. He had argued strenuously for the centrality of the land of Israel in the consciousness of the Jews. He saw that some of the comfortable Western European Jews were content with their lives in their adopted countries, and had no desire to return to Israel. The process noted by Rabbi Hagiz intensified during the eighteenth and nineteenth centuries in Western European countries where Jews were given political emancipation. The Reform movement, especially as it originated and developed among German Jews, was very anxious to have Jews live as citizens in their lands of residence. Reform Judaism was opposed to a distinctive Jewish nationalism, a Jewish homeland, a Jewish Messiah. Rabbi Alkalai, like Rabbi Hagiz before him, was disturbed by this distortion of religious tradition. Nationalism could not be wrenched away from Judaism without destroying Judaism.

The Blood Libels in Damascus and Rhodes in 1840

The perilous status of the communities in Christian and Moslem lands over the centuries was evidenced by periodic attacks against Jews and Judaism. A recurring calumny, which cost many innocent Jewish lives, was the blood libel. Non-Jews would claim that Jews had killed a non-Jewish child to use its blood for ritual purposes generally associated with the Passover festival. Although the charges were entirely fabricated, the masses of the non-Jewish population were only too happy to be stirred to action against Jews. How many Jewish lives were lost due to these vicious libels! How many Jewish hearts trembled with fear!

Historically, the Jews had little means of defending themselves against these false accusations. The non-Jews were generally hostile, for hatred of the Jews was part of their culture. They were ready to believe the most ridiculous things about Jews. Antagonism to Jews and Judaism was in the realm of deeply held superstitions. For their part, Jews were not accustomed to warfare or physical violence against others. When non-Jews attacked, they could hardly fight back. They did their best to board up their homes and strengthen their doors; and they prayed. Sometimes it was possible to win a reprieve by gaining the assistance of a powerful non-Jewish official, often by means of bribery. The history of blood libels against Jews is an ugly chapter in Christian and Moslem history; and a tragic chapter in Jewish history.

In 1840, when enlightened and emancipated Jews thought that blood libels were no longer possible, two simultaneous incidents occurred in Damascus and in Rhodes. The libels followed the classic pattern—the fabrication of charges that Jews had murdered a non-Jewish child, the stirring up of emotions and hatred. Since the nineteenth century was a period of "enlightenment," the libel did not unleash an immediate physical assault on the entire Jewish community; instead, a number of "suspects" and community leaders were arrested and held for trial. After conviction, they would receive their punishment.

Western Jews were particularly shocked by these blood libels. In their optimism, they had hoped that the civilized world had progressed so far that such barbaric behavior had become impossible. Although the libels both occurred in Moslem lands, Jews in Christian lands were deeply troubled and offended. A flurry of diplomatic activity involving leading European Jews such as Adolphe Crémieux and Moses Montefiore ultimately was successful. The Sultan was convinced that the charges against the Jews were baseless. He issued an order on behalf of his Jewish subjects, stating that they could live safely in his domains and were not to be subjected to persecution and injustice.[32]

Naturally, the Jews rejoiced at this victory. The community in Rhodes celebrated a special "Purim" to commemorate the day when their leaders, including their chief rabbi Michael Yaacov Israel, were freed from prison.

In evaluating the horrible events which had confronted him and Rhodes Jewry, Rabbi Israel preached a sermon in which he stated that the near-disaster had been due to their own sins. The members of the community, he said, had spoken ill of one another and had been querulous. In consequence, God had brought this punishment upon them so as to lead them to repent and improve their ways. Rabbi Israel, who himself had been imprisoned and tortured, did not call for any action against his oppressors. He followed the policy of acceptance, passively taking whatever came one's way as a message from the Almighty. His response conformed to the pattern of thinking of Rabbi Papo and the musar writers of the eighteenth century. [33]

Rabbi Alkalai, on the other hand, saw the blood libels as blatant evidence of Jewish powerlessness. He said that the Jews should finally have learned their lesson: it was time to leave the lands of the exile and return to their own land of Israel. If they would unite, and would trust God to help them, they would move themselves toward their own redemption. [34]

The blood libels reminded Jews of their precarious position in the non-Jewish world. Rabbi Israel argued that this helplessness was part of God's plan. Jews should accept their destiny, striving to perfect themselves religiously. Rabbi Alkalai argued that they should no longer tolerate their subservient position. Since they could not alter the attitudes of the non-Jewish world, they should establish their own country where they would be able to live in peace.

Many Western European (and American) Jews preferred another alternative. They were, for the most part, content to remain where they lived, with little desire to migrate to the land of Israel. On the other hand, they had moved away from the attitude of acceptance of God's will, of passivity, of devotion to religious study and observance. Like Rabbi Alkalai, they felt that Jews should take the initiative on their own behalf and not wait for miracles. But unlike Rabbi Alkalai, they did not see the establishment of a Jewish state as the correct response. They wanted to fight for Jewish rights in the non-Jewish societies in which they lived.

Indeed, the nineteenth century witnessed for the first time the emergence of national and international Jewish organizations dedicated to fighting for and defending Jewish rights in the non-Jewish world. These organizations were largely secular, not under the authority of rabbis and religious leaders. They developed among Jews in Europe and America, the large majority of whom were Ashkenazim.

The Board of Deputies of British Jews, founded in 1760, became a recognized agency only after the adoption of its constitution in 1835. Moses Montefiore became its president in 1838 and held the office for many years. A leader of the Sephardic community of London, Montefiore was deeply committed to the struggle for Jewish emancipation and to the protection of Jews wherever they lived. He was a wealthy man, and decided to devote his life to serving Jews rather than to increasing his fortune. He traveled to Israel seven times. He also met with various world leaders in order to represent persecuted Jews. Montefiore opposed religious reform and was committed to the historical religion of Israel based on Torah and halakhah.

The B'nai B'rith was founded in New York in 1843, in the aftermath of the blood libels. It set lofty goals for its work on behalf of the Jewish people, stating that it

has taken upon itself the mission of uniting persons of the Jewish faith in the work of promoting their highest interests and those of humanity; of developing and elevating the mental and moral character of the people of our faith; of inculcating the purest principles of philanthropy, honor and patriotism; of supporting science and art; alleviating the wants of the poor and needy; visiting and attending the sick; coming to the rescue of victims of persecution; providing for, protecting, and assisting the widow and orphan on the broadest principles of humanity.

World Jewry faced another terrible shock in 1858. A six-year-old Jewish child, Edgardo Mortara, was abducted by Catholic conversionists in Bologna, Italy. It turned out that the Mortara's Christian servant had secretly baptized the child when he was still a baby. The case was brought to Pope Pius IX, but he rejected all petitions on behalf of the boy's parents. In spite of the outcry of Jewish leaders throughout the world, the child was not returned to his parents. He was raised in the Augustinian order and became a canon in Rome and a professor of theology.

The Mortara case demonstrated the difficult situation of the Jews in the non-Jewish world. A Jewish child could be kidnapped and raised as a Catholic, and the Jews had no power to prevent this. Recourse to the Pope and other leaders proved fruitless.

But the Jewish communities of Western Europe and America were imbued with a new sense of assertiveness. They recognized the need to organize themselves so that they could more forcefully defend Jewish interests. In 1859, prompted by the Mortara case, the first national organization of Jewish congregations in the United States was founded, the Board of Delegates of American Israelites. It was devoted to the defense of Jewish rights in the United States and abroad.

Of much greater significance at the time was the establishment in 1860 of the Alliance Israélite Universelle in France. The organization published its goals, formulated by J. Carvallo and C. Netter, in June of 1860. The Alliance intended "to work everywhere for the emancipation and moral progress of the Jews; to offer effective assistance to Jews suffering from anti-Semitism; and to encourage all publications calculated to promote this aim." The Alliance became involved in diplomatic activity to help beleaguered Jewish communities and Jews suffering from persecution. It also provided assistance to Jewish refugees and emigrants.

Rabbi Alkalai praised the establishment of such organizations. Here was proof that it was possible for Jews to unite for common causes. These organizations provided the framework for Jewish self-help, education, and—of course—return to the land of Israel. He called on the leaders of the Jewish people—rabbinic and lay— to use their organizational and diplomatic strength to win support for a Jewish state in Israel.[35]

The establishment of large, secular Jewish organizations was a reflection of dramatic changes in Jewish life in the Western world during the nineteenth century. The Jews of Western Europe and the United States had considerable political, economic, educational, and social freedom. They had the opportunity to be citizens of the countries in which they lived. As a minority group, they wanted to be seen as a patriotic and constructive element of society. Although they could not be oblivious to the anti-Jewish sentiments that still existed in their societies, they had faith in the progress of civilization. Many Jews were optimistic that their situation would only improve with time.

In this atmosphere, Jews became more comfortable dealing with non-Jewish society. They grew more confident in expressing their opinions and their needs. The hold of traditional religion grew weaker, however, and many Jews were no longer satisfied to live for the world-to-come. They wanted to live good lives in this world, and were prepared to work hard to attain their goals.

That segment of the Sephardic world which was under the influence of Western liberalism increasingly left the worldview of Rabbi Papo behind. Nonetheless, it was generally unsympathetic to the ideas of Rabbi Alkalai, ideas that were far ahead of their time. It found itself in a period of transition, a time of crisis, of confrontation with modernity.

The vast majority of Sephardic Jewry lived in Moslem lands. Their confrontations with the conflicts of modernity varied, depending on the impact of European intellectual and political currents in their communities. While there were still large segments of traditionalists, there were also those who were moving away from traditional patterns of Jewish thought and observance. Throughout the Sephardic world, the nineteenth century was a period of changing perceptions. Modernity was presenting its challenges.

•10•

Sephardic Haskalah

One manifestation of the confrontation with modernity among the Jews of Europe was known as haskalah, "enlightenment." Proponents of haskalah held that Jews should study Judaism and its classic texts in a modern, scientific fashion. They argued for a modernization of education for Jews to include secular subjects. The haskalah witnessed a rebirth of literary creativity among Jews. Generally, haskalah figures were critical of the traditional, talmudic/rabbinic structure of Jewish life.

Moses Mendelssohn (1729–1786) was the guiding light of early haskalah thought. He attempted to harmonize Jewish teachings with modern philosophy. He felt that if Jews presented their religious ideas to the non-Jewish world in a sophisticated manner, the non-Jews would come to respect Judaism and appreciate the Jews. Realizing that increasing numbers of young Jews were seeking and receiving secular education, Mendelssohn wanted to demonstrate that Judaism could be respectable even to those who studied philosophy and other academic subjects.

Within the Ashkenazic world, there was considerable controversy between the proponents of haskalah and the traditionalists who opposed it. Essentially, the Jews in Europe were facing a serious dilemma: how could they adapt and survive in a Christian society which was giving them more freedom than they had ever had before? When they had been restricted to ghettos and had few civil rights, they had lived according to their traditions and found satisfaction in them. But now that they had been given the possibility of participating in the larger society around them, they had to make critical decisions. Jews who entered the non-Jewish world very often came to abandon their religious heritage. They adopted the customs and ideas of the non-Jews. After all, they wanted to be like the others, not old-fashioned or identifiably different. Traditionalists, seeing how quickly Jews assimilated into the non-Jewish culture, were alarmed that the Jews would lose their distinct religious identity. They therefore strenuously resisted any tendency that they felt would weaken the hold of biblical and rabbinic tradition. They saw the haskalah as a negative force, a direct threat to traditional authority.

While the haskalah movement itself called for modernization rather than assimilation, it did shake the foundations of traditional religious authority. In this sense, it contributed to the tendency of Jews to give up orthodox beliefs and practices.

The haskalah was a phenomenon primarily among Ashkenazic Jews. Nevertheless, it did have an impact on the Sephardic communities of Western Europe. As European cultural influence in Moselm lands increased, Sephardim in Turkey, Egypt, Morocco, and other countries also came into contact with the teachings of the haskalah.

The ideology of haskalah was generally not the same among Sephardim as among Ashkenazim, however. For the Ashkenazim, enlightenment represented a way to enter mainstream European culture in a respectable fashion. In a sense, haskalah was an apologetic for Judaism, an attempt to present it scientifically, universally. It wanted to shake off the nonmodern aspects of traditional Judaism. An underlying hope was that enlightened Jews would be able to function successfully in non-Jewish society, accepted as equals.

The Sephardim of Western Europe, though, already felt relatively comfortable in their non-Jewish milieu. They had a tradition of adaptability. They spoke the languages of the lands in which they lived; some had risen to prominence in various fields of endeavor. Their synagogues were prestigious; their services were elegant and dignified. Western Sephardim maintained their institutions according to their ancient traditions and were not inclined to "modernize." Haskalah issues were not central to their concerns.

This was even truer for the vast majority of Sephardim who lived in Moslem lands. They did not feel that the Jewish culture was in any way inferior to the culture of the Moslems among whom they lived. They had no compelling reason to abandon traditional religious patterns as a means of adapting to the non-Jewish society around them. Indeed, they functioned as autonomous communities within the broader Moslem world, and were not motivated to strive for emancipation and legal equality. [1]

Yet the ideas and tendencies of the haskalah movement did manifest themselves among Sephardim. From the second half of the nineteenth century, enlightenment ideas filtered into the Sephardic communities in Moslem lands especially through the efforts of the schools of the Alliance Israélite Universelle—bastions of French culture. The influence of European colonial powers in North Africa and the Middle East was also an important factor in Sephardic intellectual life. The challenges of haskalah could not be ignored.

Grace Aguilar: Jewish Spirituality

Grace Aguilar (1816–1847) belonged to the Sephardic community of London. Although her life was cut short by an untimely death, she left a remarkable literary legacy. Aside from a number of novels, she also wrote several works relating to Jewish religious teachings.

She was concerned that the wave of modernism was undermining the foundations of traditional religious life. Jews were seeking success in the secular world; the bond of religion was weakening. She was particularly aware of the spiritual turmoil among Jewish youth; she sought to address their religious questions and thereby strengthen their faith.

Grace Aguilar corresponded with Isaac Leeser, spiritual leader of the Spanish and Portuguese Congregation Mikveh Israel in Philadelphia, and he was of much help to her. Indeed, he edited several of her works for publication, including *The Spirit of Judaism*. This work reflected Aguilar's deep concern that Jewish youth were not receiving a proper spiritual education in Judaism. She feared that they would be attracted to Christianity, which was popularly portrayed as a religion of the spirit. In contrast, Judaism was described as a religion of numerous detailed observances. Presented as an elaborate commentary on the first paragraph of the Shema (which she transliterated in the Spanish and Portuguese style as Shemang), the book dealt with a wide range of religious topics, emphasizing the profound spirituality inherent in Judaism.

Grace Aguilar argued that if Jews understood the true power and beauty of their religion, they would proudly assert their Jewishness instead of trying to conceal it. The repetition of the Shema itself is a source of holy comfort. If recited regularly "we shall go forth, no longer striving to conceal our religion through *shame* (for it can only be such a base emotion prompting us to conceal it in free and happy England); but strengthened, sanctified by its blessed spirit, we shall feel the soul elevated within us"[2]

Aguilar stressed the need for Jews to devote themselves to the study of the Bible, the foundation of Judaism. In so doing, she made some pejorative remarks about "tradition," apparently referring to the traditional stress on fulfilling the details of the law. (Isaac Leeser, in his notes to the book, took her to task on several occasions for her detraction of "tradition.")[3] However, Aguilar can hardly be accused of being unorthodox and opposed to the observance of mitzvot. She consistently called for the faithful observance of the commandments in their details. "Instead then of seeking to find excuses for their non-performance, should we not rather glory in the minutest observance which would stamp us as so peculiarly the Lord's own, and deem it a glorious privilege to be thus marked out not only in feature and in faith, but in our civil and religious code, as the chosen of God?"[4]

It may be argued that Grace Aguilar's stress on the Bible and seeming deprecation of "tradition" was her way of trying to appeal to the religious needs of her audience. She perceived her readers as being under the influence of Christian notions of what a religion should be. By asking Jews to read the Bible, she was asking them to do something that was desirable even for Christians, who also venerated the Bible. By emphasizing the spirit of Judaism, she wished to convey to Jews seeking spirituality that they had no need whatever to turn to Christianity. But in the process of stressing the Jewish spirit, she found it necessary at times to play down the details of the laws of Judaism as passed down by tradition. These details themselves had to be framed within a context of spirituality and not be seen as ends in themselves.[5]

In *The Jewish Faith: Its Spiritual Consolation, Moral Guidance, and Immortal Hope*, completed shortly before her death, Grace Aguilar presented her arguments in the form of a series of letters from a knowledgeable Jewish woman to her beloved young friend, an orphan with little Jewish education. Aguilar felt that this style of presentation would be more interesting for her readers, especially younger readers whom she hoped to influence.

In the introduction to the book, she emphasized the need to present sophisticated religious educational materials to young people. Youth were easily influenced by outside sources; unless they had a proper understanding of Judaism, they would be tempted to abandon it. Indeed, the orphan to whom the letters in the book were addressed had been considering the possibility of converting to Christianity, believing that Christianity offered more spirituality than Judaism. The author, of course, forcefully refuted this claim; in the end, the orphan did not convert, but rather became a more devoted Jew.

Grace Aguilar expressed the conviction that it was necessary to provide Jewish education for girls as well as boys. She lamented the fact that the education of Jewish girls had not been given adequate attention. She described her book as "an humble help in supplying the painful want of Anglo-Jewish literature, to elucidate for our female youth the tenets of their own, and so remove all danger from the perusal of abler and better works by spiritual Christians."[6]

Arguing that the new knowledge and ideas brought about by the advances in science did not contradict the truth of the divinely revealed Torah, Aguilar wrote: "So simple, so easy appears to me the union of Revelation and all science, that how any mind can reject the one as contradicting the other is as utterly incomprehensible as it is fearful."[7] Scoffers who scorned the truth of religion were guilty of arrogance; they did not have a proper understanding of religion. She was obviously troubled by the increase in skepticism among Jews and by their intellectual surrender to the antireligious proponents of modern science and philosophy. If Jews received an enlightened Jewish education, they would hold fast to their own religious traditions.

Moreover, Jews were not learning the spiritual aspects of Judaism. They were taught laws and customs, but often had no insight into the deeper meanings and ideas of Jewish tradition. Grace Aguilar noted that the Spanish and Portuguese Jews tended to stress the external forms of religious ceremony, giving the impression that these forms were the essence of Judaism. While she recognized the reasons for the emphasis on forms, Grace Aguilar argued for the necessity of emphasizing the spiritual aspects of Jewish teachings. But she warned that people should not abandon religious observance, thinking that spirituality was of higher value. On the contrary, the observances gave expression to the spiritual feelings of love of God. She wrote that "every spiritual Hebrew, instead of disregarding the outward ceremonies, will delight in obeying them for the love he bears his God, welcoming them as immediate instructions from Him, even as a child obeys with joy and gladness the slightest bidding of those he loves."[8]

Grace Aguilar was troubled by the phenomenon of Jews who achieved success in general society but in the process moved away from Jewish commitment. "Many, indeed, have lately distinguished themselves in the law, and in the fine arts of the English world; but why will not these gifted spirits do something for Judaism as well as England? There is no need to neglect the interests of the latter, in attending to the need of the former. We want Jewish writers, Jewish books."[9] She was convinced that if the best and most enlightened Jewish minds devoted themselves to presenting Judaism at its best, the non-Jewish world would be duly impressed. Hatred of Jews would diminish as non-Jews came to learn about and respect Judaism and Jews.

Grace Aguilar's writings reflected major issues of modernism: the education of women, the need for spirituality, the renewed interest in the Bible, the critique of blind obedience to details of the law without understanding its deeper meanings. They also shed light on the religiosity of her reading audience: relatively unversed in Jewish learning, skeptical about the mitzvot, susceptible to the spiritual charm of Christianity. (Leeser challenged the latter point, believing that it was very rare for a Jew to convert to Christianity. As he saw the problem, Jews were simply becoming apathetic to their own spiritual heritage.)[10] Grace Aguilar's essential goal was to demonstrate that loyalty to traditional Judaism was not antipathetic to success in the modern world. By studying the classic sources of their religion and maintaining observance of the commandments, Jews would be secure in their own faith and could function more confidently in the general non-Jewish society.

Eliyahu Benamozegh: Jewish Ethics

The impact of haskalah thought was also evidenced in the writings of Rabbi Eliyahu Benamozegh (1822–1900). Born in Leghorn, Italy, to a family of Moroccan Sephardic background, Benamozegh was a major figure in Jewish intellectual life during the nineteenth century. He served as rabbi in Leghorn and was a professor of theology in the rabbinical school there. He published works in Hebrew, French, and Italian.

Rabbi Benamozegh was well steeped in rabbinic learning, including the kabbalah. He also was educated in general academic disciplines; his writings reflect his knowledge of archaeological research, philology, history, Christianity, philosophy.

Like Aguilar, Benamozegh was concerned with the relationship of the Jews to the larger Christian society in Europe. In his *In Ethical Paths,* he attempted to clarify Jewish teachings on ethics and demonstrate their superiority to the seemingly more spiritual ethics of Christianity. He too felt that Jews needed to have a better grounding in the moral teachings of their own religion in order to withstand the influence of Christian society.

Benamozegh stated that it was unfair of Christians to argue that their system of ethics was superior to Jewish ethics. After all, Christianity was based on Judaism and many of its main teachings were of Jewish origin. Moreover, the Christian claim to have superseded Judaism was not sound. Why would God—who chose Israel and gave them His Torah—suddenly change His mind and establish a new religion to replace Judaism? Since God was omniscient, such a change in plans would seem absurd. But even using Christian logic, there was no reason to believe that Christianity had become the ultimate expression of God's will. If—as Christians claimed—God had changed His mind once, then what would preclude Him from doing so again, choosing another religion to replace Christianity? In short, Christianity's argument on this issue was untenable.[11]

In describing Jewish ethics, Benamozegh noted that Judaism encompassed two factors: the national *(mediniyut)* and the ethical *(musar).* Thus, Jewish ethics is grounded in practical reality. It is not ethereal or over-idealized but is based on the real considerations of a real nation. In contrast, Christian ethics is not applicable to national life in the same way. Christians speak of humility, suffering, compassion, and other such concepts in unrealistic ways. Which nation on earth would allow itself to be attacked and not defend itself or strike back? Which nation would forgive debts or ignore insults and cruelties committed against its people? Christianity cannot adequately satisfy the natural human need and attachment for a homeland. On the other hand, Judaism is realistic in linking ethical teachings to national and practical concerns. Religion and nationality cannot be separated.[12]

In his elaboration of the Jewish ethical tradition, Benamozegh stressed the universalism of Judaism. The Torah described humanity as deriving from common ancestors, Adam and Eve. Humanity has a common destiny—the messianic time.[13] Jewish ethics shows respect for non-Jews and does not preclude them from God's love and salvation. Judaism's goal is not to punish the wicked but to bring them back to righteousness. Since Jewish faith is necessarily contingent on the performance of practical works, it provides the most realistic framework for the creation of an ethical society.[14]

Benamozegh published this work in French, intending it for both Jewish and Christian readers. For the Jews, he hoped this work would strengthen their commitment to their own tradition. For the Christians, he hoped that they would gain a new understanding of Judaism and would come to appreciate it better. He recognized the growing influence of Christianity over the emancipated and enlightened Jews; he offered his book as an anodyne to that influence. As a man of broad Jewish and general culture, Benamozegh was eminently qualified for the task he had set himself.

Rabbi Israel Moshe Hazan

One of the most influential Sephardic thinkers of the nineteenth century was Rabbi Israel Moshe Hazan (1808–1863).[15] Born in Izmir, his family moved to Jerusalem when he was still a small child. He studied there in the yeshiva of his grandfather, Rabbi Yosef Refael Hazan. In 1842 he was appointed to the rabbinical court in Jerusalem, a testimony to his scholarship and stature in the community. In 1844 he traveled as an emissary to London. He subsequently held rabbinic positions in Rome, Corfu, and Alexandria.

Rabbi Hazan was deeply committed to maintaining Judaism in its traditional form. During his stay in London, he wrote a pamphlet attacking the recently established Reform movement in England. He also joined a group of traditionalists who were opposed to the teachings of Reform.

Rabbi Hazan argued that the Jewish people should conduct themselves according to their own laws and traditions. They should not abandon their religious and national autonomy by succumbing to the temptations of emancipation and enlightenment. He complained that European Jews tended to polarize, either assimilating readily into non-Jewish culture or fiercely isolating themselves against its influence. He represented the classic Sephardic model—maintaining traditional religious autonomy while at the same time being open to the best teachings of the non-Jewish world.

In his *Nahalah le-Yisrael*, Rabbi Hazan contended that Jews should adhere to their own laws, including the laws of inheritance. The non-Jewish governments did not require Jews to abandon their own legal system; why then should they do so voluntarily? Anyone who studied Jewish history would quickly realize that "from the time of the exile of Judah from his land, [the Jews] followed the laws of the Torah of Moses their teacher! Even when they lived in foreign lands, some here and some there, they sacrificed themselves in order to fulfill all that was written in the book of the Torah."[16] This was true when Jews lived among pagans; so much more should it be true when they lived among those who believed in God, in the divinity of the Torah. Indeed, Christianity and Islam had both acknowledged the basic principles of Judaism and the sacred nature of the Jewish Bible. Judaism had taught the world vital social values, love of fellow human beings. The non-Jewish world had not asked Jews to forfeit their autonomous religious life. Therefore, the Jews should certainly maintain their own laws and traditions in all areas, including inheritance, marriage, and divorce.

Rabbi Hazan expressed rage at those who followed non-Jewish civil laws of inheritance instead of relying on the rules of Judaism. "Those Jews who seek inheritance contrary to the Torah of Moses are adjudged as heretics, Sadducees, uprooters of Torah, notorious thiefs. If you investigate them, you will find that they violate other commandments arrogantly."[17]

Calling on his fellow rabbis to fight against those who advocated following the civil law in matters of inheritance, Rabbi Hazan warned that if this section of Jewish law were forfeited, it would only lead to further undermining of the Torah and its legal authority. "Know truly that if at this time we are silent, the laws of inheritance will be completely uprooted, as though the Torah had never been written. Woe unto us! Woe unto us, what will be our end! It is as though we were almost dead, almost lost; it is as though a Torah scroll had been burnt . . . in which case all Jews in all places should rend their garments never to be resewn."[18] Considering the gravity of the threat to Jewish religious hegemony, Rabbi Hazan called on rabbis to struggle courageously against those who were willing to compromise Jewish law. He received approbation for his position from leading Sephardic rabbis in Izmir, Salonika, Istanbul, Vienna, and other communities.

Rabbi Yehudah Yaacov Nehama: Defending Tradition

The tide of modernism and Europeanization made itself felt in the domains of the Ottoman Empire during the nineteenth century. The Turkish authorities instituted a number of reforms *(tanzimat)*, indicating their desire to shake off past stagnation and become a modern society. European culture, especially in its French form, seemed particularly attractive to the Ottoman rulers.[19]

The wave of Europeanization also had an effect on the Jews of the empire. Sephardic intellectuals were receptive to French influence. Schools operated by the Alliance Israélite Universelle sprang up throughout the Ottoman Empire, the Middle East, and North Africa. They eagerly promoted the glories of French language and culture. They also introduced modern educational techniques. In short, an intellectual transformation was occurring among the Sephardim, bringing them into contact with European modernism.

Rabbi Yehudah Yaacov Nehama (1825–1899) was an influential figure in Salonika. His life and work are a reflection of the impact of haskalah on Sephardic thinkers. He wrote three major works that were destroyed in a fire and thus never published. One of these was a history of the Jewish people, one was a volume of rabbinic responsa, and one was a history of the Jews of Salonika. The scope of these works reflects Nehama's wide-ranging interests and knowledge. He was not only deeply learned in classic rabbinic literature, but was also a historian of Jewry in general and of his own community in particular. Historical research was an important feature of the Jewish enlightenment.

Two volumes of Rabbi Nehama's letters were published. They reflect his knowledge in many fields of thought. He corresponded with leading Jewish intellectuals of his time, Sephardic and Ashkenazic. His interest in books and bibliographic information was formidable.

Like Aguilar, Benamozegh, and Hazan, Nehama was well versed in contemporary culture and was also committed to maintaining the traditional structure of religious observance. In a letter written in the year 5614 (1854), he responded to Rabbi Mordecai Halevi Mortara and Rabbi Shelomo Nissim of Mantua, who had written to inform him that some members of their community were agitating to abolish the observance of the second day of festivals. (According to rabbinic law, communities outside the land of Israel are obligated to observe two festival days, whereas the communities in Israel observe one day.) Rabbi Nehama was infuriated by this suggestion, since it undermined age-old Jewish practice. He condemned those who called for reforms in Judaism, referring to the spirit of reform as a leprous plague. Such recommendations were divisive and would lead to factionalism. "My brothers and my people, beware of heeding the words of those who love reform and heresy; take heed of the custom of your ancestors and do not turn from it."[20]

Rabbi Henry Pereira Mendes

A leading religious and communal figure in American Jewish life during the late nineteenth and early twentieth centuries was Dr. Henry Pereira Mendes (1852–1937).[21] Born in Birmingham, England, he was the son of Abraham Mendes, who was minister of the Sephardic congregation there. On both his father's and his mother's side, he was the product of a long line of religious leaders.

Rabbi Mendes served as minister of the historic Congregation Shearith Israel, the Spanish and Portuguese Synagogue in New York City, the oldest Jewish congregation in North America. His service began in 1877, and he was associated with the congregation until his death sixty years later. Aside from his training in Jewish studies, he received the degree of medical doctor from New York University in 1884.

Dr. Mendes was tireless in his work on behalf of Jewish tradition. He was a founder of the Union of Orthodox Jewish Congregations of America, believing it necessary for the Orthodox community to be united. He also was a co-founder, together with his colleague Rabbi Sabato Morais of Philadelphia, of the Jewish Theological Seminary of America. He and Morais envisioned the institution as a training ground for American-bred traditional rabbis who could serve Jewish communities in the United States. When the Seminary later identified itself with the Conservative movement, Dr. Mendes dropped his association with it. His goal had been to strengthen orthodoxy and to combat reform.

An energetic communal leader and humanitarian, Dr. Mendes was also involved in the establishment of such institutions as the Young Women's Hebrew Association in New York, Montefiore

Hospital, and the Lexington School for the Deaf. He was a leader in such organizations as the Union of Orthodox Jewish Congregations of America, the New York Board of Jewish Ministers, the Federation of American Zionists, and the World Zionist Organization. He also was a prolific author of religious textbooks for children, dramatic works, poetry, books on Jewish history and ethics, and more.

Dr. Bernard Drachman, a colleague of Dr. Mendes, described him as "an ideal representative of orthodox Judaism." He praised Dr. Mendes' "absolute freedom . . . from anything approaching narrowness of sectarian bias within the Jewish community."[22]

Indeed, Dr. Mendes was a universally respected figure, whether among the Sephardim of America, the Yiddish-speaking Ashkenazim, the non-Orthodox community, or the non-Jewish community. He was urbane, highly educated, principled, hard-working. His sermons and literary works demonstrate his devotion to the Bible. He did not consider himself a scholar of Talmud and halakhah, although he certainly was comfortable studying the classic rabbinic texts.

Dr. Mendes viewed himself as a spokesman for the Sephardic outlook on Judaism. In a guest sermon which he delivered in the Sephardic synagogue on Lauderdale Road in London (July 27, 1901), he was effusive in his praise of the Sephardic religious tradition, which was able to blend loyalty to the past with an openness to new thinking. He called for "a revival of Sephardic activity, a renewal of Sephardic energy, an earnest demonstration of fidelity to God and Torah, a continued proof by our own lives that culture and fidelity can go hand in hand."[23]

Stressing the point that faithfulness to tradition could go hand in hand with modern culture, Dr. Mendes strenuously opposed Reform Judaism, believing that it was an incorrect diagnosis for the spiritual malaise of the Jewish people. Instead of breaking with tradition, Jews actually needed to come closer to it, to find peace and contentment in the age-old laws and customs of the Jewish people. Reform led to a weakening of the hold of tradition. It engendered more apathy and irreligion among Jews. If each individual did as he chose without taking the claims of Jewish law and tradition into consideration, then the structure of Jewish life would be seriously weakened. Dr. Mendes criticized this "everyone-doing-as-he-pleases-religion" as the source of ignorance, apathy, and disregard of religious restrictions.[24]

In 1891, some suggestions for ritual changes were made in his own Congregation Shearith Israel. Dr. Mendes reacted with characteristic eloquence.

I say it is a very solemn thing for this Congregation with its centuries of proud adherence to historic Judaism to approach the subject of change at all. . . . Are those who have enlisted under the banner of change distinguished for a better observance of the Sabbath? Are they in any way improved religiously? Are their homes more Jewish? Are their children more devoted to Judaism and better exponents of its teachings? . . . No new virtues have been created in the heart of the Reform Jew which are not found in the heart of the Orthodox Jew. Nor is the cultured Reformer more respected than is the cultured Orthodox brother.[25]

Dr. Mendes prevailed and the changes were averted.

Traditional Communal Framework

Religious leaders and intellectuals throughout the Sephardic diaspora advocated loyalty to Jewish tradition. Although they were well aware of the spirit of modernism and of the challenges to religious patterns, they felt that the Jewish people could best be served by remaining faithful to its own distinctive way of life. Reform was not acceptable. It was a surrender to the whims of European modernity. It could only lead to a breakdown in Jewish religious life, to assimilation.

Whereas the issues of emancipation and enlightenment led to the formation of religious movements within Ashkenazic Jewry, Sephardic Jewry did not fragment itself into Orthodox, Conservative, Reform, or other movements. Ashkenazic Jewry was torn apart by feuding among the ideological movements. It established separate communities, institutions, even cemeteries. Sephardic Jewry was spared this internecine religious struggle.

Certainly, not all Sephardic Jews adhered to all the details of traditional halakhah. Laxity in observance was growing. A lessening of reverence for rabbinic authority was also apparent in many communities. Yet the general Sephardic attitude was respectful to tradition. The religious intellectuals, as well as the masses, were desirous of maintaining a traditional religious framework for their communities. The Sephardim found a modus vivendi characterized by respect for tradition and tolerance for those whose observance of halakhah fell short. Whereas some individuals might not be personally observant, the synagogue and community structure were to operate according to halakhah.

The haskalah movement, then, did have an impact on the Sephardic world. But the Sephardic communities remained loyal to the traditional halakhic communal framework. This was not a small accomplishment.

•11•

Secular Sephardic Literature

The nineteenth and early twentieth centuries witnessed an efflorescence of Judeo-Spanish literature. Whereas the traditional literature in this language was primarily of a religious nature, the new outburst of creativity showed itself in the fields of journalism, drama, poetry, and fiction. There was also a significant effort to record and preserve traditional Judeo-Spanish songs and folklore.

The flowering of modern Judeo-Spanish literature was a clear reflection of the expanding intellectual horizons of Sephardim. The first Judeo-Spanish newspaper, *La Buena Esperansa*, was established by Raphael Uziel in 1842. Others soon followed. Over three hundred different newspapers were published throughout the Sephardic diaspora through the mid-twentieth century—in Istanbul, Izmir, Edirne, Salonika, New York; in communities in Bulgaria, Yugoslavia, Rumania, Austria, Erets Israel, Egypt, and elsewhere.[1] These newspapers are a remarkable record of Sephardic intellectual life during the modern period. Among the early figures in Sephardic journalism were Uziel, Hayyim de Castro, Yehezkel Effendi Gabbai, and Ezra Benveniste. Leading Sephardic journalists included Hayyim Carmona, David Fresco, Isaac Gabbai, Elia Carmona, Alexander Benguiat, Abraham Galante, and Moise Gadol.

Many of the newspapers were operated independently by their publishers and editors. They were often critical of the established religious and communal leadership. A common theme was the call for progress, modernization, and advancement. The newspapers not only brought news of world events to their readers; they also provided entertainment, political and social commentary, practical advice, editorial opinions, translations of famous literary works, and much more. The editors saw their newspapers as agents of education and enlightenment for their readers, leading

them into the modern world. Sephardic intellectuals were attracted to write for these publications and to express their
thoughts on the burning issues of the day.

If the literary explosion was evident in Judeo-Spanish journalism, it was also manifested in the field of Judeo-Spanish drama.
Hundreds of plays were written in this language; many others
were translated into it, mainly from French and Hebrew. Drama
became a major feature of Sephardic cultural life, and dramatic
performances attracted enthusiastic audiences. Although the
players were amateur actors, at least some dramatic companies
did achieve a quasi-professional level of production.[2]

As might be expected, a large number of plays related to Jewish
religious themes. Purim plays were very popular, as were dramatic
presentations based on the biblical story of Joseph and his
brothers. Heroes of the Jewish people, such as Rabbi Yitzhak
Abravanel and Captain Dreyfus, also were depicted in Judeo-
Spanish drama. Yet there were also plays dealing with the problems and circumstances of contemporary life. The repertoire
included comedies and tragedies, full-scale productions, and
monologues.

Some of the plays described conflicts and tensions stemming
from the clash between modernism and traditional religious values. Abraham Galante (1873–1961) wrote a dramatic work entitled *Rinu,* based on an actual event which had occurred on the
island of Rhodes.[3] Interestingly, all of the characters in the play
are Greek Christians, not Jews. The story tells about a woman
who falls in love with the man next door—who happens to be
married and the father of two children. When he rejects her, she
takes revenge by killing his son. The crime is discovered; the
criminal is apprehended, tried in court, and sentenced to be
executed. During the play, the main characters ponder the question of whether they should follow their emotions spontaneously
or whether they should remain faithful to their religious tradition.
The play is thoughtful and challenging.

It is significant that Galante chose to present his Sephardic
audiences with an emotionally powerful story drawn from contemporary non-Jewish life. Obviously, he felt that Sephardim
could and should focus their attention on the world around them,
and not dwell only on Jewish themes and personalities. More
important, Galante confronted his audience with emotional and
moral conflict. He felt that it was appropriate to discuss such
issues in a public forum. Published in 1906, *Rinu* is a cultural

monument of the intellectual ferment which was taking place in Sephardic communities. The influences of Western culture and of modern education were coming into conflict with traditional religious and communal values.

Elia Carmona

One of the towering figures of Judeo-Spanish literature was Elia Carmona (1869–1931).[4] A prolific and versatile author, he wrote dozens of novels, many of them inspired by popular French novels. He also wrote Judeo-Spanish poetry.

Carmona published a periodical devoted to humor and satire, *El Jugeton,* founded in 1908. On the eighteenth anniversary of this newspaper, he issued an autobiographical pamphlet entitled *Como nacio Elia Carmona* ("Elia Carmona's Upbringing"). This work provides insight into Carmona's life as well as into the general cultural condition of Sephardic Jewry at that time.

He opens his autobiography with a letter to his readers, thanking them for their support over the years. He explains that the book will describe the main events of the fifty-five years of his life. "In this story which I am presenting to you today, you will not encounter robberies, nor murders; but facts and various curious accounts, so that you will see how patience brings one to a good end, and how a human being must not be discouraged in the course of his life."

Carmona relates that he was born in the neighborhood known as Ortakoy in Istanbul. His family was prominent and prosperous. At age six, he went to the community Talmud Torah and at age eleven was enrolled in the school of the Alliance Israélite Universelle, which was directed by Gabriel Aryeh. During his childhood, the financial condition of his family worsened; his father had to work as a ticket man for the tramway company. At age fifteen, Carmona's father informed him that he would have to quit school in order to earn some money to help the family. Elia obtained a position as teacher of French for the children of a Turkish official. This only lasted several months, since a French official in Istanbul wanted his own son to have the job.

Elia Carmona then found employment working for a Sephardic Jew who sold matches and papers for making cigarettes. Carmona's mother disapproved, feeling that the job was beneath the dignity of the family. A Turkish official who was a friend of the Carmona family told Elia's mother: "Where is the law that records that a banker is great and a peddler is small? Each man must work to earn his bread with honor." He then told the young Carmona: "The job you wish to do is satisfactory in order for you to earn your bread by the sweat of your brow, with honor. You are not stealing, you are not doing anything dishonorable; you are doing that which you want to do, and you have nothing to be ashamed of." But Elia's mother still frowned on this endeavor. Nevertheless, the young man set up a stand and went into business.

One of the elder members of the Carmona clan learned of Elia's job and told him that it reflected badly on the prestige of the family. He made it clear that Elia had to find another kind of work. Carmona writes: "It is known that the respect which there once was for the elders of the family is not as it is now. I turned all red and promised him that I would not continue anymore in this job, asking him to find me another position as he might choose." The elder Carmona found Elia a position in the printery of a Judeo-Spanish newspaper, *El Tiempo*. Although the young man earned very little, he became a good worker and learned the printing trade.

At that time, David Fresco was the director of the newspaper *El Telegrafo*. When Fresco began a polemic against the chief rabbi of Turkey, Rabbi Moshe Alevy, the rabbi had Fresco's newspaper closed. But Fresco obtained an order from the Turkish government allowing him to reopen. However, eight days later, another order came from the Sultan ordering Fresco to leave his position as editor. Fresco started a new publication, *El Instructor,* and hired some of the workers from *El Tiempo*. Ultimately, Carmona went to work for him.

But Carmona's wages were quite low and he grew dissatisfied. He decided to look for work elsewhere. He went to Salonika, but was not successful in finding a position. He then went to Izmir, but was also frustrated in his goal. Some people had advised him to try his luck in Paris, and he decided to do so. But when his mother learned of his plan, she snared him back to Istanbul.

Carmona's mother suggested that Elia write stories, have them printed, and then sell them for profit. In fact, his mother told him stories which he elaborated into fictional works; thus began his career as a publisher of fiction. "Having noticed that the person who reads Spanish knows neither Turkish nor French, I began to write in a popular language so that children as well as adults could understand, and thereby my little stories began to have much success." He entered a business relationship with the publishers Arditti and Castro, and they printed a number of his stories. Carmona sought new sources for ideas for his works:

I went to see plays in order to get more ideas. I took a little from here and a little from there, and I put together stories. . . . For three years our partnership went very well. One day, we submitted a new novel to the censor, and we were told that we had to wait perhaps three months before it would be approved. What was I to do for three months? I told my friend, Mr. Isaac Arditti, that we had many extra books in stock and that I would travel to Rodosto [Tekirdag] to sell them—and that is what I did. In four days, I received a hundred liras of orders for our printery and sold twenty liras of books of the stories. From there I went to Corlu, where I did little business. Then I went to Edirne. I was there for ten days and received eighty liras for printery jobs and fifty liras for the books I sold.

During this period (1901), Carmona's father died. Not long after his father's death, Carmona finally got married. One year later, his tale continues, "the censors told me that from then on I would not be allowed to write in my books about killing, robbing, or love. I thought of going to Alexandria to publish my novels there. My mother and my wife finally agreed to this. I arrived in Alexandria on the night of Purim 5662 [1902]." Carmona was fascinated by Alexandria, where he saw electric lights for the first time. He quickly made contact with Turkish Jews who were living in Alexandria, and arranged for a Sephardic printer to issue his novels. But things did not go well. Carmona then moved to Cairo, where he received general encouragement—but no real help.

For thirty nights, I had no place to go to sleep and practically nothing to eat. I looked for food in the garbage. I had reached the point where I seriously considered committing suicide. But as I arrived at the river, I remembered the words of my mother, who had told me that I should go in peace and return in peace and in good health. This thought made me hesitate. I could not kill myself. I would not cause my mother such pain. I turned back and began walking.

Fortunately, a philanthropist took an interest in Carmona and gave him a considerable sum of money in order to help him in his career. He decided to purchase a stock of costume jewelry in Alexandria, in the hope of increasing his capital. But within four months, he was ruined once again. He had just enough money left to buy passage back to Istanbul.

Having returned home to his wife and mother, Carmona planned to go back into the printing business. He went to work for David Fresco, but then came up with the idea of starting a newspaper of his own, a humorous publication which would make people laugh and raise their spirits. On July 24, 1908, David Fresco jubilantly brought the news to his printery that Sultan Abdul Hamid had restored the Turkish constitution (he had suspended it in 1878) and thus there would be no more censorship. Carmona immediately found a partner, Abraham Behar, and applied for the necessary licenses to open a newspaper; fifteen days after the proclamation of the Constitution, Carmona founded *El Jugeton.*

Had Carmona done nothing else than publish *El Jugeton,* his literary achievement would have been noteworthy. His was one of the longest-lasting Judeo-Spanish newspapers. His wit, independence, and sense of irony won him an appreciative audience. He was not reluctant to criticize the "establishment," nor was he hesitant to poke fun at himself.

But Carmona's writings included many other works, most of them in the area of fiction.[5] His novels were filled with excitement, adventures, crimes, romance, unlikely coincidences. His purpose was to entertain his audience, so he chose to write colorful and fast-moving stories.

A good example of his work is his novel *Los dos hermanicos,* published in Istanbul in 1921 and listed as his twenty-ninth novel. It related a story which ostensibly occurred in Istanbul in 1913. The story is about a brother, Mushon, and a sister, Estreyica, who were orphaned when quite young. Mushon is kidnapped by a non-Jewish neighbor who wants to raise him as a Christian. The novel relates the trials and tribulations of each of the siblings during their period of separation from each other. Mushon, for example, is miserable in the Christian home in which he is being raised. He decides to run awway. "No! I can no longer tolerate this life! It is true that I have no father or mother, but I do have a nation! . . . My nation will protect me, my nation will give me to eat!" He escapes from the Christian family and begins to live on the streets together with other poor children. The youngsters beg for alms and somehow manage to sustain themselves. During World War I, there are shortages of food and other necessities in Turkey, and many poor people—adults and children—are compelled to beg in the streets for assistance. After the war, a Jewish woman establishes an orphanage for Jewish children. By a fortunate coincidence, Mushon and Estreyica are both brought to the orphanage and are happily reunited.

Another novel, *La novia agunah*, was published in Istanbul in 1922. The story is set in Istanbul. A certain wealthy Jew is celebrating the engagement of his only daughter to the son of a pious rabbi. Everyone rejoices over the match—except the bridegroom. He is very poor and does not like the idea of marrying a rich wife, feeling he will always be dependent on her and her family. Before the marriage takes place, he flees, hoping to go to Paris to become wealthy on his own. But the ship on which he is traveling is wrecked near Corsica. As he struggles to swim to shore, a non-Jewish criminal, who has already reached shore safely, tells him that he will save him only if he hands over his ring and all his valuables. Of course, the young man agrees. Once the thief has taken the valuables, though, he throws the young man back into the ocean to drown. But the victim somehow manages to make it to shore alive. Having no money and nowhere to go, he decides to stay in Corsica and try to earn a living there.

Meanwhile, everyone in Istanbul hears that the ship has been wrecked. One of the young man's friends tells the community that the bridegroom was on the ship. The bride then becomes an *aguna*, a woman not free to marry anyone else because there is no absolute proof that her bridegroom has died and thus she is still bound to him. After about eight years, the thief comes to Istanbul and tells the story of the shipwreck. On the basis of his account, the rabbinic court, after due deliberation, decides that the young man is dead and that the bride should be permitted to marry someone else. A new bridegroom is found and the wedding day arrives.

But then the original bridegroom comes to Istanbul. He is dressed in European-style clothes, his face is clean-shaven, and he speaks Italian. He arrives at the wedding just before it begins, and protests that the ceremony may not take place since it has never been proven that the first bridegroom is actually dead. The rabbis call the thief and have him tell the newcomer the story. But the young man confronts the thief and tells what really happened. Then he marries the bride. The second bridegroom is married to the young man's orphaned cousin. Everyone lives happily ever after.

Carmona's works were written in a flowing, simple style, inter-

spersed with Judeo-Spanish proverbs and folk sayings. His stories, though featuring Jewish heroes, were not at all of a religious
nature. On the contrary, he did not hesitate to portray characters
who were not religiously observant. His literary output was
dramatic evidence of the development of secular literature among
the Judeo-Spanish Sephardic communities.

Angel Pulido

In August 1903, the Spanish senator, Angel Pulido, was traveling on a boat from Belgrade when he met some Sephardic Jews
who were conversing in Judeo-Spanish. The Spaniard was impressed by the discovery that the roots of the Sephardim in Spain
were so deep and lasting that they had continued to speak a
medieval Spanish language. He struck up a friendship with a
Sephardic fellow passenger, Dr. Enrique Bejerano, director of the
Sephardic school in Bucharest. Bejerano was a dignified man,
erudite, conversant in a number of languages. (He was the first
Sephardic Jew to become an academic correspondent to the
Academy of the Spanish Language.) Pulido's conversation with
Bejerano was an important turning point for the senator. He was
filled with the desire to learn more about Sephardim, to meet and
speak with them, to reclaim them for Spain. Pulido went on to
write a book about the Sephardim which he entitled *Españoles
sin patria* ("Spaniards Without a Country").[6]

This book, published in Madrid in 1905, is itself a cultural
monument to the Sephardic life of that time. Pulido included
correspondence he had received from Sephardic intellectuals and
communal leaders throughout the Judeo-Spanish-speaking
world—Turkey, Greece, the Balkans, Morocco, Erets Israel,
South America, the United States. He also included many photo-
graphs of Sephardic personalities. While some are garbed in
traditional clothing, others are dressed in the European fashion.
The pictures themselves reflect the cultural changes which were
occurring among the Sephardim.

Pulido's book demonstrates clearly that there was a significant
group among the Sephardim who were devoted to intellectual
concerns other than religion. They were proud of their heritage
as Sephardim; they worked to improve the cultural lot of the
masses; they often felt frustrated that progress—as they envisioned it—was slow in coming. Writers, educators, journalists,

communal activists—these men and women represented a new era for Sephardic intellectual life.

Pulido praised those Sephardim who collected and published Judeo-Spanish folklore. This activity symbolized a cultural awareness of the significance of the language and folk traditions of the Sephardim. Folk sayings, proverbs, ballads, and folk tales could sometimes be traced back to medieval Spain. These collections, therefore, not only preserved folk traditions for posterity, but also served as a direct connection between the Sephardim and Spain. Among the important Sephardic researchers in this area whom Pulido cited were Abraham Danon, Abraham Galante, and José Benoliel.

Pulido's interest in the Sephardim captured the imagination of a number of Spanish scholars, who also began to collect and study Judeo-Spanish materials. Spanish historians started to research and write about the Sephardic experience in medieval Spain. As Christian Spain became more fascinated with the Sephardim, even inviting them to return to live there, some Sephardim were becoming more fascinated with their Iberian roots. This tendency was dominant, for example, in the thinking of the Sephardic scholar and historian Mair José Benardete (1895–1989), whose history of the Sephardim was significantly entitled *The Hispanic Culture and Character of the Sephardic Jews*. Benardete, born in Turkey, lived most of his life in New York. He argued with conviction that Sephardic Jews could only understand their culture by reestablishing their links with Spain. The more they understood Spain, the more they would come to understand their own distinctive identity.[7]

Pulido's interest in the Sephardim of his time extended to the history of the various Sephardic communities. This coincided with a growing interest in Sephardic history among the Sephardim themselves which had accompanied the flowering of Judeo-Spanish literature. Solomon Rosanes (1862–1938), a Bulgarian-born intellectual, wrote a six-volume history in Hebrew of the Jews in the Turkish Empire. Abraham Galante, born in Budrum, Turkey, wrote numerous studies on the Sephardic communities in Turkey. Other writers, too, devoted themselves to historical studies of the Sephardic experience.[8]

La America

During the last decades of the nineteenth century and the early decades of the twentieth, many Sephardic communities experienced significant demographic changes. With the inroads of Western thought came the notions of progress and of individual success. Young people were beginning to believe that they could improve their lot in life by breaking away from the traditional communal and occupational patterns which characterized Sephardic society in the Ottoman Empire, the Middle East, and North Africa. Many chose to migrate to other lands, to try their hands at a new life. Sephardic colonies sprouted up in South Africa, the Congo, Rhodesia, and Latin America. Some Sephardim moved to cities in France and elsewhere in Western Europe. Others migrated to Erets Israel. In the early twentieth century, relatively large numbers of Sephardim found their way to the United States, lured by dreams of fortune and success.

With the migration of thousands of Sephardim, mostly young, the native communities obviously were affected in various ways. The stability of the old societies was shaken to a certain extent. The elders could no longer be sure that the younger generation would remain to maintain the community. Traditional authority was weakened, since people who did not wish to submit to it now had the opportunity to leave and settle elsewhere. Moreover, the young people who left their communities usually sent back money regularly to help support their parents and relatives. The inflow of money from abroad served to heighten the desirability of migrating, or at least of encouraging family members to do so.

From 1890 to 1924, it has been estimated that approximately thirty thousand Sephardic Jews arrived in the United States from the countries of the Levant. Most settled in New York, mainly on the Lower East Side.[9] The lot of the Sephardim, like the lot of most new immigrants, was difficult. They lived in tenements in overcrowded neighborhoods; they were poor; they were unfamiliar with the English language and the patterns of America life. They had to adapt relatively quickly to a society which was radically different from the one they had left.

Sephardic immigrants to New York had even more problems than the far more numerous Yiddish-speaking Ashkenazic newcomers. The established New York Jewish community provided many services for the new immigrants, particularly through the Hebrew Immigrant Aid Society. Help was provided in the areas of housing, employment, and social adjustment to American life. Classes in English were offered. But virtually all of these services were originally geared to Yiddish-speakers. The Sephardim, who spoke Judeo-Spanish (or Judeo-Arabic or Judeo-Greek), were almost completely ignored. In fact, many complained that they had not even been recognized as being Jewish, but had been assumed to be Italians, Greeks, or Arabs. The historic Spanish and Portuguese Synagogue of New York City (Congregation Shearith Israel) did become involved in assisting the Sephardic newcomers. A settlement house on the Lower East Side, operated by the synagogue's sisterhood, provided numerous services for the Sephardic community downtown. Dr. Henry Pereira Mendes was helpful in this work. His assistant, Rabbi David de Sola Pool, was particularly active in efforts to assist the Sephardic immigrants.

The Sephardim on the Lower East Side were far from being a monolithic group. They formed various burial and self-help societies based on their cities of origin in the Old World. Religious and cultural life was hampered by the lack of communal organization. There were many immigrants, all struggling for their livelihoods; Sephardic leaders had difficulty trying to mold the immigrants into a harmonious, efficient community.

In May 1910, Moise Salomon Gadol arrived in New York from his native Bulgaria. Aged thirty-six, Gadol was a highly educated Sephardic Jew who had done well for himself in the "old country." He came to New York to visit some relatives and to learn about life in America. He was shocked to find such harsh conditions on the Lower East Side. He was particularly distressed by the plight of the Sephardic immigrants. He decided to remain in New York and to publish a newspaper in Judeo-Spanish for the benefit of his community. He named it *La America*. The first issue came out on November 11, 1910. Except for various interruptions in publication, *La America* appeared weekly on Fridays until July of 1925 when it closed.

Gadol was a fiery editor, filled with enthusiasm and energy. He saw himself as a leader of his people, providing them with news, facts, guidance, inspiration. He was a staunch proponent of Zionism. He argued tirelessly for a united, harmonious Sephardic community in New York—indeed in the entire United States. He defended the honor of Sephardim when he thought it was slighted by others. He sought to promote unity and understanding between Ashkenazim and Sephardim and to protect the dignity of the Jewish people against those who maligned them.

Fiercely independent, Gadol saw himself as engaged in a great spiritual battle, trying to uplift the Sephardic masses to share his visionary ideals. In 1912 he wrote:

We will not be afraid of anything, we will go to this war with open arms until death, as faithful soldiers, for the honor of our nation. Our weapons are not cannons, knives or guns, but rather the smallest and most powerful weapon in the world. Our weapon is one small pen, the point of which wrote and will always write only the truth, which will break the hearts of the charlatans and intriguers. . . . We will not lose hope before seeing that day which certainly will come, when it will be known that truth always triumphs. [10]

Gadol respected traditional Jewish religious values and observances, although he himself could not be described as being scrupulously careful in his personal religious observance. His printery was sometimes open on the Sabbath. He, like so many of his Sephardic readers, was caught in the struggle to adapt to modernity. It was not easy to balance the claims of tradition with the demands of advancement in a non-Jewish society.

Gadol was a cultural giant among Sephardim during the period in which *La America* was published. Yet, since he was such a passionate proponent of his own ideas, he was not too popular among those who differed with him. The masses of workers were not overly responsive to his idealistic calls for a united communal structure, for improved religious schools and synagogues, and for his other projects.

In spite of Gadol's failure to achieve many of his practical goals, his newspaper served as a vital outlet for Sephardic intellectual life in America. Sephardic leaders, thinkers, essayists, and poets found in *La America* a means of reaching a significant audience. *La America* was an example of the journalistic creativity which characterized Sephardic communities throughout the Judeo-Spanish-speaking world.

Poetry

Judeo-Spanish poetry had two frameworks: religious and secular. Religious poetry was composed throughout the generations. Popular poetic works included humorous poems in honor of Purim, serious poems relating to holy days or biblical themes, and poems relating to religious life-cycle events such as birth and marriage. Secular poetry also had a long tradition in Judeo-Spanish, especially in the realm of ballads and folk songs. The *romancas* dealt with love themes. This folk poetry portrayed human emotions and passions and used imagery evoking the beauties of nature. It had a long tradition, going back to the Sephardic experience in Spain. Outside the genre of the *romancas*, poems on nonreligious themes were uncommon until the late nineteenth century. Then there was an outburst of literary activity which included poetic writings on general as well as religious themes.

Among the Judeo-Spanish poets who wrote on secular themes were Alexandro Perez, born in Izmir but active as a writer in Salonika, Barukh Mitrani of Edirne, E. Navon of Istanbul, Laura Papo Capon of Sarajevo, M. Papo of Ruschuk, S. Salem, A. Taragano of Salonika, and M. D. Gaon of Jerusalem. Many writers had their poems published in the various newspapers, and some issued small collections of poems published separately.[11]

The rising sense of Jewish nationalism found expression in Sephardic poetry of the modern period. In a poem published in 1913, Yosef Uziel wrote movingly of the love of the children, i.e., the Jews, for their mother, the land of Israel. Although the Jewish people have been scattered to the four corners of the earth by their enemies, they continue to long for a return to their mother, their homeland. The mother must not worry; her children are returning, a miracle is happening. The children of Israel are coming back to their mother, Zion.[12]

A booklet of Judeo-Spanish poems by Yitzhak de Boton of Tel Aviv was issued in 1935. De Boton's poems express unreserved enthusiasm for Zionism, for the return of the Jews to their ancestral homeland. In one of his poems, he wrote:

Let us all work without exception
to obtain sooner the realization
more quickly than the Jewish people desires
to live in Palestine and to speak the Hebrew language.[13]

In a poem lamenting the sadness of the the Ninth of Ab, the day when both the First and Second Temples in Jerusalem had been destroyed by enemies, de Boton called on his brothers in the captivity to put an end to the exile, break the chains of slavery, and courageously go to Palestine (p. 15). In a poem addressed to anti-Semites, the poet stated that the more the Jews were oppressed, the stronger became their resistance (p. 30).

Continue your savage work
O barbarous anti-Semite!

In this way you will give more courage
to the great people of Israel.

In his enthusiasm for the rebirth of Jewish sovereignty in the land of Israel, he wrote a poem lauding the establishment of the Hebrew University in 1925. He described the event as an indication of the beginning of the long-awaited redemption (pp. 38–39).

It should be noted that the Sephardim themselves did not create a sharp division between religious and "secular" themes. Very religious and traditional Jews sang love ballads and enjoyed poetry which had not been composed specifically for religious purposes. Likewise, poetry on religious themes remained popular among the masses of Sephardim, even those whose religious observance had declined in the face of modernism.

An interesting illustration of this is found in the *Pirkei Avot* of Rabbi Reuben Eliyahu Israel of Rhodes. Published in 1924, this book included the Hebrew text and a Judeo-Spanish translation of the classic rabbinic collection, *The Ethics of the Fathers*, as well as a brief commentary. In the back of the volume, Rabbi Israel published several poems of a philosophical nature. He also offered maxims to help his male readers understand women! For example: "He who takes a wife in order to obtain her large dowry writes a divorce to his repose"; "Intelligence is the beauty of men, and beauty is the intelligence of women"; "Examine carefully the companion you choose, because the error is one minute but the remorse is a lifetime"; "Praise a woman's beauty in her presence and she will forgive all your sins." The fact that a noted rabbi could include such maxims in a rabbinic work is itself indicative of the lack of strict barriers between religious and "secular" themes.[14]

The burst of literary creativity in Judeo-Spanish which began in the mid-nineteenth century started to wane seriously during the 1930s. Sephardim were adapting more and more to the countries in which they lived, and the younger generations preferred to speak the language of the land rather than Judeo-Spanish. The rise of Turkish nationalism and a constitutional government led to the Turkification of the new generations of Sephardim in Turkey, so that Turkish gradually replaced Judeo-Spanish as their mother tongue. Since Turkey was the major center of Judeo-Spanish life, the weakening of the language there sounded the death-knell for Judeo-Spanish literary creativity.

Moreover, important Sephardic communities were decimated by the vicious Nazis and their collaborators during World War II. Bastions of Judeo-Spanish life—such as Salonika, Rhodes, Monastir, and Sarajevo—were destroyed. The culture which those communities had fostered for centuries entered its own dying stages.

Yet, looking back at the Judeo-Spanish legacy, one can see vibrance, spiritual energy, humor, love, idealism. Through the newspapers, drama, fiction, poetry, and other works, Judeo-Spanish authors left their impress on the destiny of their people.

•12•

Religious Responses to Modernity

Modern times presented new challenges to the traditional structure of Sephardic life. The influences of haskalah thought and the rise of secular literature have been discussed in the previous two chapters. Related to these patterns was the growing desire among educated Sephardim to appear to be cultured and progressive, in the European sense of these terms. Abraham Cappon, an intellectual and author from Sarajevo, wrote that "in our times, thank the Lord, the desire to advance in the ways of culture is not less among the Jews of the Orient than among Jews of the entire world."[1]

Often enough, "progress" was associated with breaking away from traditional religious beliefs and observances. Rabbinic authority was questioned. A growing number of people felt they had the right to do as they pleased, without needing to defer to the rules and regulations of halakhah. While the masses of Sephardim certainly remained traditional throughout the nineteenth century, there were clear signs of change. Some Jews did not properly observe the Sabbath and other holy days. Some grew careless in their observance of the dietary laws. Some men shaved their beards; some women dressed in the European styles, even leaving their heads uncovered.[2]

The drive for "progress" also led a number of Sephardic educators to call for reforms in the traditional educational system. In general, the Sephardic communities of Moslem lands provided formal education for boys, but very little for girls. The boys were taught many things by rote, and often their schooling ended by the age of thirteen or fourteen. Educational techniques varied, depending on the ability of the teachers. While some children benefited from the instruction of gifted and idealistic teachers, many studied under the tutelage of less than inspiring instruc-

179

tors. The "progressive" educators called for the use of modern educational techniques, the hiring of qualified and trained teachers and administrators, and the study of secular as well as Jewish subjects in an organized curriculum.

The schools of the Alliance Israélite Universelle had a significant impact on the Sephardim of Moslem lands. These schools were modern and "progressive." They stressed secular culture in general, and French culture in particular. Some religious traditionalists viewed the Alliance schools as a threat to the religious structure of the community. The Alliance seemed more interested in conveying knowledge than in teaching piety. Yet the Alliance schools served to stimulate the more traditional schools to make improvements in their own programs of study.

An example of the struggle between traditionalists and modernists occurred in the community of Rhodes late in the nineteenth century.[3] In 1882, Moshe Franco established a primary school which he named "Progress." The school taught Hebrew, Turkish, and French, and its teachers were all committed to modern education. The rabbis of the city opposed the new school from its inception. Indeed, their pressure was so great that the school was soon forced to close. One of the teachers, Jacques Abravaya, continued to work for the establishment of a modern school in Rhodes under the aegis of the Alliance Israélite Universelle. But he was unable to achieve his goal. In July 1890, Abravaya wrote to the Alliance office in Paris, seeking a position in a school away from Rhodes. He was "discouraged to see the constantly increasing hostility of the Jews of Rhodes" toward modern education, and he no longer was willing to struggle against the community. In 1895, Abraham Galante—who had received much of his own education in Rhodes—founded a grammar school in the city. It offered a curriculum with Hebrew, Turkish, and French languages. Yet this school, too, did not gain widespread communal support. In 1899, Galante met with several other Sephardic educators to establish a new school. In 1901, the school became affiliated with the Alliance Israélite Universelle. In 1902, a school for girls was also opened in Rhodes under the sponsorship of the Alliance. Once these schools were established, the wave toward modern education increased, and the resistance of the traditionalists declined. In fact, the traditionalists began to utilize modern methods in their own schools.

In this context, it is important to note the contributions to Jewish education of Nissim Behar (1848–1931). Born in Jerusalem, Behar graduated from the Alliance teachers institute in Paris and went on to head the Alliance school in Istanbul from 1873 to 1882. He introduced the method of teaching Hebrew by only speaking Hebrew *(Ivrit be-Ivrit)*. He later headed an Alliance school in Jerusalem, where his modern methods of education were emulated by schools throughout the country. But the rabbinic establishment of Jerusalem was hostile to him, since the rabbis did not condone his educational innovations. In 1901, the Alliance sent Behar to New York to represent its interests in America.

Behar became a public figure in American Jewish life. He also devoted considerable effort to advancing the education of Sephardim on the Lower East Side. He spoke to them in their native Judeo-Spanish language. He was tireless in his commitment to them. Nissim Behar stands out as a cultural hero of his time.[4]

The Sephardic world was blessed with religious traditionalists who recognized the challenge posed by modernism but were not afraid to confront it directly. Instead of retreating into the safety and security of the old patterns, these spiritual leaders strove to inculcate traditional piety while being open to and appreciative of what modernism had to offer.

In Salonika, for example, the large communal school known as Talmud Torah ha-Gadol was headed by Rabbi Moshe Yaacov Otolenghi. In the spring of 1886, a special event was held in order to encourage the public to contribute clothing for the school's students. The ceremony was attended by the leading Jewish dignitaries of the community, as well as the local committee of the Alliance Israélite Universelle. Rabbi Otolenghi delivered a sermon in which he praised the accomplishments of the school. Aside from the academic skills which the children learned, they also received a loving and caring education. The teachers were like parents in their devotion and dedication to the students. Rabbi Otolenghi noted with pride that education was flourishing in Salonika. The older schools were still operating, and new schools were being opened. Graduates of the Talmud Torah ha-Gadol were beginning to assume positions of educational leadership. "We have the good hope—and I say that we are almost certain—that ignorance will dwindle little by little until it disappears forever; when it disappears, idleness and poverty will also disappear. Then honesty and civilization will go forth from our nation, the people chosen from all the nations."[5]

Rabbi Otolenghi's belief in progress was characteristic of the spirit of modernity in his time. Yet the expressed goal of Rabbi Otolenghi and his colleagues was to revive Jewish religious learning among the young of the community so that it would once more be possible to say: "For from Salonika will the Torah go forth."[6] His intention was to create Torah students who were also well trained according to modern standards.

Rabbi Yehudah Nehama worked with Rabbi Yaacov Kovo, the chief rabbi of Salonika, to institute reforms in the educational methods of the Talmud Torah school. When the Alliance opened a school in Salonika, Rabbi Nehama supported it enthusiastically, teaching in the school and cooperating with other teachers to develop a proper curriculum. He recognized the need to teach the children in an enlightened way; but he also recommended that they be given instruction in practical crafts so that they could obtain gainful employment when they were older.[7]

Attitude Toward Secular Education

Attitudes toward the teaching of secular subjects in Jewish schools were an important source of conflict during the latter half of the nineteenth century. Traditionally, Jewish students were taught Hebrew, Bible, Jewish laws, and other religiously oriented subjects. They also learned some rudimentary arithmetic and other basic information that they would need in order to earn a living. But with the advent of modernism came the realization that students needed a much stronger secular education in order to succeed in the world at large. Indeed, the Alliance Israélite Universelle school system stressed the importance of secular studies and encouraged students to delve as deeply as possible into the wisdom of European, especially French, culture.

While some traditional religionists opposed the incorporation of secular studies in the curricula of Jewish schools, the trend was toward the acceptance of such subjects. A number of rabbinic responsa of the nineteenth century shed light on the ensuing controversies.

In 1855, Rabbi Yitzhak Bengualid of Tetuán responded to a question related to this issue from the Jewish community of Gibraltar. The government of Gibraltar had offered to subsidize the schools under its aegis in the amount of one-third of their annual budgets. The Jewish community had declined the subsidy, desiring to support its own school by itself. But as time passed and the financial burden of operating the school increased, some Gibraltan Jews had proposed that the community should take advantage of the government's offer. The question addressed to Rabbi Bengualid asked whether it was appropriate, according to halakhah, for Jews to take money from the government in order to operate their own school. In responding to this question, Rabbi Bengualid articulated the Gibraltar community's concern that Torah education ought to be financed only by Jews. It would not be appropriate to let the non-Jewish government pay part of the educational expenses, he wrote. Since those who provided financial support for Torah education shared in the spiritual reward of the Torah study, the Jewish community ought to maintain jealously all aspects of such education for its members. However, added Rabbi Bengualid, it would be appropriate for the community to take government funds to subsidize non-Torah subjects offered in the school. In particular, he specified that the teacher who taught the children how to write (in the vernacular) could be paid from such funds. But non-Torah subjects were to be taught in classrooms other than those used for the study of Torah subjects.[8] It is obvious from this responsum that for Rabbi Bengualid and the community of Gibraltar, the primacy of Torah study was axiomatic. But it is also clear that the teaching of the vernacular was viewed as a normal and legitimate function for a Jewish school.

Rabbi Israel Moshe Hazan argued forcefully that studying the language of the land in which one lived was necessary. Not only was such study required, but it should be conducted under religious Jewish auspices, under the supervision of the rabbis of the school. Rabbi Hazan noted that this system was working well in the Jewish school of Corfu.

He quoted a statement in the name of the great sage Hai Gaon (939–1038) which had been found in the Genizah in Cairo. Hai Gaon had ruled that it was permissible to teach Jewish children Arabic writing and arithmetic, along with their Torah studies. But it was not permissible to teach writing and arithmetic unaccompanied by Torah studies. In other words, the secular subjects were to be taught in the context of Torah education, under religious supervision.

Rabbi Hazan maintained that Jews should study secular knowledge, taking what was valuable from Greek (and other) wisdom. Other nations did have truths and had discovered important knowledge about nature; Jews were obliged to study these truths. The Bible taught that God gave the earth to all human beings, not only to Jews. Therefore, all humans had the potential of advancing human knowledge and understanding.[9]

Rabbi Eliyahu Hazan

Rabbi Eliyahu Hazan (1846–1908) was born in Izmir into a prominent Sephardic rabbinic family. For several years, he served as an emissary to North Africa on behalf of the Jewish community of Jerusalem. In 1874 he was appointed rabbi in Tripoli, and in 1888 he was elected chief rabbi of Alexandria. Rabbi Hazan was a prolific author and gained a fine reputation for his erudition and religious leadership.

His philosophy of education is reflected in a responsum dealing with the Jewish school of Tripoli.[10] Rabbi Hazan noted that he had accepted the call to serve the community of Tripoli reluctantly, since he would have preferred to remain in Jerusalem. Yet, he had felt a moral responsibility to provide religious leadership to that large community. He had found the level of religious education among the Jews of the city to be quite low. There was no central school building. Instead, the students received religious instruction in the synagogues—which were not properly equipped to serve as classrooms. Moreover, each teacher had from sixty to seventy students, a situation which was certainly not conducive to maximum educational progress.

The major problem for Jewish religious education in the community, Rabbi Hazan indicated, was that many parents removed their children from the Jewish educational system. The wealthier ones sent their children to be educated in Europe, where they learned secular knowledge. Other parents enrolled their children in a Christian school in Tripoli, believing that they would receive a better education there than in the Jewish classes.

Rabbi Hazan decided to establish a large school, where competent teachers could instruct the children in Torah studies. The school also taught Italian and Arabic, languages needed in Tripoli. But some critics arose who argued that it was forbidden according to halakhah to teach foreign languages. Rabbi Hazan wondered why his critics had been silent when Jewish children were studying Italian and French in the Christian school, but were now so vocal in their criticism of such studies under Jewish auspices!

Rabbi Hazan wrote a responsum in which he demonstrated that the study of foreign languages was not only not forbidden by Jewish law but was actually required: no one could be appointed to the Great Court in Jerusalem in ancient times unless he was proficient in many languages. In order to gain this proficiency, it was necessary to be instructed in languages from an early age. Thus, the sages of Israel saw to it that their children received language instruction. They obviously would not have done so if studying foreign languages had been prohibited.

Moreover, he continued, the modern situation required that Jews know the languages of the lands in which they lived. Otherwise, they would not be able to function successfully in society. Indeed, the Bible itself indicated the vital importance of knowing foreign languages. In the Book of Esther, it was recorded that Mordecai had overheard two men plotting to murder the king. Had Mordecai not understood Persian, he would not have been able to save the king's life, and Haman might not have been led to his downfall.

Rabbi Hazan argued further that Jews should be not only educated in languages, but that they should also study the wisdom of the non-Jews. On the one hand, such wisdom presented no danger to people who were steeped in Judaism; on the other, individuals who studied only Torah but had bad personality characteristics were capable of doing improper deeds. Rabbi Hazan stated that the study of secular knowledge should take place under religious auspices so as to ensure that no heretical ideas were taught. The subjects themselves were not a problem; the concern was with the attitudes and beliefs of the teachers. In other words, secular education for Jewish students was fine, as long as the teachers were under religious Jewish guidance.

The Torah, Rabbi Hazan continued, stated that the nations of the world would be impressed with the great wisdom of the people of Israel. If the Jews did not even know how to speak the languages of the non-Jews, however, the Israelites would not appear to be wise, but rather would be deemed to be foolish. Certainly, Jews were not allowed to study heretical texts which could undermine their faith; but this prohibition had nothing to do with the study of languages. A text whose contents are forbidden may not be read even in Hebrew. On the other hand, appropriate texts may be read in any language.

In Rabbi Hazan's view, the current situation of the Jews demanded that they be proficient in the languages of the non-Jewish societies in which they lived. This requirement applied equally to rabbinic scholars and to lay people, including children. If the Jewish school did not instruct children properly in this knowledge, then it was doing a disservice to the Jewish people. Moreover, Jewish parents would refuse to send their children to the Jewish school. If some pietists felt they could live their lives without needing to know the vernacular languages of the non-Jews, they had no right to impose their position on the rest of the community. Most Jews could not and would not abide by such a policy, especially when Jewish law did not require it.

Rabbi Hazan concluded his responsum with a request that his critics cease their attacks on him and his new school. The critics were not arguing on sound halakhic grounds, but were letting their personal feelings obstruct their proper judgment.

A number of leading Sephardic rabbis sent letters of approval to Rabbi Hazan in support of his position.[11] Rabbi Abraham Ashkenazy agreed that the study of non-Jewish languages was vital, but stated that the students should only be taught those languages which they specifically would need in order to make a living. He also emphasized that the instructors should be religious Jews, who would teach with the proper spirit of piety.

Rabbi Abraham Haggiag of Tunis concurred with Rabbi Hazan, stating that the Jewish students in Tunis studied Italian. Jewish schools were obligated to give this instruction in order to help the students to advance themselves. The alternative was that Jewish parents would send their children to non-Jewish schools, believing that the Jewish schools were not providing a proper education. Rabbi Haggiag noted that even the wealthy members of his community were sending their children to the Jewish school now that it provided instruction in Italian.

Rabbi Abraham Palache of Izmir wrote that the Jewish schools of Istanbul had introduced the study of languages. Although there had been initial resistance from some pietists, the practice had become widely accepted and approved. Indeed, the schools in Izmir followed the same policy.

When Rabbi Eliyahu Hazan became chief rabbi of Alexandria in 1888, he found that the Jewish schools of the city emphasized the teaching of languages (Arabic, French, and Italian as well as Hebrew). He felt it was necessary, though, for the Jewish community also to provide vocational training. In 1897, a school was opened which included sections for tailoring and carpentry. Eventually, the Alliance Israélite Universelle adopted the school and expanded its curriculum. The school's enrollment, though, remained relatively small.[12]

Rabbi Reuben Eliyahu Israel

Rabbi Reuben Eliyahu Israel was the last official chief rabbi of the Jewish community of Rhodes.[13] A descendant of a long line of rabbinic scholars, Rabbi Israel as a young man had served as a religious functionary in Rhodes for eighteen years. He then became rabbi of the Sephardim of Craiova, Rumania, where he served for over twenty-four years. He returned to Rhodes in 1922, and served as chief rabbi until his death in 1932.

Rabbi Israel had received traditional rabbinic training and was well-steeped in Talmud and rabbinic literature. He was also receptive to modern educational ideas. Rabbi Israel was knighted by King Victor Emmanuel of Italy.

While serving in Craiova, Rabbi Israel argued for the need to improve the Jewish educational system. The Jewish school had few boys and no girls attending. Most Jewish children were enrolled in Christian schools. The Jewish school provided inadequate instruction in Hebrew language, generally taught by rote. Rabbi Israel called for instruction in conversational Hebrew, believing that the language was a link between Jews and their own culture. It was especially important to be able to speak Hebrew because the Jews in the land of Israel were using Hebrew. This language was the bond that could tie all Jews together.

Recognizing that many students (and adults) did not have a good knowledge of Hebrew, Rabbi Israel translated Psalms and Proverbs into Judeo-Spanish. He also published Judeo-Spanish translations of various hymns sung on the High Holy Days, as well as a translation of the *Ethics of the Fathers*. He wanted Jews to understand the contents of the Hebrew texts which they were reading and chanting.

Rabbi Israel stressed the importance of teaching Jewish history. In one of his sermons, he noted: "We have a sacred obligation to study profoundly our history, in order to know who we are." In the same sermon, he displayed knowledge of non-Jewish art and culture.

Recognizing the forces of modernism, Rabbi Israel opposed the notion of insulating Jewish children in an intellectual ghetto. On the contrary, he believed that children should receive a modern education that would inculcate piety and general culture. If Jews received a proper education, they would in fact be more faithful to their own religious heritage. Rabbi Israel expressed unhappiness with several individuals in Rhodes who had attacked the authority of the Bible based on some things they had read in works of modern biblical criticism. He properly noted that the critics had relied on non-Jewish commentaries, but were ignorant of the Jewish sources and commentaries. They spoke from incomplete knowledge. Rabbi Israel agreed that the modern era required Jews to be open to new scholarship and insights; yet this did not at all mean that traditional beliefs and observances should be cast aside thoughtlessly. He was confident that the tools of modern education could only enhance traditional Jewish education, strengthening Jewish commitment to Torah.

During the period of his service as chief rabbi, the Italian government established a rabbinical college in Rhodes. This college, founded in December 1928, was organized as a modern seminary. Rabbinical students were expected to gain a mastery of the Bible and its commentaries, Hebrew language and grammar, Talmud, codes of Jewish law, Jewish history, Hebrew literature, and religious philosophy. Candidates were given oral examinations and were required to write a dissertation. Beyond the requirements in Jewish studies, students were obligated to study secular subjects under Italian professors. The Rabbinical College of Rhodes was accredited by the Italian government and was required to meet all of the academic standards for state schools. The college attracted students from throughout the Sephardic world, quickly gaining an international reputation for educational excellence. Regrettably, it was closed in 1938 by the Fascist Italian government.

The fact that a modern-style rabbinical school could flourish in Rhodes was testimony to the receptivity to innovation in educational methods among Sephardic religious leaders, including Rabbi Reuben Eliyahu Israel. Graduates of the college became rabbis and teachers in many communities, further spreading its educational philosophy.

Halakhah and Modernity

The changing political, social, and intellectual conditions among the Sephardim obviously were reflected in the works of leading authorities on halakhah. The issues which the rabbis considered, and the manner in which they approached them, give an indication of the religious climate of their times.

Rabbi Hayyim Palache (1788–1869) was born in Izmir into a distinguished rabbinic family. His maternal grandfather was

Rabbi Yosef Hazan, author of *Hikrei Lev,* a collection of responsa. Rabbi Palache grew to become one of the leading rabbis in Izmir, becoming chief rabbi in 1865. He was the author of seventy-two works, although many were not published. His writings covered the entire range of rabbinic scholarship.

Rabbi Palache was a strong opponent of the study of philosophy, even religious philosophy. He chastised those who studied philosophy, stating that it would have been better had they devoted themselves entirely to Torah studies, including the regular study of musar works. Studying philosophy was not only a waste of time, but it could also lead to intellectual confusion and heresy.[14] Rabbi Palache was an advocate of musar study, believing that only through such means could moral excellence be achieved. A strict pietist, he accepted upon himself a number of halakhic stringencies and kabbalistic practices. A traditional halakhist/kabbalist, he was not enthusiastic about the modernizing changes that were beginning to take place during the course of his lifetime.

For one thing, he lamented the fact that some individuals spoke disparagingly of rabbis and rabbinic students.[15] Anti-rabbinic criticism was, of course, not a new phenomenon in Jewish history, but Rabbi Palache believed the sin to be a feature of his own time. Since so much of Jewish practice rested on rabbinical authority, those who disparaged rabbis were undermining the commitment to normative halakhic observance.

Rabbi Palache approved of debate and criticism within the context of rabbinic studies. That is, rabbinic sages and students had the right to present arguments and disagreements in matters of halakhah. Internal debate of this kind was acceptable because all parties involved were searching for the halakhic truth. They worked within the halakhic system and their questions were vital to the halakhic process.[16] However, those who raised challenges to halakhic authority in order to tear it down were committing a serious transgression.

The desire to uphold rabbinic authority was also evidenced in the responsa of Rabbi Yitzhak Bengualid of Tetuán. He was asked a question by Sephardim in London.[17] The members of the historic Shaar Hashamayim Congregation had made a rule forbidding the establishment of worship services within a six-mile radius of the synagogue. Violators were punishable by *herem* (excommunication). The purpose of this rule was to maintain the central authority at Shaar Hashamayim so that splinter groups would be unable to establish their own congregations anywhere in the vicinity of the original synagogue. It happened that some members of Shaar Hashamayim began to attend an early-morning service at an Ashkenazic synagogue within the six-mile radius, although afterward they also went to Shaar Hashamayim. Were they violating the community's rule, since they were praying elsewhere within six miles of their own synagogue? Rabbi Bengualid pointed out that these individuals were not violating the rule and were not subject to the punishment of *herem*. They had valid reasons for attending the Ashkenazic synagogue and they showed their loyalty to Shaar Hashamayim by also attending services there. In the course of his discussion, though, Rabbi Bengualid noted that there were some Sephardim in London who were arguing for the abolition of the second day of holidays, a basic practice established by the sages for the Jews of the diaspora. He sharply rebuked the dissenters, stating that their opinion was contrary to halakhah and that they were separating themselves from the proper ways of the Torah.

In another responsum, Rabbi Bengualid's defense of rabbinic authority provided him the opportunity to express his notion of rabbinic responsibility.[18] It had been the practice of the Jews of Gibraltar and Tangiers, as well as of other cities, to bake their bread in large communal ovens. They did so even when the ovens were owned by non-Jews, and when non-Jews, too, used the ovens for baking their own food. A certain rabbi had declared that Jews were not permitted to bake bread in these ovens, since non-kasher food was also baked in them. Rabbi Bengualid rejected the rabbi's opinion, justifying the traditional practice. In the course of his discussion, he stated that it was obligatory to defend the policy of the previous generations of rabbis who had allowed this practice, since they had been greater sages than the rabbis of the current generation. To stop their policy would lead to severe hardship for the Jewish people: how could they live without bread? It was not proper to enforce stringent interpretations which would hurt the public; one could be strict with himself, but should not impose his strictness on others. Rabbi Bengualid stated that "the recommended idea is to behave with them [the public] with kindness, compassion, and with words which their hearts will accept."

One reaction to the advance of modernism was to reemphasize commitment to traditional rabbinic learning. Significant halakhic works were composed in order to present rabbinic scholarship to the public in a systematic way. Among the works that had a significant impact in the Sephardic world was the monumental *Sedei Hemed,* by Rabbi Hayyim Hizkiah Medini (1832–1904). This was a multivolume encyclopedia which included an alphabetical list of various halakhot, rules of rabbinic methodology, detailed halakhic discussions on major areas of Jewish law, and more. The *Sedei Hemed* was of great importance among Ashkenazim as well as Sephardim. Other halakhic works which gained influence in the Sephardic diaspora were *Ben Ish Hai*, by Rabbi Yosef Hayyim of Baghdad (ca. 1833–1909), and *Kaf ha-Hayyim*, by Rabbi Yaacob Sofer of Baghdad (1870–1939).

A number of halakhic authorities energetically confronted modern problems in a direct way. Recognizing that new conditions had arisen, these rabbinic scholars applied traditional principles of halakhah in a spirit of creativity and innovation. A major example of this type of halakhic leader was Rabbi Eliyahu Hazan.[19]

Rabbi Hazan had a halakhic disagreement with Rabbi Yitzhak Abulafia, chief rabbi of the Jewish community of Damascus, on the following case. A grandfather had arranged for the marriage of his granddaughter and had agreed to pay a penalty if the bride did not show up for the wedding. The agreement was made in a legally binding fashion and included the stipulation that the grandfather would be obligated to make payment if the wedding were called off.

As things turned out, the granddaughter refused to marry the man chosen by the grandfather. He tried to persuade her, but was unsuccessful. Finally, realizing that he could not change her mind, he allowed her to marry another man whom she wished to marry. But then the original bridegroom demanded that the grandfather pay him the sum he had promised in the event that the wedding did not take place. The grandfather refused. He claimed that he had done everything possible to convince his granddaughter to marry the first bridegroom, but that she had refused to do so. He felt that he should not be held responsible for his granddaughter's totally unreasonable decision; he could not have foreseen that she would defy his authority.

Rabbi Abulafia ruled in favor of the grandfather. The essence of his argument was that the grandfather could not have expected his granddaughter to reject the marriage which had been arranged for her. He cited a medieval rabbinic authority who had dealt with a similar case and likewise ruled that the fine need not be paid; it was so rare for a daughter to defy the authority of the one who arranged her marriage that the parent/grandparent could not be held responsible for her abnormal behavior.

Rabbi Hazan disagreed with Rabbi Abulafia's approach. He quoted the opinion of Rabbi Hayyim Yosef David Azulai, who indicated that halakhic decisions had to take changing times into account. If conditions now were different from conditions in previous eras, one could not rely on the previous sources to solve today's problems. By extension, Rabbi Hazan argued, it was no longer a rarity for daughters or granddaughters to choose their own spouses, defying decisions made by parents or grandparents. Medieval sources were dealing with a different reality; they ruled according to the mores and assumptions prevalent in their time. Modern rabbis, argued Rabbi Hazan, had to take into consideration the real situation in their own time. Therefore, the grandfather certainly should have realized that his granddaughter might very well reject the marriage he had arranged. It was not a farfetched concern, but a practical, realistic one which he was obliged to consider when he entered the agreement.[20]

Rabbi Hazan showed his awareness of modern conditions and his desire to address new problems in a responsum dealing with the issue of *agunot*, women who were separated from their husbands but not permitted by halakhah to remarry. The *agunah* problem was indeed an ancient one. For example, if a husband died leaving no children, then his widow was bound by halakhah to her husband's brother. He could either marry her *(yibum)* or free her to marry someone else *(halitsah)*. The widow, thus, was tied to her brother-in-law. If he refused to give her the *halitsah*, or if he could not be found, then she could never remarry. She was an *agunah*. A similar dilemma faced a woman whose husband refused to grant her a divorce *(get)*. She could not remarry without first receiving the divorce. The classic problem was aggravated in the modern era by the availability of civil divorce. Now a couple could get divorced civilly, but since this action had no status or validity according to Jewish law, the wife would still not be able to remarry without obtaining a *get*. As a result, unscrupulous men were able to blackmail their former wives, demanding payment for the delivery of a Jewish divorce.

Rabbi Hazan realized that a solution to the *agunah* problem required the consensus of the leading rabbinic authorities of the time. No one person could solve it on his own. Nevertheless, he felt obliged to offer a solution in the hope that other rabbis would give it serious consideration and act on it. He recommended that during the wedding ceremony, the bridegroom should make a statement indicating that the marriage was conditional. That is, if in the future he and his wife were divorced civilly, he would give her a *get* within a specified time; if he failed to do so, then the marriage would be considered null and void retroactively. While recognizing that many rabbinic authorities would not approve of this solution, he also noted that there were great authorities who had subscribed to it. Since the contemporary situation was so critical, Rabbi Hazan felt it was proper to rely on those authorities who agreed to such a procedure.[21]

In another responsum, Rabbi Hazan dealt with an issue which had recently come up regarding ritual circumcision. One of the traditional procedures of the circumcision was *metsitsah,* drawing out the blood. The ancient practice had been for the mohel (the person performing the circumcision) to draw out the blood orally. In modern times, however, with the greater concern for hygienic methods, some parents objected to the traditional form of *metsitsah.* A mechanical device had been developed which could draw out the blood in a more sanitary fashion.

Rabbi Hazan noted that the traditional method was perfectly proper and should be maintained by those who wished to perform the mitzvah in the best fashion. Yet, he believed each rabbi should decide—case by case—what policy to adopt. If a rabbi felt that a family would forfeit the mitzvah of circumcision altogether if he insisted on oral *metsitsah,* then it was preferable to allow the use of the mechanical device. Since *metsitsah* was not absolutely essential for the circumcision, one could use a more hygienic means, taking a lenient halakhic position due to the exigencies of the times.[22]

Another modern halakhic issue related to the practice of cremation. Halakhah forbids cremation, mandating that the dead be buried in the earth. While Jews had been very careful to observe this law in the past, some who had broken away from the observance of halakhah were now violating it. Rabbi Hazan ruled that it was forbidden to bury in a Jewish cemetery the ashes of someone who had been cremated. The purpose of the prohibition was to demonstrate communal repudiation of cremation, thereby discouraging others from following this terrible practice of sinners. Rabbi Hazan expressed his total opposition to cremation in a letter to Rabbi Eliyahu Benamozegh. He argued that those who requested that their remains be cremated were defying an ancient and sacred Jewish practice; their request demonstrated their insensitivity to Jewish law and tradition. Nevertheless, the near kin of the person who was cremated could observe the various laws of mourning if the cremation had been performed without their approval. They could recite Kaddish and chant a Haftarah in memory of the deceased, as well as observe those laws of mourning which were for the honor of the mourners rather than for the deceased.[23]

Rabbi Benzion Uziel

One of the great luminaries of modern Jewry was Rabbi Benzion Meir Hai Uziel (1880–1953). He was born in Jerusalem, where his father had served as head of the rabbinical court of the Sephardic community as well as president of the community council. In 1911, Rabbi Uziel was appointed chief rabbi of the city and district of Jaffa, where he worked closely with the Ashkenazic rabbi of the district, Rabbi Abraham Yitzhak Kook. In 1921, Rabbi Uziel was appointed chief rabbi of the Jews of Salonika, and in 1923 he returned to Israel to serve as chief rabbi of Tel Aviv. In 1939 he became Rishon le-Zion, the Sephardic Chief Rabbi of the land of Israel. In addition to being a dynamic leader and activist, he was a prolific author, having composed a number of influential works in halakhah and Jewish thought.

In an address given on 12 Kislev 5697 (1936), Rabbi Uziel called for the establishment of an authoritative rabbinic body along the lines of the ancient Sanhedrin.[24] He declared that the reconstituted Sanhedrin would provide uniform halakhic leadership to world Jewry, strengthening religious commitment among Jews everywhere. In the face of growing disaffection with religion, the Sanhedrin would be a powerful voice for unity and revival. But Rabbi Uziel had a broad vision of rabbinic responsibility. Rabbis were to establish justice, not merely to rule on specific halakhic questions that came their way. They were to deal with the great public issues of the time and give creative leadership to the Jewish people. Rabbi Uziel believed that rabbinic decisors were not bound by the precedents established by sages of previous generations. Going back to the model of the Great Court in ancient Jerusalem, Rabbi Uziel noted that its authority "was restricted only to the time in which it sits on the chair of judgment. But the decisions of the Great Court are not established as law and do not obligate the judges who will come after them to judge and to teach like them."[25] Rabbi Uziel followed the principle established by Maimonides that halakhic decisions should be made on the basis of rigorous intellectual inquiry, not merely by relying on the opinions of great sages.

In addressing modern problems, Rabbi Uziel demonstrated his erudition, compassion, and love of Israel. For example, in his zeal to strengthen Jewish settlement in the land of Israel, he ruled that grafted *etrogim* (citrons) grown in Israel were acceptable for use on the festival of Succoth. Although this was a matter of halakhic controversy, Rabbi Uziel posited that Israeli-grown etrogim should be given precedence over any others, since by purchasing them one would thereby support the Jewish farmers in Israel.[26]

Like Rabbi Hazan, Rabbi Uziel was deeply troubled by the *agunah* problem. He agreed with Rabbi Yaacov Moshe Toledano of Alexandria, who had recommended that at the time of the wedding the bridegroom should be required to make a clear statement that his betrothal of his wife was based on the approval of the rabbinic court of the city. This statement would enable the rabbinic court, if circumstances should warrant it, to invalidate the marriage retroactively at some future date. In spite of considerable rabbinic opposition to this idea, Rabbi Uziel defended it and recommended its implementation.[27]

Rabbi Uziel's concern with modern issues led him to consider what was then a hypothetical case: the legal status of testimony given by non-Jews in a state governed by Jewish law. He prefaced his discussion with the following remarks:

One of the greatest yearnings of the people of Israel is the reestablishment of Jewish justice according to the laws of the Torah. And one of the most important goals of the redemption is to establish our system of justice as it was in ancient times. Therefore, when justice returns to our power, and Jewish judges sit on the chairs of judgment, and the Torah rules in all matters among people—will we then be able to accept the testimony of a non-Jew and pass judgment based on it? It is impossible to answer this question in the negative, because it would not be civil justice to disqualify as witnesses those who live among us and deal with us honestly and fairly. Weren't we ourselves embittered when the lands of our exile invalidated us as witnesses? If in the entire enlightened world the law has been accepted to receive the testimony of every person without consideration of religion or race, how then may we make such a separation?[28]

He went on to present a halakhic case for allowing non-Jews to serve as witnesses in courts which operated according to Jewish law.

Rabbinic scholars such as Rabbi Eliyahu Hazan and Rabbi Benzion Uziel provided halakhic insight with which to deal with modern problems. Their contributions to modern halakhic literature were truly monumental.

• 13 •

Israel and the Nations

The Jewish people underwent cataclysmic crises during the modern period. Enlightenment and emancipation in Europe created enormous challenges for the maintenance of traditional Jewish religious life. Jews developed various responses to modernity—some antagonistic, some conciliatory, some enthusiastic. The spread of European ideas into the Moslem lands in which most Sephardim lived introduced tensions within Sephardic life there as well.

Moreover, the Jewish world underwent major demographic changes during the late nineteenth and early twentieth centuries. Massive pogroms in Russia led to a huge migration of Russian Jews, mainly to the United States. During the 1880s, large numbers of Eastern European Jews went to America, hoping for a better and safer life. Within the Sephardic world, there was also a significant increase in population movements. Thousands emigrated to the United States. Also, many Sephardim and Ashkenazim migrated to the land of Israel, sharing the dream of reestablishing a Jewish homeland there. During this period of migration, Jews from the "old countries" found new homes in Latin America, Canada, Africa, and Australia.

Jewish communities which had been relatively self-contained for centuries were now facing powerful changes. The historic, traditional authority structures were breaking down.

For centuries, Jews had ambivalent feelings regarding the "outside" world of the non-Jews. On the one hand, they had suffered so much oppression and humiliation in Christian and Moslem lands that it was impossible for them not to have some bitterness toward the non-Jewish world. Although Jews in Moslem lands generally were not subject to the same degree of physical brutality as Jews in Christian lands, they still lived an abnormal existence.

197

A Christian traveler through Egypt in the 1830s reported that "the Jews are held in the utmost contempt and abhorrence by the Muslims." Although the situation of the Jews, he said, was less oppressive than formerly, they "scarcely ever dare to utter a word of abuse when reviled or beaten unjustly by the meanest Arab or Turk."[1] A generation later, another observer noted that

the Muslim hates no other religion as he hates that of the Jews. . . . Even now that all forms of political oppression have ceased, at a time when such great tolerance is shown to the Christian population, the Arabs still bear the same contemptuous hatred of the Jews. It is a commonplace occurrence, for example, for two Arabs reviling each other to call each other Ibn Yahudi (or "son of a Jew") as the supreme insult . . . it should be mentioned that in these cases, they pronounce the word Yahudi in a violent and contemptuous tone that would be hard to reproduce.[2]

A common Moslem epithet for Jew was *tchifut*, a derogatory term meaning avaricious and mean.[3] Living in a society where hostility against them was common and where they suffered serious legal disabilities, the Jews of Moslem lands tried their best to be unobtrusive. A nineteenth-century French traveler, Victor Guerin, noted that the Jews of Rhodes, "fashioned by long centuries of servitude, bend themselves under their yoke with supple and docile faces."[4]

In 1840, the Jews of Rhodes and Damascus both faced the malicious blood libel. That such an incredible lie could willingly be believed by the masses of non-Jews is itself testimony to the hostile environment in which Jews lived.

The specter of the blood libel continued to haunt Jews. When a rabbinic conference was scheduled to be held in Cracow in 1903, Rabbi Eliyahu Hazan wrote to a number of rabbis in advance, proposing that the agenda include a public repudiation of the blood libel charges. During the previous few years, he said, several Jewish communities had been victimized by such libels, and it was necessary to demonstrate the falseness of these charges once and for all. Rabbi Hazan noted that even in Egypt "a land of liberty and freedom, our enemies scorn us with this abominable libel." He stated that the libel was believed not only by the masses of ignorant people, but also by the educated classes.

Non-Jews had been raised with this hateful idea since infancy, and it was deeply rooted within them. Rabbi Hazan recommended, therefore, that the rabbinic conference begin with a solemn ceremony in a synagogue in Cracow. With rabbinic delegates from around the world present, as well as government officials, the holy ark should be opened and the rabbis should take the Torah scrolls into their arms. Then they should pronounce under oath that the blood libel was absolutely false and had no foundation whatsoever. No Jew at any time or in any place had ever been guilty of such a charge, since murder is reprehensible according to the laws of the Torah. Rabbi Hazan believed that a solemn public ceremony of this kind might have an effect at least on the more educated non-Jews, and possibly even on the lower classes. [5]

Rabbi Hazan's suggestion was accepted by the conference committee and the ceremony took place in the ancient synagogue of Cracow. Thousands of people crowded into the synagogue. Rabbi Hayyim Leibush Horowitz, the head of the rabbinic court in Cracow, addressed the gathering, stating that it was a sacred occasion when rabbis gathered in order to strengthen the faith of the Jewish people and to combat the growing trends of religious apathy and assimilation. He then went on to inveigh against the blood libel, declaring its absolute falseness and demanding that the non-Jewish world stop fabricating this charge against the Jews.

It is not for our sake, not for us. Our aim today is for all of humanity, not for ourselves—to cleanse all of humanity of the great sin of suspecting the innocent. We ask all the rabbis to call out in the name of God and to take an oath that this libel which stems from the source of ignorance and viciousness is a false libel, an untrue charge; so that it can be completely eliminated from the world forever.

Rabbi Eliyahu Hazan then reiterated that the blood libel was a lie. Over the years, non-Jewish rulers had recognized the falsity of the blood libel. Rabbi Hazan mentioned the decree issued by the Sultan (after the blood libels of 1840) which stated that the charges were false, and that Jews should be spared from such unjust libels in the future. He expressed the hope that this evil would vanish like smoke so that "we will live together with all the nations in love, friendship and fellowship. For we all have one Father, and one God created us." He went on to state that the

Jews had always been a faithful and law-abiding group in the countries in which they lived.

Some criticism was raised against this ceremony by a certain rabbi who believed that it had been unnecessary for the rabbis to take an oath regarding the blood libel. It was so obviously false that the oath was not needed; therefore, the rabbis who took the oath had used God's name in vain. To this charge, Rabbi Hazan responded that he himself had spoken with educated non-Jews who believed that it was part of Jewish tradition for Jews to use blood of non-Jewish children for ritual purposes. Rabbi Hazan argued that it was necessary to do something very dramatic and powerful to set aside this deep prejudice among non-Jews. Many great rabbis had agreed with Rabbi Hazan that it was justified to take the oath since it was for the sanctification of God's name.[6] Obviously, anti-Jewish sentiment had not disappeared with the rise of modernity. Jews still were subjected to overt and subtle discrimination. As they tried to make peace with the non-Jewish world, hoping that modernity would bring true enlightenment and tolerance, they nevertheless could not be oblivious to the hatred against them which still existed.

Israel and Humanity

During the nineteenth century, Rabbi Eliyahu Benamozegh attempted to present Judaism in universalistic terms. He believed that Christians and Moslems misunderstood Judaism, and that their misunderstanding led to hatred and suspicion. If only they had a true idea of Judaism, they would be more sympathetic and respectful. Rabbi Benamozegh wrote a number of works presenting Jewish ethical and philosophical teachings. His works were aimed both at Jewish and non-Jewish readers.

One of his important books, written in French, was *Israel and Humanity*. He opened his discussion by noting that religion was threatened by the increasing secularism of society. All religions were engaged in an internal struggle between traditionalism and modernism; the conflict between faith and reason was ubiquitous.

Rationalism, he said, was not capable of fulfilling the true needs of humanity. Spiritual life was vital for human well-being. Christianity and Islam, both of which grew from Jewish sources, had dominated much of the world for many centuries. But Judaism had remained relatively obscure. However, Judaism contained universal features and had a message for humanity. The problem was that Judaism was known to the world largely through the teachings of Christianity and Islam. At times it was presented favorably; at other times it was presented unfavorably. But real Judaism, from its own point of view, had not been revealed to humanity. Judaism had not had the opportunity to explain its own ideals to the world.[7] This book was an attempt to do so.

Rabbi Benamozegh described the Jewish notion that humanity was actually one family, created by one God. God loved all His children, but gave the people of Israel the special responsibility of maintaining and teaching the Torah. "In the heavens there is but one God, one Father for all humanity; and on earth there is a family of nations, among whom Israel is the *behor* [first-born], destined to teach and give as an inheritance the true faith to humanity."[8] The Torah of Moses was given to the Jews, and the Torah of the children of Noah was given to the non-Jews.

The ancient Israelites had the concept of one God, a universal and eternal deity. Judaism's pure monotheism precluded the Christian idea of a trinity. Although the people of Israel practiced the laws of the Torah among themselves, their goal was to introduce spiritual ideas to others as well. That Judaism was outward-looking and had a universal message was evidenced by the many proselytes who joined the Jewish people. The people of Israel were influenced by the non-Jewish world, but only absorbed those things which did not compromise essential Jewish identity. Jewish tradition benefited greatly from the contributions of proselytes and their descendants. According to a kabbalistic teaching, Jews were scattered among the nations in order to gather the sparks of truths which were spread among them, and to assimilate these truths into Judaism. Moreover, this process drew non-Jews closer to Judaism. Jews were obligated to spread religious teachings to the nations, but at the same time to preserve their own identity. Thus, Judaism forbade intermarriage with non-Jews even though it recognized a responsibility toward them.[9]

The Jews were able to communicate their religion to non-Jews in terms which the people of the surrounding culture could understand. They drew on the general intellectual and spiritual culture of their societies.

Long before Greek philosophers dealt with metaphysical topics, the people of Israel had already established the belief in the unity of God. How was it possible for people who were not experts in philosophy to arrive at such an elevated understanding of God, surpassing the understanding of the greatest of Greek philosophers? Israel's achievement was the result of "intuition," or better stated, of revelation.

The belief in one God led to a belief in the unity of science, the unity of the laws of the natural universe. Since everything had been created by one God, the laws of nature were unified and consistent. Moreover, the belief in one God necessitated the belief that God was the creator of all human beings, not only of Israel. Even idolaters had some notion of the unique and universal God; the Israelites taught that the one God was God of all the universe, of all humanity. God's providence is universal. All righteous people, Jews and non-Jews, have a portion in the world-to-come.[10]

Rabbi Benamozegh pointed out that Jewish law protected the interests of non-Jews. The Noahide laws, principles revealed by God through the Torah, were intended for the non-Jews. By fulfilling these basic laws of morality, non-Jews would live righteous and good lives; society would be just and upright.[11]

Thus, according to Rabbi Benamozegh, Judaism provided a proper basis for a moral and happy society for all people, not just for Jews. The Israelites had the special responsibility of teaching these basic principles of morality and justice to the world, just as the first-born in antiquity had the responsibility of providing spiritual guidance to his family.

Maintaining Uniqueness and Universality

Rabbi Benamozegh stressed the need for Israel to maintain its distinctiveness and its universality simultaneously. This was not an easy task. Since the Jewish people was so small numerically, there was always the risk of assimilation. Isolationism had its proponents. They argued that in order to remain distinctive, the Jews needed to cut themselves off as much as possible from the much larger non-Jewish society. Rabbi Benamozegh rejected this position, believing it was not true to the genius of Judaism.

Rabbi Benzion Uziel, writing in the twentieth century, also considered the dilemma of balancing uniqueness and universality. He insisted that Jews needed to know their own religious charter, their goals.[12] This national charter would guide them in all their relationships, since it would give them the transcendent vision which would allow them to overcome any difficulties. Judaism was all-encompassing.

Rabbi Uziel noted that there were some who argued that Judaism should be practiced privately; in public, Jews should conduct themselves as "human beings." Such an attitude was absurd. The very goal of Judaism is to make the Jew into the finest possible human being. Non-Jews who saw Jews who were truly fulfilling the teachings of Judaism would be much impressed with their humanity and righteousness. A Jew who thought religion should be a private matter, not for application in the world at large, was making a horrible error. He simply did not understand the real message of Judaism.

On the other hand, Rabbi Uziel pointed out, there were Jews who claimed that Judaism was only a faith. This position, too, was erroneous. It ignored the fact that the people of Israel constituted a nation with a distinctive national character. It was incorrect to divorce Jewish faith from Jewish nationalism; the Torah did not do so, nor did the sages throughout the generations. The Jews were a nation with a deep connection to their own historic homeland.

Rabbi Uziel criticized yet another erroneous approach to Judaism—the notion that it could only survive if Jews isolated themselves from the rest of society. Those who relegated Jewish life to the synagogues and study halls were constricting the real message of Judaism. The Torah was capable of confronting all cultures and all peoples without retreating. Jews who had a deep understanding of Torah did not have to fear that it would be unable to withstand pressures from non-Jewish culture. On the contrary, the Torah was God's word and could stand up to any possible confrontation. A living culture has no fear of borrowing and integrating concepts from other cultures; it can do so without losing its own identity. Jews can learn from the non-Jewish world and still remain faithful to their own distinctive mission of holiness and righteousness. Moreover, a living culture naturally wants to share its ideas with others. Judaism has a message from which others could learn. To constrict Judaism to a ghetto mentality was unacceptable. Indeed, it was a sign of failure, an indication that Jews felt their teachings could not be shared with others.

The goal of Judaism, said Rabbi Uziel, is holiness. But holiness did not entail isolation from the real world. On the contrary, Jews were called upon to maintain holiness in the practical everyday world, in thought and deed. Moreover, their holiness would be incomplete if they separated themselves from human society, closing themselves off from the new scientific and philosophical ideas of the age. Rather, their responsibility was to draw what was good and valuable from modern thought and to integrate it into the mainstream of Jewish life. This process would not compromise the essence of Judaism, the quest for holiness. The task of the Jewish nation was to work, to build, to improve itself; to make the world better; to raise others to the highest level of human perfection through peace and love; to be sanctified in the service of God, both in thought and deed; to be a blessing to themselves and to all the nations; to be a holy nation to God, the creator of the universe and of humanity.

Conversion to Judaism

The modern period witnessed a dramatic increase in intermarriages involving Jews with non-Jewish partners. Questions arose frequently about the possibility of converting non-Jewish fiancees or spouses to Judaism, and about converting children born of a non-Jewish mother and a Jewish father.

Rabbinic attitudes varied concerning the issue of conversion. One viewpoint was that no one should be accepted as a convert to Judaism unless he or she fully intended to live according to halakhah, observing all the commandments incumbent on Jews. Yet, in reality, many of those who wished to convert to Judaism were not converting from strictly religious and ideological motivations. They simply wanted to be Jews so that they could share the same religious culture as their spouses and could raise their children within the Jewish fold. Their decision for conversion was often practical and sociological rather than idealistic and theological.

Other rabbis argued that it was permissible to accept converts whose motivation for conversion was for the sake of marriage. Rabbi Uziel argued that it was actually incumbent upon rabbis to perform conversions for non-Jewish individuals married to Jews, even when it was expected that the convert would not be strictly observant of Jewish law. Rabbi Uziel believed that such conversions were mandated since they would serve to remove the sin of intermarriage and would enable the children born of such relationships to remain within the Jewish community.[13] Rabbi Eliyahu Hazan also had had a liberal attitude toward conversion.[14]

Zionism

During the nineteenth century, Rabbi Yehudah Alkalai had argued for the reestablishment of Jewish sovereignty in the land of Israel. Through his writings, preachings, and activities, he was a precursor of the Zionist movement organized by Theodor Herzl. Other Sephardic voices could also be heard which expressed the longing for a return to Israel. These included the poet Emma Lazaraus as well as Rabbi Henry Pereira Mendes.

Zionist groups existed in numerous Sephardic communities during the half-century before the establishment of the State of Israel in 1948. Nonetheless, the Sephardic love for and attachment to Israel was based more on historic religious feelings than on the political and organizational work of the Zionist movement. The masses of Sephardim in Africa and Asia held the traditional Jewish belief that God would one day restore the Jews to their own land. Over the generations, thousands had left their homes to migrate to the Holy Land. During the twentieth century, the numbers increased greatly. And when the State of Israel was actually established, there was a massive migration of Jews from Africa and Asia. A messianic fervor was associated with this migration.

Rabbi Benzion Uziel was a forceful advocate of Zionism, of the reestablishment of Jewish sovereignty in the land of Israel. His writings were imbued with a profound love of the land of Israel and a sincere desire that Jews from throughout the world would return to their historic homeland. The Holy Land was a central feature of Jewish national existence, and it had been promised by God to Abraham, Isaac, and Jacob and their descendants forever. Rabbi Uziel praised the modern Jewish pioneers, the *halutsim*, who followed the example of their ancestors in reclaiming the land of Israel for the Jewish people. They were heroic in their ideals and in their work; they were prepared to fight against many enemies. They were paving the way for the redemption of Israel, which would also bring peace and joy to the entire world. [15]

Rabbi Uziel pointed out that there was an eternal bond between the people of Israel and the land of Israel. Although many peoples had conquered Israel over the centuries, none had been able to keep the land as a permanent home. The land itself rejected foreign rulers. When England issued its White Paper restricting Jewish immigration into Israel, Rabbi Uziel concluded that England had written its own decree, expelling itself from Israel.

England and the Arab nations which wanted control of the land were driven out, and the people of Israel were able to establish their own sovereignty. "According to the measure which they had wished to expel Israel from its land—so it was measured for them that they be expelled from the land in haste and confusion. And who caused this, if not the God of Israel who sanctified the land with His holiness and who keeps His covenant with His chosen people."[16]

God's providence was evident in the establishment of the Jewish state. Not only did the Jews repulse the huge Arab attack; not only did they defeat armies which were far larger and better trained. But Arab countries sent Jews from their own countries to Israel. Yemenite and Iraqi Jews had come in great numbers; Jews from other Arab countries would also come. This could only have occurred through God's benevolence.[17]

A problem which bothered some religious Jews was: If the rise of the State of Israel was an act of God's providence, why were most of the Zionist leaders and workers not religious Jews? Why would God have chosen nonreligious people to effect His will? Rabbi Uziel responded by saying that God wanted all Jews to follow the ways of the Torah. Those who had drifted away from religious life needed to do *teshuvah* (repentance). God motivated the nonreligious Jews to be involved in Zionism as a way of bringing them closer to their people, to spare them from assimilation. In this way, they would have the possibility of doing a complete repentance. "With this faith, we approach them [the nonreligious] with love, and we draw them closer to the love of Judaism, the Torah and its holiness. . . . Is it at all permissible for us to turn away from any effort which involves the redemption of our people and our land simply because secular Jews have engaged in it?"[18] Religious Jews should certainly remain faithful to their beliefs and traditions; yet they should not reject their nonreligious fellow Jews.

Indeed, Rabbi Uziel maintained that religious Jews should be involved in all facets of life in Israel, participating in the full range of civic and governmental activities. In this way, they could bring all Jews closer to the ways of Torah. Numerical strength would bring an increase in overall influence. Rabbi Uziel was much in favor of the approach of Mizrachi, the movement of religious Zionism. He said that Mizrachi had been founded by great sages, people of deep faith. "We will walk in their path, though it be difficult and dangerous. This path of God is long, but we are not free from exerting all our strength to reach our goal."[19]

Rabbi Uziel's vision of Zionism was messianic. The State of Israel was to be a flourishing country, a place where the Jews of the world would come to settle. It was to be built on the ideals of Judaism. The Jewish people would be able to live happily and at peace, serving God, following the teachings of the Torah, creating a model society of righteousness and justice. But the reestablishment of Jewish sovereignty in the land of Israel was not only for the benefit of Jews. All the peoples of the world would be blessed with peace. The non-Jewish nations which had poured forth such hatred against Jews for so many painful centuries would now cease their hatred. In a true sense, the redemption of the world—not just of Israel—would be reflected in the changed attitude toward the Jewish people among the non-Jewish nations. When there had been hatred of Jews, the world had not been redeemed. When this hatred was eliminated, the non-Jews would themselves begin to experience peace, blessing, and redemption.

The world has not yet achieved the fulfillment of Rabbi Uziel's vision. Israel is still a state struggling for peaceful survival. Anti-Jewish sentiment is still widespread throughout the world. The messianic vision of peace, love, righteousness, and harmony has not been realized as quickly as Rabbi Uziel had hoped it would be.

But the hope lives on.

Epilogue

Throughout this book, we have confronted Sephardic thinkers dealing with the issues of rationalism and anti-rationalism; acceptance of God's decrees and rebellion; halakhic authority and kabbalistic inquiry. We have considered the forces of mysticism and messianism, traditionalism and modernism. We have witnessed a diversity of approaches and attitudes; and we have been convinced of the sincerity and integrity of those whose ideas we have studied.

Many of the Sephardic intellectuals discussed in this work are relatively unknown and unappreciated. Yet their teachings are of profound interest and of lasting value and inspiration. For centuries they have been voices in exile. Perhaps now, in this generation when there are signs of the end of Israel's long exile, their voices will once again be heard.

Notes

CHAPTER 1

1. The life of the Jews in Spain is described by Eliyahu Ashtor, *The Jews of Moslem Spain*, 3 vols. (Philadelphia, 1973, 1979, 1984); and Yitzhak Baer, *A History of the Jews in Christian Spain*, 2 vol. (Philadelphia, 1971).

2. Yitzhak Abravanel, *Mayenei ha-Yeshua* (Stettin, 1860), introduction.

3. Yitzhak Abravanel, Commentary on *Nevi-im Rishonim* (Jerusalem, 1955), introduction to Kings.

4. Yosef ha-Cohen, *Emek ha-Bakhah* (Jerusalem, 5716), pp. 62 f.

5. Hayyim Hillel Ben-Sasson, "Kinah al Gerush Sefarad," *Tarbits* 3 (Tishri 5722): 63.

6. Eliyahu Capsali, *Likutim Shonim mi-Sefer Debei Eliyahu*, ed. M. Lattes (Padua, 1869), p. 72.

7. Yehudah Abravanel's poem is found in Simon Bernfeld, *Sefer ha-Demaot*, vol. 2 (Berlin, 1924), pp. 262 f. The spiritual crisis of the exiles is discussed by Yitzhak Abravanel, *Yeshuot Meshiho* (Königsberg, 1861), introduction. See also Yosef Yaavets, *Hasdei Hashem*, in *Kol Sifrei Rav Yosef Yaavets*, vol. 2 (Jerusalem, 5694), p. 13. (Subsequent references to Rabbi Yaavets' writings are from this volume.)

8. S. D. Goitein, *Jews and Arabs* (New York, 1974), p. 67.

9. M. de Thevenot, as quoted by Alfred Rubens, *A History of Jewish Costume* (New York, 1973), p. 33.

10. Yaavets, *Or ha-Hayyim*, pp. 7–8.

11. *Hasdei Hashem*, p. 36.

12. *Maamar ha-Ahdut*, p. 20.

13. *Hasdei Hashem*, p. 37.

14. *Maamar ha-Ahdut*, p. 27.

15. Abraham Gabison, *Omer ha-Shikha* (Jerusalem, 5733), p. 3b.

16. Moshe Almosnino, *Yedei Moshe*, vol. 1 (Tel Aviv, 5740), pp. 31–32.

17. Ibid., p. 270.

18. Eliyahu de Vidas, *Reishit Hokhmah* (Jerusalem, 5732), p. 79a.

19. Yosef Hayim Yerushalmi, "Clio and the Jews: Reflections on Jewish Historiography in the 16th Century," in *American Academy for Jewish Research Jubilee Volume*, ed. Salo W. Baron and Isaac E. Barzilay (Jerusalem, 1980), vol. 2, p. 624.

20. Samuel Usque, *Consolation for the Tribulations of Israel*, trans. Martin Cohen (Philadelphia, 1965), p. 39.

CHAPTER 2

1. *Or ha-Hayyim*, p. 26. See also Baer, *History of the Jews in Christian Spain*, vol. 2, pp. 442–43 and 509.

2. *Or ha-Hayyim*, pp. 64–65.

3. Ibid., p. 27.

4. Ibid., p. 65.

5. Ibid., p. 86.

6. Ibid., pp. 91, 96.

7. Ibid., pp. 79, 115.

8. Almosnino, *Yedei Moshe*, vol. 1, p. 27.

9. Ibid., p. 62.

10. David Ibn Abi Zimra, *Responsa* (New York, 1967), vol. 2, no. 1303.

11. Moshe ben Nahman (Nahmanides), *Vikuah*, in *Kitvei Rabbeinu Moshe ben Nahman*, ed. Charles Chavel, vol. 1 (New York, 1963), pp. 306–8.

12. Yitzhak Abravanel, *Yeshuot Meshiho*, introduction.

13. Shemuel ha-Naggid, introduction to the Talmud.

14. Abraham ben Moshe Maimon, *Maamar al Odot Derashot Hazal*, printed at the beginning of Yaacov ben Habib's *Ein Yaacob* (New York, 5731).

15. Maimonides, introduction to *Perek Helek*.

16. Abraham Ibn Migash, *Kevod Elohim* (Jerusalem, 5737), p. 51b, chap. 24. See also p. 57b for an expression of the value of secular knowledge.

17. Ibid., pp. 93a–b.

18. See Joseph Hacker, "The Intellectual Activity of the Jews of the Ottoman Empire during the 16th and 17th Centuries," in *Jewish Thought in the Seventeenth Century*, ed. I. Twersky and B. Septimus (Cambridge, 1987), pp. 118–19.

19. Yehudah Zarco, *Lehem Yehudah*, ed. A. M. Haberman (Jerusalem, 1970). See also M. Angel, *The Jews of Rhodes* (New York, 1978), p. 62.

20. Meir ben Gabbai, *Sefer Avodat ha-Kodesh* (Lvov, 1848), pp. 32a–34b.

21. Moshe Almosnino, *Regimiento de la Vida* (Amsterdam, 5489), pp. 1–13.

22. *Sefer Avodat ha-Kodesh*, p. 3a.

23. *Hasdei Hashem*, pp. 26–27.

24. Yehudah Abravanel (Leone Ebreo), *The Philosophy of Love*, trans. F. Friedeberg-Seeley and Jean H. Barnes (London, 1937), pp. 71–72. See also M. Angel, "Judah Abravanel's Philosophy of Love," *Tradition* 15 (1975): 81–88.

25. The elegies are found in *Seder Arba Taaniot ke-Minhag Sefaradim*, 5638, pp. 182–85.

26. R. J. Zwi Werblowsky, "Tikun Tefilot le-Rabi Shelomo ha-Levi Alkabets," *Sefunot* 6 (5722): 152–53.

27. Quoted by Gershom Scholem, *Sabbatai Sevi* (Princeton, 1973), p. 18.

28. Ibid., p. 19. See Scholem's articles on Rabbi Abraham ha-Levi in *Kiryath Sepher* 2 (1925) and 7 (1931). See also Baer, *History of the Jews in Christian Spain*, vol. 2, pp. 430–31.

29. Scholem, *Sabbatai Sevi*, p. 18.

30. For a discussion of Abravanel's messianic works, see Benzion Netan-yahu, *Abravanel* (Philadelphia, 1968). An interesting discussion of Sephardic messianism is found in Gerson Cohen, "Messianic Postures of Ashkenazim and Sephardim," *Leo Baeck Memorial Lectures,* vol. 9 (New York, 1967), pp. 117–56. See also Y. H. Yerushalmi, "Messianic Impulses in Joseph Ha-Kohen," in *Studies in Sixteenth Century Jewish Thought,* ed. B. D. Cooperman (Cambridge, 1983), pp. 460–87; and in the same volume, Shalom Rosenberg, "Exile and Redemption in Jewish Thought in the Sixteenth Century: Contending Conceptions," pp. 399–430.

31. Quoted by Hayyim Hillel Ben-Sasson, "Galut u-Geula be-Enav shel Dor Golei Sefarad," in *Yitzhak Baer Jubilee Volume* (Jerusalem, 5721), p. 218.

32. Abraham Saba, *Tseror Hamor* (Venice, 5327), commentary on Bereishit, p. 4a.

33. Meir Benayahu, "Hidushah shel ha-Semikhah bi-Tsefat," in *Yitzhak Baer Jubilee Volume,* pp. 248–69. See also Y. Baer, *Galut* (New York, 1947), p. 69; and Levi ben Habib, *Responsa* (Lemberg, n.d.), section following p. 110.

34. See Ben-Sasson, "Galut u-Geula be-Enav shel Dor Golei Sefarad," p. 223.

35. Almosnino, *Yedei Moshe,* vol. 1, pp. 34, 129.

36. Shemuel de Medina, *Responsa* (Lemberg, 1862), *Hoshen Mishpat,* no. 12.

37. H. J. Zimmels, "The Contributions of the Sephardim to the Responsa Literature Till the Beginning of the Sixteenth Century," in *The Sephardi Heritage,* ed. Richard Barnett (New York, 1971), p. 394.

38. Solomon Rosanes, *Divrei Yemei Yisrael be-Togarmah,* vol. 1 (Tel Aviv, 5690), p. 63. See also p. 90.

39. See Hayyim Bentov, "Shitat Limud ha-Talmud be-Yeshivot Saloniki ve-Turkiah," *Sefunot* 13 (5731): 5–102. The method of Rabbi Confanton is discussed on pp. 31 f. See also Yitzhak Confanton, *Darkhei ha-Talmud* (Jerusalem, 5741).

40. Yosef Hacker, "Lidmutam ha-Ruhanit shel Yehudei Sefarad be-Sof ha-Meah he-Hamesh Esrei," *Sefunot* 17 (5743), esp. pp. 47 f.

41. Gershom Scholem, "Derush al ha-Geulah le-Rabi Shelomo le-Beit Turiel," *Sefunot* 1 (5717): 62–79.

42. R. J. Zwi Werblowsky, *Joseph Caro* (Philadelphia, 1977), p. 286.

43. See M. Angel, *The Rhythms of Jewish Living: A Sephardic Approach* (New York, 1986), p. 99.

44. Joseph Dan, *Jewish Mysticism and Jewish Ethics* (Seattle, 1986), p. 97.

45. Eliezer Azikri, *Sefer Hareidim* (Jerusalem, 5718), p. 214.

46. Ibid., p. 215.

47. Moshe Cordovero, *Sefer Gerushin* (Shklov, 5551), p. 3a.

48. Moshe Cordovero, *The Palm Tree of Deborah,* trans. Louis Jacobs (London, 1960), p. 69.

49. Dan, *Jewish Mysticism and Jewish Ethics,* pp. 100–101.

50. *Palm Tree of Deborah*, pp. 52–53.

51. See, for example, the lists of pious practices suggested by various sages, printed as appendices to Solomon Schechter, "Safed in the Sixteenth Century," *Studies in Judaism*, second series (Philadelphia, 1908), pp. 292 ff.

CHAPTER 3

1. For a discussion of the disputation and its ramifications, see M. Angel and H. P. Salomon, "Nahmanides' Approach to Midrash in the Disputation of Barcelona," *American Sephardi* 6 (1973): 41–51; Cecil Roth, "The Disputation of Barcelona," *Gleanings* (New York, 1967), pp. 34–61; Baer, *History of the Jews in Christian Spain*, vol. 1, pp. 150–57; Martin Cohen, "Reflexions on the Text and Context of the Disputation of Barcelona," *Hebrew Union College Annual* 35 (1954): 157–92.

2. For a general study of the conversos, see Cecil Roth, *A History of the Marranos* (New York, 1966); see also Yosef H. Yerushalmi, *From Spanish Court to Italian Ghetto* (New York, 1971), chap. 1.

3. Roth, *History of the Marranos*, chaps. 2–5.

4. Ibid., chap. 7. See also B. Netanyahu, *The Marranos of Spain* (New York, 1966), esp. pp. 75, 95, 212–13; I. S. Revah, "Les Marranes," *Revue des Etudes Juives* 118 (1959–60): 29–77; Roth, *Gleanings*, pp. 122 f., 131; Samuel Schwarz, *Os Cristaos-Novos em Portugal no Seculo XX* (Lisbon, 1925); Lucien Wolf, *Jews in the Canary Islands* (London, 1926); Cyrus Adler, "Trial of Jorge de Almeida," *Publications of the American Jewish Historical Society* 4, pp. 29–79.

5. Roth, *History of the Marranos*, pp. 100–102.

6. Baer, *History of the Jews in Christian Spain*, vol. 2, pp. 350 f.; Schechter, "Safed in the Sixteenth Century," pp. 222 f.

7. *Mashmia Yeshua* (Salonika, 1526), pp. 6abc, 27c, 33d; Netanyahu, *Abravanel*, pp. 202 f.; idem, *Marranos of Spain*, pp. 177–203.

8. Quoted by Hayyim Hillel Ben-Sasson, "Dor Golei Sefarad al Atsmo," *Zion* 26 (1961): 41.

9. Roth, *History of the Marranos*, p. 388.

10. Simha Assaf, "Anusei Sefarad u-Portugal be-Sifrut ha-Teshuvot," *Zion* 5 (1933): 22.

11. See *Tefilat kol Peh*, ed. B. Israel Ricardo (Amsterdam, 1950), pp. 217–19; see also Roth, *History of the Marranos*, p. 141.

12. Netanyahu, *Marranos of Spain*. See also Moises Orfali Levi, *Los Conversos Españoles en la Literatura Rabinica* (Salamanca, 1982).

13. Shemuel Aboab, *Sefer Devar Shemuel* (Venice, 1702), no. 45.

14. Yaacov Sasportas, *Ohel Yaacov* (Bnei Brak, 5746), no. 3.

15. See Asaf, "Anusei Sefarad u-Portugal," p. 34.

16. de Medina, *Responsa, Even ha-Ezer*, no. 10. See also the discussion in *Los Conversos Españoles*, Levi, pp. 34 f. A different opinion was offered by Yomtov Zahalon, *Responsa* (Jerusalem, 5745), no. 148.

17. Elias Artom and H. Cassuto, eds., *Sefer Takanoth Candia* (Jerusalem, 1943), pp. 147–48.

18. de Medina, *Responsa, Even ha-Ezer*, no. 112.

19. Hayyim Sutehon, *Erets Hayyim* (Jerusalem, 5668), no. 139. About the priestly status of returning conversos who claimed to be *cohanim*, see Eliyahu Mizrahi, *Mayim Amukim* (Salonika, 5570), no. 3.

20. Levi ben Habib, *Responsa*, "Maamar al ha-Semikhah," p. 26.

21. Yosef Kaplan, "Ha-Yehudim ha-Portugalim be-Amsterdam: me-Hayyim bi-Shemad le-Shivah le-Yahadut," in *Moreshet Yehudei Sefarad ve-ha-Mizrah*, ed. Y. Ben-Ami (Jerusalem, 5742), p. 118.

22. Abraham Elmaleh, *Ha-Rishonim le-Zion* (Jerusalem, 1970), p. 47.

23. Alexander Altmann, "Eternality of Punishment: A Theological Controversy within the Amsterdam Rabbinate in the Thirties of the Seventeenth Century," *Proceedings of the American Academy for Jewish Research* 40 (1972): 17 f. For more on Mortera, see H. P. Salomon's doctoral dissertation, an edition of Mortera's Treatise on the Truth of the Law of Moses (Coimbra, Acta Universitatis Conimbrigensis, 1988).

CHAPTER 4

1. For a description of the migration patterns of the conversos, see Roth, *History of the Marranos*, pp. 195 f.

2. Ibid., chaps. 8–11.

3. See, for example, Sasportas, *Ohel Yaacov*, no. 59. An example of the spiritual struggles of the conversos is described by Constance Rose, *Alonso Nunez de Reinoso: The Lament of a 16th Century Exile* (Cranbury, N.J., 1971), esp. pp. 91 f. See also Cecil Roth, "The Strange Case of Hector Mendes Bravo," *Hebrew Union College Annual* 18 (1943–44): 221–45.

4. de Medina, *Responsa, Yoreh Deah*, no. 199.

5. Ibn Abi Zimra, *Responsa*, vol. 1, no. 187.

6. Cecil Roth, *Manasseh ben Israel* (Philadelphia, 1934), pp. 46–47, 70 f., 100 f.

7. Jacob Petuchowski, *The Theology of Haham David Nieto* (New York, 1970), pp. 33 f.

8. Isaac Reggio, ed., *Behinath ha-Kabbalah* (includes *Kol Sakhal*) (Goeritz, 1852).

9. Imanuel Aboab, *Nomologia*, 5389.

10. David Nieto, *Ha-Kuzari ha-Sheni hu Mateh Dan* (Jerusalem, 5718).

11. See Yosef Kaplan, *Mi-Notsrut le-Yahadut: Hayyav u-Paolo shel ha-Anus Yitzhak Orobio de Castro* (Jerusalem, 5743).

12. See Yerushalmi's biography of Cardoso, *From Spanish Court to Italian Ghetto*.

13. Quoted by Yerushalmi, ibid., p. 404.

14. Ibid., p. 49.

15. I thank H. P. Salomon for referring me to works on Herrera. See Alexander Altmann, "Lurianic Kabbala in a Platonic Key: Abraham Cohen Herrera's *Puerta del Cielo*," *Hebrew Union College Annual* 53 (1982): 317–55; Ralph Melnick, *From Polemics to Apologetics* (Assen, 1981), chap. 3.

16. Mair José Benardete, *Hispanic Culture and Character of the Sephardic Jews* (1952; reprinted, New York, 1982), esp. chap. 4.

17. Cecil Roth, "Immanuel Aboab's Proselytization of the Marranos," *Jewish Quarterly Review* 23 (1932): 133.

18. Fernand Braudel, *The Mediterranean*, vol. 2 (New York, 1973), p. 823.

CHAPTER 5

1. Jacob Katz, "Post-Zoharic Relations between Halakhah and Kabbalah," in *Jewish Thought in the Sixteenth Century*, ed. B. D. Cooperman (Cambridge, 1983), pp. 283 f. See also his article, "Halakhah and Kabbalah as Competing Disciplines of Study," in *Jewish Spirituality from the Sixteenth Century Revival to the Present*, ed. Arthur Green (New York, 1987), pp. 34–63.

2. Joseph Dan, "Manasseh ben Israel's *Nishmat Hayyim* and the Concept of Evil in Seventeenth Century Jewish Thought," in *Jewish Thought in the Seventeenth Century*, ed. I. Twersky and B. Septimus (Cambridge, 1987), p. 74.

3. Bernard Cooperman, "Eliyahu Montalto's 'Suitable and Incontrovertible Propositions': A Seventeenth Century Anti-Christian Polemic," ibid., pp. 488 f.

4. Moshe Idel, "Differing Conceptions of Kabbalah in the Early Seventeenth Century," ibid., pp. 150 f.

5. Scholem, *Sabbatai Sevi*, pp. 54 f. and 64 f. See also Jacob Katz's article in the Hebrew section of *Studies in Jewish Religious and Intellectual History Presented to Alexander Altmann*, ed. Siegfried Stein and Raphael Loewe (Alabama, 1979), p. 94.

6. Yaacov Hagiz, *Halakhot Ketanot* (Jerusalem, 5734), 2:7.

7. Shalom Rosenberg, "Emunat Hakhamim," in *Jewish Thought in the Seventeenth Century*, p. 334.

8. See Dan, "Manasseh ben Israel's *Nishmat Hayyim*," ibid., pp. 63 f.; in the same volume, see the article by Bracha Sack, "The Influence of Cordovero on Seventeenth Century Jewish Thought," pp. 365–79.

9. Joseph Dan, "No Evil Descends from Heaven," in *Jewish Thought in the Sixteenth Century*, p. 103.

10. See Scholem, *Sabbatai Sevi*. Much of the historical discussion in the text is drawn from this work.

11. Sasportas, *Ohel Yaacov*, in the *Tsitsat Novel* printed in the back of the volume, p. 84b.

12. Ibid., p. 85a.

13. Scholem, *Sabbatai Sevi*, pp. 394, 706.

14. Ibid., p. 583.

15. *Tsitsat Novel*, p. 85a.

16. Yerushalmi, *From Spanish Court to Italian Ghetto*, p. 319.

17. Scholem, *Sabbatai Sevi*, p. 758.

18. Hayyim Benveniste, *Kenesset ha-Gedolah, Orah Hayyim* (Jerusalem, n.d.), *Hilkhot Tisha b'Ab ve-Shaar Taaniyot*, pp. 281 f.

19. *Ohel Yaacov*, no. 70. See also no. 68.

20. Yerushalmi, *From Spanish Court to Italian Ghetto*, p. 341.

21. Aboab, *Devar Shemuel*, no. 375.

22. Dan, *Jewish Mysticism and Jewish Ethics*, pp. 106–108.

23. Elisheva Carlebach, "Rabbi Moses Hagiz: The Rabbinate and the Pursuit of Heresy, Late Seventeenth–Early Eighteenth Centuries" (Ph.D. diss., Columbia University, 1986), p. 129.

24. Ibid., pp. 94 f.

25. Ibid., pp. 231 f.

26. Moshe Hagiz, *Mishnat Hakhamim* (Brooklyn, 5719), nos. 236, 309, 558.

27. Ibid., nos. 104, 105, 106, 111, 114, 495.

28. Carlebach, "Rabbi Moses Hagiz," p. 254.

29. Moshe Hagiz, *Sefer Leket ha-Kemah* (Bnei Brak), 5743, introduction.

30. *Mishnat Hakhamim*, nos. 519, 548, 552, 580.

31. Ibid., nos. 589, 626.

32. Ibid., no. 53.

33. Ibid., nos. 54, 55.

34. Ibid., no. 88.

35. Ibid., nos. 124, 125, 126.

36. Ibid., nos. 671, 672, 673.

37. Ibid., nos. 729, 730.

38. Ibid., no. 713.

39. Ibid., nos. 119, 144.

40. Carlebach, "Rabbi Moses Hagiz," p. 462.

CHAPTER 6

1. M. D. Gaon, *Yehudei ha-Mizrah be-Erets Israel*, vol. 1 (Jerusalem, 1937), pp. 83 f.

2. Ibid., pp. 89–90.

3. Carlebach, "Rabbi Moses Hagiz," pp. 29–31.

4. Yitzhak Baer, *Galut* (New York, 1947), p. 114.

5. Ibid., pp. 112–113.

6. Moshe Hagiz, *Sefat Emet* (Amsterdam, 5647), p. 17a.

7. M. Benayahu, *Rabbi Hayyim Yosef David Azulai* (Jerusalem, 1959), pp. 25–27.

8. Aharon Bohbot, ed., *Rabbi Hayyim Abulafia, Zimrat ha-Arets*, composed by Rabbi Yaacov Berav (Jerusalem, 5747).

9. Ibid., pp. 130 f.

10. Yaacov Nacht, *Mekor Hayyim* (Drohobycz, 1898), p. 48.

11. Ibid., pp. 24 f.

12. Abraham Yaari, *Sheluhei Erets Israel* (Jerusalem, 5711).

13. Benayahu, *Rabbi H. Y. D. Azulai*, chap. 2.

14. André Chouraqui, *Between East and West* (Philadelphia, 1968), pp. 71 f.

15. Yaari, *Sheluhei Erets Israel*, pp. 174–75.

16. Angel, *Jews of Rhodes*, pp. 68 f.

17. Moshe Israel, *Masat Moshe*, vol. 1 (Constantinople, 5495), *Yoreh Deah*, no. 8. See also Abraham Yaari, "Rabbi Moshe Israel u-Shelihuto ba-ad Erets Israel," *Sinai* 13 (1949): 149–65; Simon Markus, *Toledot ha-Rabbanim mi-Mishpahat Israel me-Rodos* (Jerusalem, 1935), pp. 8–30.

18. Angel, *Jews of Rhodes*, pp. 49 f.

19. Hagiz, *Mishnat Hakhamim*, no. 713.

20. M. Y. Israel, *Shenoth Yamin*, vol. 1 (Izmir, 5620), p. 130b.

21. Eliyahu Israel, *Shenei Eliyahu* (Livorno, 5566).

22. Introduction to *Masat Moshe*, vol. 3 (Constantinople, 5502).

CHAPTER 7

1. For information about these rabbis, see Angel, *Jews of Rhodes*, pp. 68 f.

2. For more on Ibn Abi Zimra, see Israel Goldman, *The Life and Times of Rabbi David Ibn Abi Zimra* (New York, 1970); for more on de Medina, see Morris Goodblatt, *Jewish Life in Turkey in the 16th Century* (New York, 1952).

3. The first edition of the *Me'am Lo'ez* was published in Constantinople, 1730. It went into various subsequent editions. A Hebrew translation by Shemuel Yerushalmi was published in Jerusalem, 5727–32. Aryeh Kaplan undertook an English translation under the title *The Torah Anthology*, the first volume being issued in New York, 1977. An edition of the *Me'am Lo'ez* (Genesis) was produced in Madrid, 1964, 1969, 1970, under the editorship of David Gonzalo Maeso and Pascual Pascual Recuero. See also M. D. Gaon, *Maskiyut Levav al Me'am Lo'ez* (Jerusalem, 5693).

4. Eliezer Papo, *Pele Yoets* (Jerusalem, 5747), section on *taanit.*

5. Louis Landau, "Yahaso shel R. Yaacov Huli el ha-Shabtaut," *Peamim* 15 (1983): 58–66.

6. For example, see Abraham Yaari, *Ha-Defus ha-Ivri be-Kushta* (Jerusalem, 5727).

7. *Me'am Lo'ez* on Exodus 34:1–3.

8. See Gershom Scholem, *On the Kabbalah and Its Symbolism* (New York, 1965), pp. 116 f.

9. Chouraqui, *Between East and West*, pp. 71 f.

10. H. Y. D. Azulai, *Shem ha-Gedolim* (Warsaw, 1876).

11. The travel account is found in J. D. Eisenstein, *Ozar ha-Masaot* (Tel Aviv, 1969), p. 241.

12. Eliyahu ha-Cohen, *Midrash Talpiot* (Tchernowitz, 1860), p. 73a.

13. Israel, *Masat Moshe*, vol. 3, *Yoreh Deah*, no. 4.

14. Eliyahu Israel, *Kol Eliyahu* (Livorno, 1792), no. 5.

15. Benayahu, *Rabbi H. Y. D. Azulai*, p. 110.

16. Ibid., p. 165.

17. Chouraqui, *Between East and West*, p. 63.

18. Michael Molho, *Usos y costumbres de los Sefardíes de Salónica* (Madrid, 1950), p. 155.

CHAPTER 8

1. Dan, *Jewish Mysticism and Jewish Ethics*, chap. 2.
2. These lists are printed in Schechter, *Studies in Judaism*, second series, pp. 292 f.
3. Dan, *Jewish Mysticism and Jewish Ethics*, pp. 100–101.
4. H. Y. D. Azulai, *Kikar la-Aden* (Livorno, 5561), sec. 29.
5. Raphael Berdugo, *Rav mi-Peninim* (Casablanca, 1969), p. 29. I thank Dr. Henry Toledano for making the works of Rabbi Berdugo available to me.
6. Azulai, *Lev David*, pp. 43–45, and 121 f. See also H. Y. D. Azulai, *Avodat ha-Kodesh* (Warsaw, 1879), p. 6.
7. M. H. Luzzatto, *Mesilat Yesharim*, trans. Shraga Silverstein (New York, 1980), p. 174.
8. Benayahu, *Rabbi H. Y. D. Azulai*, p. 142.
9. Papo, *Yaalzu Hasidim*, sec. 155; see also the closing paragraphs of the book.
10. Abraham Meshi-Zahav, *Mesilot ha-Hayyim* (Jerusalem, 5734), p. 24.
11. *Lev David*, p. 10.
12. See Eliezer Papo, *Orot Elim* (Jerusalem, 5723), p. 142; also Benayahu, *Rabbi H. Y. D. Azulai*, p. 156.
13. *Mesilat Yesharim*, pp. 42, 194, 334.
14. *Pele Yoets*, section on *musar*.
15. Ibid., sections on *laaz* and *mezakeh*.
16. See his Torah commentary, *Or ha-Hayyim*, on Genesis 1:1.
17. Eliyahu ha-Cohen, *Shevet Musar* (Lublin, 5642), p. 99a.
18. Ibid., p. 99b.
19. *Mesilat Yesharim*, p. 98.
20. *Or ha-Hayyim* on Deuteronomy 11:26.
21. Ibid., on Genesis 2:3.
22. Ibid., on Deuteronomy 21:14; see also on Numbers 23:21.
23. Ibid., on Deuteronomy 8:1.
24. *Yaalzu Hasidim*, sec. 100.
25. *Shevet Musar*, p. 27b.
26. Benayahu, *Rabbi H. Y. D. Azulai*, p. 147.
27. H. Y. D. Azulai, *Hasdei Avot*, published with Moshe Alsheikh's commentary on Avot (Przemysl, 5674), on the phrase *lo ha-midrash ikar ela ha-maaseh*.
28. *Pele Yoets*, section on *halakhah*.
29. *Mesilat Yesharim*, p. 216.
30. Ibid., pp. 26, 332.
31. *Or ha-Hayyim* on Genesis 2:15. For Rabbi Benattar's halakhic approach, see Hayyim Bentov, "Al Yetsirato ha-Halkhatit shel R. Hayyim Benattar u-Peiluto be-Morocco," *Peamim* 17 (1983): 36–52.
32. *Lev David*, chap. 14.
33. Dan, *Jewish Mysticism and Jewish Ethics*, p. 83.
34. *Shevet Musar*, introduction and first chapter.
35. Ibid., chap. 4.

36. Ibid., chap. 13.

37. H. Y. D. Azulai, *Simhat ha-Regel* (Jerusalem, 5719), p. 21b.

38. *Mesilat Yesharim*, p. 272.

39. *Yaalzu Hasidim*, sec. 11, 15, 18, 52, 53, 155; see also *Pele Yoets* on *yuhara*.

40. *Pele Yoets*, section on *bekhiah*.

41. Ibid., section on *shir*.

42. Eliezer Papo, *Hesed la-Alafim, Orah Hayyim* (Jerusalem, 5745), no. 262.

43. *Pele Yoets*, section on *hashva-ah*.

44. *Rav mi-Peninim*, p. 32.

45. *Or ha-Hayyim* on Leviticus 17:10.

46. Ibid., on Exodus 39:32.

47. Ibid., on Leviticus 19:13.

48. *Rav mi-Peninim*, pp. 11, 44.

49. Benayahu, *Rabbi H. Y. D. Azulai*, p. 167.

50. *Orot Elim*, pp. 139–40.

51. *Pele Yoets*, section on *sanegoriah*.

52. Ibid., section on *ger* and *lashon hara*.

53. Eliyahu ha-Cohen, *Midrash Talpiot*, p. 110b.

54. Eliezer b. Yomtov Papo, *Damesek Eliezer* (Jerusalem, 5736), p. 8, section on *dor holekh*.

55. Benayahu, *Rabbi H. Y. D. Azulai*, pp. 145–46.

CHAPTER 9

1. *Pele Yoets*, section on *ger*.

2. Ibid., section on *tsaar*.

3. Ibid., section on *ahavat ish ve-ishah*.

4. Ibid., section on *ashirut* and *aniyut*.

5. *Yaalzu Hasidim*, sec. 499.

6. Ibid., sec. 550.

7. Ibid., see the *Maamar ha-Kavod*.

8. *Pele Yoets*, section on *galut*.

9. Ibid., section on *piryah ve-rivyah*.

10. Ibid., section on *bat*; also, *Yaalzu Hasidim*, sec. 1, 100.

11. Solomon Gaon, "Rabbi Yehudah Alkalai," in *The Rebirth of Israel*, ed. Israel Cohen (London, 1952), pp. 138–47.

12. A letter from Rabbi Alkalai to Moses Sachs (1866) in Isaac Werfel, ed., *Kitvei ha-Rav Yehudah Alkalai* (Jerusalem, 5704), vol. 2, p. 529. Subsequent references to Rabbi Alkalai's works are from this edition of his collected works, unless otherwise indicated.

13. *Goral Hashem*, vol. 2, p. 426; *Mevaser Tov*, vol. 1, pp. 287–88.

14. *Goral Hashem*, vol. 2, pp. 427, 440; *Mevaser Tov*, vol. 1, p. 289.

15. *Kol Koreh*, vol. 1, pp. 251–52.

16. *Minhat Yehudah*, 1843, p. 180.

17. *Goral Hashem*, vol. 2, p. 440.

18. *Kol Koreh*, vol. 1, p. 249.

19. Ibid., p. 247.

20. *Darkhei Noam*, vol. 1, p. 22.

21. *Kol Koreh*, vol. 1, pp. 244–46.

22. Ibid., p. 255.

23. *Sefer Hayyim*, vol. 2, pp. 350, 354.

24. *Petah ke-Huda shel Mahat*, vol. 1, p. 284.

25. *Goral Hashem*, vol. 2, p. 438.

26. *Shalom Yerushalayim*, vol. 1, p. 77.

27. Ibid., pp. 81 f.; *Kol Koreh*, vol. 1, p. 242.

28. *Kol Koreh*, vol. 1, p. 244.

29. *Darkhei Noam*, vol. 1, pp. 12–13.

30. *Meoded Anavim*, vol. 2, p. 486.

31. *Kibbuts Galuyot*, vol. 2, pp. 545–46.

32. Angel, *Jews of Rhodes*, pp. 37–39. See also M. Franco, *Essai sur l'histoire des Israélites de l'Empire Ottoman* (Paris, 1897), pp. 158–60; Lucien Wolf, *The Life of Sir Moses Montefiore* (New York, 1881), pp. 22–26; Paul Goodman, *Moses Montefiore* (Philadelphia, 1925), pp. 64–69; Albert Hyamson, *The Sephardim of England* (London, 1951), pp. 152, 251.

33. Israel, *Shenoth Yamin*, vol. 1, p. 130b. For an interesting responsum relating to the blood libel in Rhodes, see Hayyim Palache, *Hikekei Lev*, vol. 3 (Salonika, 5609), *Hoshen Mishpat*, no. 25.

34. *Shalom Yisrael*, vol. 1, p. 35.

35. *Meoded Anavim*, vol. 2, p. 479.

CHAPTER 10

1. See David Benveniste, "Rabbi Yehudah Yaacov Nehama: Mevaser Tekufat ha-Haskalah be-Saloniki," in *The Sephardic and Oriental Jewish Heritage*, ed. Issachar Ben-Ami (Jerusalem, 1982), p. 30. See also José Faur, *Harav Yisrael Moshe Hazan: ha-Ish u-Mishnato* (Jerusalem, 5738), esp. pp. 3–17.

2. Grace Aguilar, *The Spirit of Judaism* (Philadelphia, 5602), p. 9.

3. See, for example, Leeser's comments on pp. vii, 21, 100, and 104.

4. Ibid., pp. 225–26.

5. See the discussion of Grace Aguilar's thought in Philip M. Weinberger, *The Social and Religious Thought of Grace Aguilar* (New York, 1970); see also Beth-Zion Lask Abrahams, "Grace Aguilar: a Centenary Tribute," *Jewish Historical Society of England Transactions* 16 (1952): 137–48.

6. Grace Aguilar, *The Jewish Faith: Its Spiritual Consolation, Moral Guidance and Immortal Hope* (Philadelphia, 1864), p. 10.

7. Ibid., p. 124.

8. Ibid., p. 221.

9. Ibid., p. 264.

10. *Spirit of Judaism*, pp. viii, 165.

11. Eliyahu Benamozegh, *Bi-Shvilei Musar* (Jerusalem, 1966), pp. 21–27.

12. Ibid., pp. 28–30, 33.

13. Ibid., pp. 120–21.

14. Ibid., pp. 124–25, 132–33, 148, 166.

15. See Faur, *Harav Yisrael Mosheh Hazan.*

16. I. M. Hazan, *Nahalah le-Yisrael* (Alexandria, 1862), pp. 53–54.

17. Ibid., p. 55.

18. Ibid., p. 61.

19. The changes in the taxation system are reflected in Rabbi Michael Yaacov Israel, *Yad Yemin* (Izmir, 1859), *Hoshen Mishpat,* no. 25; and Hayyim Palache, *Hikekei Lev* (Izmir, 5609), *Hoshen Mishpat,* no. 6.

20. Yehudah Yaacov Nehama, *Mikhtevei Dodim mi-Yayin,* vol. 1 (Salonika, 5653), pp. 48–49. See also Benveniste, "Rabbi Yehudah Yaacov Nehama."

21. For information on Dr. Mendes, see David de Sola Pool, *H. Pereira Mendes: A Biography* (New York, 1938); David de Sola Pool and Tamar de Sola Pool, *An Old Faith in the New World* (New York, 1955), pp. 192–201; and Eugene Markovits, *Henry Pereira Mendes: Builder of Traditional Judaism in America,* (doctoral diss., Yeshiva University, 1961). See also Markovitz, "Henry Pereira Mendes: Architect of the Union of Orthodox Jewish Congregations of America," *American Jewish Historical Quarterly* 55, no. 3, pp. 364–84.

22. B. Drachman, "Forty Years of Loyal Service," *Orthodox Union* 7, no. 6.

23. See Markovits, "Henry Pereira Mendes: Builder of Traditional Judaism," p. 250.

24. Ibid., p. 86.

25. Dr. Mendes' remarks are found in the archives of Congregation Shearith Israel, and are quoted in M. D. Angel, "Thoughts About Early American Jewry," *Tradition* 16 (1976): 21.

CHAPTER 11

1. See M. D. Gaon, *A Bibliography of the Judeo-Spanish Press* (Jerusalem, 1965); Michael Molho, *Literatura Sefardita de Oriente* (Madrid and Barcelona, 1960), pp. 327–37; Haim Vidal Sephiha, *L'Agonie des Judeo-Espagnols* (Paris, 1977), pp. 97–106. See also Avner Levy, "Alexander Benguiat u-Terumato le-Itonut ve-ha-Sifrut ha-Yafah be-Ladino," in *The Sephardi and Oriental Jewish Heritage,* ed. Issachar Ben-Ami (Jerusalem, 1982), pp. 205–12.

2. Elena Romero, *El Teatro de los Sefardies Orientales,* 3 vol. (Madrid, 1979); E. Romero, *Repertorio de Noticias sobre el Mundo Teatral de los Sefardies Orientales* (Madrid, 1983). See also M. D. Angel, "Judeo-Spanish Drama: A Study of Sephardic Culture," *Tradition* (1981): 182–85; and idem, "The Sephardic Theater of Seattle," *American Jewish Archives,* 1973, pp. 156–60.

3. Abraham Galante, *Rinu* (Cairo, 1906).

4. Marc D. Angel, "Elia Carmona: Judeo-Spanish Author," *Jewish Book Annual* 44 (1986): 132–40.

5. Robyn Loewenthal, *Elia Carmona's Autobiography* (doctoral diss., University of Nebraska, Lincoln, 1984).

6. Angel Pulido Fernandez, *Españoles sin patria* (Madrid, 1905).

7. Benardete, *Hispanic Culture and Character of the Sephardic Jews.*

8. See the works of the authors mentioned. Also, Moise Franco, *Essai sur l'Histoire des Israélites de l'Empire Ottoman* (Paris, 1897).

9. Marc D. Angel, *La America: The Sephardic Experience in the United States* (Philadelphia, 1982), p. 6.

10. Ibid., p. 114.

11. Molho, *Literatura Sefardita de Oriente*, pp. 297–300. See also Samuel Armistead and Joseph Silverman, *The Judeo-Spanish Ballad Chapbooks of Yacob Abraham Yona* (Berkeley, 1971).

12. Molho, *Literatura Sefardita de Oriente*, pp. 317–18.

13. Yitzhak de Boton, *Cuadreno de Poesias* (Tel Aviv, 5695). Page references in the text refer to this booklet.

14. See Marc D. Angel, "The Pirkei Abot of Reuben Eliyahu Israel," *Tradition* 11 (1971): 92–98.

CHAPTER 12

1. Abraham Cappon, *El Angustiador* (Sarajevo, 1914), author's prologue.

2. See, for example, Israel, *Shenoth Yamin*, vol. 1, pp. 42a and 126b; Yitzhak Farhi, *Tsuf Devash* (Jerusalem, 5689), pp. 33 f.

3. Angel, *Jews of Rhodes*, pp. 78–80.

4. On Nissim Behar, see Z. Szajkowski, "The Alliance Israélite Universelle in the United States, 1860–1949," *Publications of the American Jewish Historical Society* 39 (1950): 406–43; Benardete, *Hispanic Culture and Character of the Sephardic Jews*, pp. 197–99; Angel, *La America*, pp. 25–26 and passim; M. D. Gaon, *Yehudei ha-Mizrah be-Erets Israel*, vol. 2 (Jerusalem, 1938), pp. 151–59; Joseph Papo, *Sephardim in Twentieth Century America* (Berkeley, 1987), pp. 335–49; idem, "Nissim Behar—A Sephardic Innovator," *Midstream* 33 (1987): 44–46.

5. Moshe Yaacov Otolenghi, *La Halbashah* (Salonika, 1886), p. 7.

6. Ibid., p. 2.

7. Benveniste, "Rabbi Yehudah Yaacov Nehama," p. 32.

8. Yitzhak Bengualid, *Vayomer Yitzhak* (Jerusalem, 5738), no. 99.

9. I. M. Hazan, *Shearith ha-Nahalah* (Alexandria, 1862), pp. 11–14, 24.

10. Eliyahu Hazan, *Taalumot Lev* (Jerusalem, 5746), vol. 1, *Yoreh Deah*, no. 4.

11. Ibid., appended at the end of Rabbi Hazan's responsum.

12. Louis Landau, *Jews in Nineteenth Century Egypt* (New York, 1969), pp. 76–77; see also pp. 94–95 on Hebrew education in Alexandria. Rabbi Hazan removed his own son from the Alliance school in Cairo because a teacher had struck the child. See pp. 309–10.

13. Angel, *Jews of Rhodes*, pp. 85–88.

14. Hayyim Palache, *Tokhahat Hayyim*, vol. 1 (Jerusalem, 5738), pp. 11 f.

15. H. Palache, *Kaf ha-Hayyim* (Jerusalem, 5736), p. 157a; see also pp. 28a, 35b.

16. H. Palache, *Hikekei Lev*, vol. 1 (Salonika, 5600), *Orah Hayyim*, no. 6.

17. Bengualid, *Vayomer Yitzhak*, no. 105. For a similar case, see Raphael Berdugo, *Mishpatim Yesharim*, vol. 2 (Cracow, 5651), no. 125.

18. *Vayomer Yitzhak*, no. 50.

19. See Zvi Zohar, "Halakhic Responses of Syrian and Egyptian Rabbinical Authorities to Social and Technological Change," in *Studies in Contemporary Jewry*, ed. Peter Medding, vol. 2 (Bloomington, 1986), pp. 18–51.

20. *Taalumot Lev*, vol. 1. *Even ha-Ezer*, no. 2; Abulafia, *Penei Yitzhak*, vol. 1, *Even ha-Ezer*, no. 17, pp. 113 f.

21. *Taalumot Lev*, vol. 3, no. 49.

22. Ibid., no. 21.

23. Ibid., no. 33.

24. B. Uziel, *Mikhmanei Uziel* (Tel Aviv, 1939), p. 358.

25. Ibid., pp. 371, 376, 382, 391.

26. B. Uziel, *Mishpetei Uziel* (Tel Aviv, 5695), vol. 1, *Orah Hayyim*, no. 24. For a discussion of Rabbi Uziel's halakhic approach, see Hayyim David Halevy, *Asei Lekha Rav*, vol. 8 (Tel Aviv, 5748), no. 97. A slightly abridged English translation of this essay by M. Angel is in *Tradition* 24 (1989): 1–20.

27. See Halevy's discussion, pp. 320 f.

28. *Mishpetei Uziel* (Tel Aviv, 5700), *Hoshen Mishpat*, no. 17.

CHAPTER 13

1. Landau, *Jews in Nineteenth Century Egypt*, p. 18.

2. Ibid., pp. 18–19.

3. Angel, *Jews of Rhodes*, p. 36.

4. Victor Guerin, *Voyage dans l'Ile de Rhodes* (Paris, 1856), p. 66.

5. *Taalumot Lev*, vol. 4, no. 21.

6. Ibid., no. 22.

7. Eliyahu Benamozegh, *Israel ve-ha-Enoshut*, trans. Simon Markus (Jerusalem, 1967), pp. 19–22, 25.

8. Ibid., pp. 31–32.

9. Ibid., pp. 49 f., 54.

10. Ibid., pp. 69, 76 f., 85, 94, 97, 104.

11. Ibid., pp. 173 f.

12. B. Uziel, *Hegyonei Uziel*, vol. 1 (Jerusalem, 5713), pp. 121 f. See also Angel, *Rhythms of Jewish Living*, pp. 151 f.

13. B. Uziel, *Mishpetei Uziel* (Jerusalem, 5724), *Even ha-Ezer*, nos. 18, 20; see also M. Angel, "Another Halakhic Approach to Conversion," *Tradition* 12 (1972): 107–113.

14. *Taalumot Lev*, vol. 3, nos. 28–31.

15. *Hegyonei Uziel*, vol. 1, p. 105.

16. Ibid., p. 154.

17. Ibid., p. 157.

18. Ibid., p. 329.

19. Ibid., p. 330. See also a series of articles on Rabbi Uziel's thought by Nissim Yosha in *Bamaarakhah*, the journal of the Sephardic Community of Jerusalem, nos. 300–306.

Bibliography

Aboab, Imanuel. *Nomologia*. Amsterdam, 5389.

Aboab, Shemuel. *Devar Shemuel*. Venice, 1702.

Abravanel, Yehudah (Leone Ebreo). *The Philosophy of Love*. Translated by F. Friedeberg-Seeley and Jean H. Barnes. London, 1937.

Abravanel, Yitzhak. *Mayenei ha-Yeshua*. Stettin, 1860.

————. *Perush al Nevi-im Rishonim*. Jerusalem, 1955.

————. *Yeshuot Meshiho*. Königsberg, 1861.

Adler, Cyrus. "Trial of Jorge de Almeida." *Publications of the American Jewish Historical Society* 4 (1896): 291–79.

Aguilar, Grace. *The Jewish Faith: Its Spiritual Consolation, Moral Guidance and Immortal Hope*. Philadelphia, 1864.

————. *The Spirit of Judaism*. Philadelphia, 1842.

Alkabets, Shelomo. *Sefer Berit Halevy*. Jerusalem, 5730.

Alkalay, Yehudah. *Kitvei ha-Rav Yehudah Alkalay*. Edited by Isaac Werfel. Jerusalem, 5704.

Angel, Marc D. "Another Halakhic Approach to Conversion." *Tradition* 12 (1972): 107–13.

————. "Elia Carmona: Judeo-Spanish Author." *Jewish Book Annual* 44 (1986): 132–40.

————. *The Jews of Rhodes*. New York, 1978.

————. "Judah Abravanel's Philosophy of Love." *Tradition* 15 (1975): 81–88.

————. "Judeo-Spanish Drama: A Study of Sephardic Culture." *Tradition* 21 (1981): 156–60.

————. *La America: The Sephardic Experience in the United States*. Philadelphia, 1982.

————. "The Pirkei Abot of Reuben Eliyahu Israel." *Tradition* 11 (1971): 92–98.

————. *The Rhythms of Jewish Living: A Sephardic Approach*. New York, 1986.

————. "The Sephardic Theater of Seattle." *American Jewish Archives* 25 (1973): 156–60.

————. "Thoughts About Early American Jewry." *Tradition* 16 (1976).

Armistead, S., and Silverman, J. *The Judeo-Spanish Ballad Chapbooks of Yacob Abraham Yona*. Berkeley, 1971.

Artom, Elias, and Cassuto, H., eds. *Sefer Takanot Candia*. Jerusalem, 1943.

Ashtor, Eliyahu. *The Jews of Moslem Spain*. 3 vols. Philadelphia, 1973, 1979, 1984.

Assaf, Simha. "Anusei Sefarad u-Portugal be-Sifrut ha-Teshuvot." *Zion* 5 (1933): 19–61.

Attias, Moshe. *Sefer Shirot ve-Tishbahot shel ha-Shabtaim*. Tel Aviv, 5708.

Azikri, Eliezer. *Sefer Hareidim*. Jerusalem, 5718.

Azulai, Hayyim Yosef David. *Avodat ha-Kodesh*. Warsaw, 1879.

———. *Hasdei Avot*. Przemysl, 5674.

———. *Kikar la-Aden*. Livorno, 5561.

———. *Lev David*. Jerusalem, 5734.

———. *Shem ha-Gedolim*. Warsaw, 1876.

———. *Simhat ha-Regel*. Jerusalem, 5719.

Baer, Yitzhak. *Galut*. New York, 1947.

———. *A History of the Jews in Christian Spain*. Philadelphia, 1971.

Benamozegh, Eliyahu. *Bi-Shevilei Musar*. Jerusalem, 1966.

———. *Israel ve-ha-Enoshut*. Jerusalem, 1967.

Benardete, Mair J. *Hispanic Culture and Character of the Sephardic Jews*. New York, 1982.

Benayahu, Meir. "Hidushah shel ha-Semikhah bi-Tsefat." In *Y. Baer Jubilee Volume*, pp. 248–69, Jerusalem, 5721.

———. *Rabbi Hayyim Yosef David Azulai*. Jerusalem, 1959.

Bengualid, Yitzhak. *Vayomer Yitzhak*. Jerusalem, 5738.

Ben-Sasson, Hayyim H. "Dor Golei Sefarad al Atsmo." *Zion* 26 (1961): 23–64.

———. "Galut u-Geulah be-Enav shel Dor Golei Sefarad." In *Y. Baer Jubilee Volume*, pp. 216–227. Jerusalem, 5721.

———. "Kinah al Gerush Sefarad." *Tarbits* 3 (5722): 59–71.

Bentov, Hayyim. "Al Yetsirato ha-Hilkhatit shel R. Hayyim Benattar u-Peiluto be-Morocco." *Peamim* 17 (1983): 36–52.

———. "Shitat Limud ha-Talmud be-Yeshivot Saloniki ve-Turkiah." *Sefunot* 13 (5731): 5–102.

Benveniste, David. "Rabbi Yehudah Yaacov Nehama: Mevaser Tekufat ha-Haskalah be-Saloniki." In *The Sephardic and Oriental Jewish Heritage*, edited by Issachar Ben-Ami, pp. 25–34. Jerusalem, 1982.

Benveniste, Hayyim. *Kenesset ha-Gedolah, Orah Hayyim*. Jerusalem, n.d.

Berdugo, Raphael. *Mishpatim Yesharim*. Vol. 2. Cracow, 5651.

————. *Rav mi-Peninim*. Casablanca, 1969.

Bernfield, Simon. *Sefer ha-Demaot*. Vol. 2. Berlin, 1924.

Bohbot, Aharon, ed. *Rabbi Hayyim Abulafia, Zimrat ha-Arets*. Jerusalem, 5747.

Boton, Yitzhak de. *Cuadreno de Poesias*. Tel Aviv, 5695.

Braudel, Fernand. *The Mediterranean*. Vol. 2. New York, 1973.

Capsali, Eliyahu. *Likutim Shonim mi-Sefer Debei Eliyahu*. Edited by M. Lattes. Padua, 1869.

Cappon, Abraham. *El Angustiador*. Sarajevo, 1914.

Cardozo, Yitzhak. *Maalot ha-Ivrim*. Translated by Yosef Kaplan. Jerusalem, n.d.

Carlebach, Elisheva. "Rabbi Moses Hagiz: The Rabbinate and the Pursuit of Heresy, Late 17th-Early 18th Centuries." Ph.D. dissertation. Columbia University, 1986.

Carmona, Elia. *Como Nacio Elia Carmona*. Istanbul, 1927.

————. *Los Dos Hermanicos*. Istanbul, 1921.

————. *La Novia Agunah*. Istanbul, 1922.

Chouraqui, André. *Between East and West*. Philadelphia, 1968.

Cohen, Gerson. "Messianic Postures of Ashkenazim and Sephardim." In *Leo Baeck Memorial Lectures*, vol. 9, pp. 117–56. New York, 1967.

Cohen, Martin. "Reflexions on the Text and Context of the Disputation of Barcelona." *Hebrew Union College Annual* 35 (1954): 157–92.

Confanton, Yitzhak. *Darkhei ha-Talmud*. Jersualem, 5741.

Cooperman, Bernard. "Eliyahu Montalto's 'Suitable and Incontrovertible Propositions': A Seventeenth Century Anti-Christian Polemic." In *Jewish Thought in the Seventeenth Century*, edited by I. Twersky and B. Septimus, pp. 469–97. Cambridge, Mass., 1987.

Cordovero, Moshe. *The Palm Tree of Deborah*. Translated by Louis Jacobs. London, 1960.

————. *Sefer Gerushin*. Shklov, 5551.

Dan, Joseph. *Jewish Mysticism and Jewish Ethics*. Seattle, 1986.

————. "Manasseh ben Israel's *Nishmat Hayyim* and the Concept of Evil in Seventeenth Century Jewish Thought." In *Jewish Thought in the Seventeenth Century*, edited by I. Twersky and B. Septimus, pp. 63–76. Cambridge, Mass., 1987.

————. "No Evil Descends from Heaven." In *Jewish Thought in the Sixteenth Century*, edited by B. D. Cooperman, pp. 89–105. Cambridge, Mass., 1983.

Eisenstein, J. D., ed. *Ozar ha-Masaot*. Tel Aviv, 1969.

Elazar, Samuel, ed. *El Romancero Judeo-Español*. Sarajevo, 1989.

Elmaleh, Abraham. *Ha-Rishonim le-Zion*. Jerusalem, 1970.

Farhi, Yitzhak. *Tsuf Devash*. Jerusalem, 5689.

Faur, José. *Harav Yisrael Moshe Hazan: ha-Ish u-Mishnato*. Jerusalem, 5738.

Franco, Moïse. *Essai sur l'Histoire des Israélites de l'Empire Ottoman*. Paris, 1897.

Gabbai, Meir ben. *Sefer Avodat ha-Kodesh*. Lvov, 1848.

Gabison, Abraham. *Omer ha-Shikhah*. Jerusalem, 5733.

Galante, Abraham. *Rinu*. Cairo, 1906.

Gaon, M. D. *Bibliography of the Judeo-Spanish Press*. Jerusalem, 1965.

———. *Yehudei ha-Mizrah be-Erets Israel*. 2 vols. Jerusalem, 1937–38.

Gaon, Solomon. "Rabbi Yehudah Alkalai." In *The Rebirth of Israel*, edited by Israel Cohen, pp. 138–47. London, 1952.

Goitein, S. D. *Jews and Arabs*. New York, 1974.

Goldman, Israel. *The Life and Times of Rabbi David Ibn Abi Zimra*. New York, 1970.

Goodblatt, Morris. *Jewish Life in Turkey in the Sixteenth Century*. New York, 1952.

Goodman, Paul. *Moses Montefiore*. Philadelphia, 1925.

Guerin, Victor. *Voyage dans l'Île de Rhodes*. Paris, 1856.

Habib, Levi ben, *Responsa*. Lemberg, n.d.

Habib, Yaacov. *Ein Yaacov*. New York, 5731.

Hacker, Yosef. "The Intellectual Activity of the Jews of the Ottoman Empire during the 16th and 17th Centuries." In *Jewish Thought in the Seventeenth Century*, edited by I. Twersky and B. Septimus, pp. 95–135. Cambridge, Mass., 1987.

———. "Lidmutam ha-Ruhanit shel Yehudei Sefarad be-Sof ha-Meah he-Hamesh Esrei." *Sefunot* 17 (5743): 21–95.

Ha-Cohen, Eliyahu. *Midrash Talpiot*. Tchernowitz, 1860.

———. *Shevet Musar*. Lublin, 5642.

Ha-Cohen, Yosef. *Emek ha-Bakhah*. Jerusalem, 5716.

Hagiz, Moshe. *Mishnat Hakhamim*. Brooklyn, 5719.

———. *Sefat Emet*. Amsterdam, 5746.

———. *Sefer Leket ha-Kemah*. Bnei Brak, 5743.

Hagiz, Yaacov. *Halakhot Ketanot*. Jerusalem, 5734.

Halevy, Hayyim David. *Asei Lekha Rav*. Vol. 8. Tel Aviv, 5748.

Hasida, Yisrael Yitzhak. *Ribi Hayyim Palache u-Sefarav*. Jerusalem, 5728.

Hazan, Eliyahu. *Taalumot Lev*. Jerusalem, 5746.

Hazan, Israel Moshe. *Nahalah le-Yisrael*. Alexandria, 1862.

———. *Shearit ha-Nahalah*. Alexandria, 1862.

Huli, Yaacov. *Me'am Lo'ez.* Constantinople, 1730.

Hyamson, Albert. *The Sephardim of England.* London, 1951.

Ibn Abi Zimra, David. *Responsa.* New York, 1967.

Ibn Migash, Abraham. *Kevod Elohim.* Jerusalem, 5737.

Idel, Moshe, "Differing Conceptions of Kabbalah in the Early Seventeenth Century." In *Jewish Thought in the Seventeenth Century,* edited by I. Twersky and B. Septimus, pp. 137–200. Cambridge, Mass., 1987.

Israel, Eliyahu. *Kol Eliyahu.* Livorno, 5552.

———. *Shenei Eliyahu.* Livorno, 5566.

Israel, Michael Yaacov. *Shenoth Yamin.* Vol. 1. Izmir, 5620.

———. *Yad Yemin.* Izmir, 1859.

Israel, Moshe. *Masat Moshe.* 3 vols. Constantinople, 5495, 5502.

Kaplan, Aryeh, trans. *The Torah Anthology.* New York, 1977.

Kaplan, Yosef. *Mi-Notsrut le-Yahadut: Hayyav u-Paolo shel ha-Anus Yitzhak Orobio de Castro.* Jerusalem, 5743.

———. "Ha-Yehudim ha-Portugalim be-Amsterdam: me-Hayyim bi-Shemad le-Shivah le-Yahadut." In *Moreshet Yehudei Sefarad ve-ha-Mizrah,* edited by Issachar Ben-Ami, pp. 115–34. Jerusalem, 5742.

Katz, Jacob. "Halakhah and Kabbalah as Competing Disciplines of Study." In *Jewish Spirituality from the Sixteenth Century Revival to the Present,* edited by Arthur Green, pp. 34–63. New York, 1987.

———. "Lish-elat ha-Kesher bein ha-Shabtaut le-bein ha-Haskalah ve-ha-Reforma." In *Studies in Jewish Religious and Intellectual History Presented to Alexander Altmann,* pp. 83–100. University, Ala., 1979.

———. "Post-Zoharic Relations between Halakhah and Kabbalah." In *Jewish Thought in the Sixteenth Century,* edited by B. D. Cooperman. pp. 283–307. Cambridge, 1983.

———. "The Semikhah Controversy in Safed." *Zion* 16 (1951): 28–45.

Landau, Louis. *Jews in Nineteenth Century Egypt.* New York, 1969.

———. "Yahaso shel R. Yaacov Huli el ha-Shabtaut." *Peamim* 15 (1983): 58–66.

Levi, Moises Orfali. *Los Conversos Españoles en la Literatura Rabinica.* Salamanca, 1982.

Levy, Avner. "Alexander Benguiat u-Terumato le-Itonut ve-ha-Sifrut ha-Yafah be-Ladino." In *The Sephardic and Oriental Jewish Heritage,* edited by I. Ben-Ami. Jerusalem, 1982.

Loewenthal, Robyn. "Elia Carmona's Autobiography." Ph.D. dissertation, University of Nebraska, 1984.

Luzzatto, Moshe Hayyim. *Mesilat Yesharim.* New York, 1980.

Markovits, Eugene. "H. P. Mendes: Architect of the Union of Orthodox

Jewish Congregations of America." *American Jewish Historical Quarterly* 55 (March 1966): 364–84.

———. "H. P. Mendes: Builder of Traditional Judaism in America." Doctoral dissertation, Yeshiva University, 1961.

Markus, Simon. *Toledot ha-Rabbanim mi-Mishpahat Israel me-Rodos.* Jerusalem, 1935.

Medina, Shemuel de. *Responsa.* Lemberg, 1862.

Melnick, Ralph. *From Polemics to Apologetics.* Assen, 1981.

Meshi-Zahav, Abraham. *Mesilot ha-Hayyim.* Jerusalem, 5734.

Mirsky, Aharon, Grossman, A., and Kaplan, Y., eds. *Galut ahar Golah.* Jerusalem, 5748.

Mizrahi, Eliyahu. *Mayim Amukim.* Salonika, 5570.

Molho, Michael. *Literatura Sefardita de Oriente.* Madrid, 1960.

———. *Usos y Costumbres de los Sefardies de Salonika.* Madrid, 1950.

Moshe ben Nahman. *Kitvei Rabbeinu Moshe ben Nahman.* Edited by Charles Chavel. New York, 1963.

Nacht, Yaacov. *Mekor Hayyim.* Drohobycz, 1898.

Nehama, Yehudah Yaacov. *Mikhtevei Dodim mi-Yayin.* Salonika, 5653.

Netanyahu, Benzion. *Abravanel.* Philadelphia, 1968.

———. *The Marranos of Spain.* New York, 1966.

Nieto, David. *Ha-Kuzari ha-Sheni hu Mateh Dan.* Jerusalem, 5718.

———. *The Rod of Judgment.* Translated by L. Loewe. London, 1842.

Otolenghi, Moshe Yaacov. *La Halbashah.* Salonika, 1886.

Palache, Hayyim. *Hikekei Lev.* Vols. 1 and 3. Salonika, 5600 and 5609.

———. *Kaf ha-Hayyim.* Jerusalem, 5736.

———. *Tokhahat Hayyim.* Jerusalem, 5738.

Papo, Eliezer. *Hesed la-Alafim, Orah Hayyim.* Jerusalem, 5745.

———. *Orot Elim.* Jerusalem, 5723.

———. *Pele Yoets.* Jerusalem, 5747.

———. *Yaalzu Hasidim.* Bnei Brak, 5730.

Papo, Eliezer ben Yomtov. *Damesek Eliezer.* Jerusalem, 5736.

Papo, Joseph. *Sephardim of Twentieth Century America.* Berkeley, 1987.

Petuchowski, Jacob. *The Theology of Haham David Nieto.* New York, 1970.

Pool, David de Sola. *H. Pereira Mendes: A Biography.* New York, 1938.

———. and Pool, Tamar de Sola. *An Old Faith in the New World.* New York, 1955.

Pulido, Angel. *Españoles sin Patria.* Madrid, 1905.

Reggio, Isaac, ed. *Behinath ha-Kabbalah.* Goeritz, 1852.

Revah, I. S. "La Religion d'Uriel da Costa, Marrane de Porto." *Revue de l'Histoire de Religions,* 1962, pp. 45–76.

⸻. "Les Marranes." *Revue des Études Juives* 118 (1959–60): 29–77.

Ricardo, B. Israel, ed. *Tefilat kol Peh.* Amsterdam, 1950.

Romero, Elena. *El Teatro de los Sefardies Orientales.* Madrid, 1979.

⸻. *Repertorio de Noticias sobre el Mundo Teatral de los Sefardies Orientales.* Madrid, 1983.

Rosanes, Solomon. *Divrei Yemei Yisrael be-Togarmah.* Vol. 1. Tel Aviv, 5690.

Rose, Constance. *Alonso Nunez de Reinoso: The Lament of a 16th Century Exile.* Cranbury, N.J., 1971.

Rosenberg, Shalom. "Exile and Redemption in Jewish Thought in the Sixteenth Century." In *Studies in Sixteenth Century Jewish Thought,* edited by B. Cooperman, pp. 399–430. Cambridge, Mass., 1983.

Roth, Cecil. *Gleanings.* New York, 1967.

⸻. *A History of the Marranos.* New York, 1966.

⸻. "Immanuel Aboab's Proselytization of the Marranos." *Jewish Quarterly Review* 23 (1932): 121–62.

⸻. *Manasseh ben Israel.* Philadelphia, 1934.

⸻. "The Strange Case of Hector Mendes Bravo." *Hebrew Union College Annual* 18 (1943–44): 221–45.

Sack, Bracha. "The Influence of Cordovero on 17th Century Jewish Thought." In *Jewish Thought in the Seventeenth Century,* edited by I. Twersky and B. Septimus, pp. 365–79. Cambridge, Mass., 1987.

Salomon, H. P. "Rabbi Saul Levi Mortera's Treatise on the Truth of the Law of Moses." Doctoral dissertation, Coimbra, Acta Universitatis Conimbrigensis, 1988.

⸻ and Angel, M. D. "Nahmanides' Approach to Midrash in the Disputation of Barcelona." *American Sephardi* 6 (1973): 41—51.

Sasportas, Yaacov. *Ohel Yaacov.* Bnei Brak, 5746.

⸻. *Zizat Nobel Zebi.* Edited by I. Tishby. Jerusalem, 1954.

Schechter, Solomon. "Safed in the Sixteenth Century." In *Studies in Judaism,* second series, pp. 202–306. Philadelphia, 1908.

Scholem, Gershom. "Derush al ha-Geulah le-Rabi Shelomo le-Beit Turiel." *Sefunot* 1 (5717): 62–79.

⸻. *Major Trends in Jewish Mysticism.* New York, 1967.

⸻. *On the Kabbalah and Its Symbolism.* New York, 1965.

⸻. *Sabbatai Sevi.* Princeton, 1973.

Schwarz, Samuel. *Os Cristaos-Novos em Portugal no Seculo XX.* Lisbon, 1925.

Sutehon, Hayyim. *Erets ha-Hayyim.* Jerusalem, 5668.

Szajkowski, Z. "The Alliance Israélite Universelle in the United States,

1860–1949." *Publications of the American Jewish Historical Society* 39 (1950): 406–43.

Usque, Samuel. *Consolation for the Tribulations of Israel.* Translated by Martin Cohen. Philadelphia, 1965

Uziel, Benzion. *Hegyonei Uziel.* Vol. 1. Jerusalem, 5713.

———. *Mikhmanei Uziel.* Tel Aviv, 1939.

———. *Mishpetei Uziel.* Tel Aviv, 5695, 5700, 5724.

Vidas, Eliyahu de, *Reishit Hokhmah.* Jerusalem, 5732.

Weinberger, Philip. *The Social and Religious Thought of Grace Aguilar.* New York, 1970.

Werblowsky, R. J. Zwi. *Joseph Caro.* Philadelphia, 1977.

———. "Tikun Tefilot le-Rabi Shelomo ha-Levi Alkabets." *Sefunot* 6 (5722): 137–82.

Wolf, Lucien. *Jews in the Canary Islands.* London, 1926.

———. *The Life of Sir Moses Montefiore.* New York, 1881.

Yaari, Abraham. *Ha-Defus ha-Ivri be-Kushta.* Jerusalem, 5727.

———. *Sheluhei Erets Israel.* Jerusalem, 5711.

Yaavets, Yosef. *Kol Sifrei Rav Yosef Yaavets.* Jerusalem, 5694.

Yerushalmi, Yosef Hayim. "Clio and the Jews: Reflections on Jewish Historiography in the 16th Century." In *American Academy for Jewish Research Jubilee Volume,* edited by Salo Baron and I. Barzilay, vol. 2, pp. 607–38. Jerusalem, 1980.

———. "Messianic Impulses in Joseph ha-Kohen." In *Studies in Sixteenth Century Jewish Thought,* edited by B. D. Cooperman, pp. 460–87. Cambridge, Mass., 1983.

———. *From Spanish Court to Italian Ghetto.* New York, 1971.

Zahalon, Yomtov. *Responsa.* Jerusalem, 5745.

Zarco, Yehudah. *Lehem Yehudah.* Edited by A. M. Haberman. Jerusalem, 1970.

Zimmels, H. J. "The Contributions of the Sephardim to the Responsa Literature Till the Beginning of the Sixteenth Century." In *The Sephardi Heritage,* edited by Richard Barnett. New York, 1971.

Zohar, Zvi. "Halakhic Responses of Syrian and Egyptian Rabbinical Authorities to Social and Technological Change." In *Studies in Contemporary Jewry,* edited by Peter Medding, vol. 2, pp. 18–51. Bloomington, 1986.

Angel, Marc D., *A New World: An American Sephardic Memoir*, Albion-Andalus Books, Boulder, 2019.

———. *Foundations of Jewish Spirituality: The Inner Life of the Jews of the Ottoman Empire*, Jewish Lights, Woodstock, 2006.

———. *Loving Truth and Peace: The Grand Religious Worldview of Rabbi Benzion Uziel*, Jason Aronson, Northvale, 1999.

———. *Maimonides, Spinoza and Us: Toward an Intellectually Vibrant Judaism*, Jewish Lights, Woodstock, 2009.

———. and Angel, Hayyim, *Rabbi Haim David Halevy: Gentle Scholar and Courageous Thinker*, Urim Publications, Jerusalem and New York, 2006.

———. Ed., *The Essential Pele Yoetz: An Encyclopedia of Ethical Jewish Living*, Sepher-Hermon Press, New York, 1991.

Benamozegh, Elijah, *Israel and Humanity*, trans. Maxwell Luria, Paulist Press, New York, 1995.

Benbassa, Esther, and Rodrigue, Aron, *Sephardi Jewry: A History of the Judeo-Spanish Community, 14th-20th Centuries*, University of California Press, Berkeley, 2000.

Naar, Devin E., *Jewish Salonica*, Stanford University Press, Stanford, 2016.

Rodrigue, Aron, *French Jews, Turkish Jews*, Indiana University Press, Bloomington, 1990.

———. *Jews and Muslims: Images of Sephardi and Eastern Jewries in Modern Times*, University of Washington Press, Seattle, 2003.

———. and Stein, Sarah, *A Jewish Voice from Ottoman Salonica: The Ladino Memoir of Sa'adi Besalel a-Levi*, Stanford University Press, Stanford, 2012.

Zohar, Zvi, *HaRav Uziel Uvnei Zemano*, Vaad leHotsaat Kitvei HaRav Uziel and the University of Tel Aviv, Tel Aviv, 2009.

———. *Rabbinic Creativity in the Modern Middle East*, Bloomsbury, London and New York, 2013.

———. *The Luminous Face of the East: Studies in the Legal and Religious Thought of Sephardic Rabbis of the Middle East*, HaKibbutz HaMeuhad Press, Tel Aviv, 2001.

Index

Abduction of Jewish child, Mortara case, 147–48
Abdul Hamid, 169
Aboab, Imanuel, 62, 66; *Nomologia*, 62, 81
Aboab, Shemuel, 51, 76
Aboab de Fonseca, Yitzhak, 54
Abraham ben Moshe Maimon, 20
Abravanel, Bienvenida, 110
Abravanel, Yehudah, 6, 25, 26; *Dialoghi d'Amore*, 25
Abravanel, Yitzhak, 4–6, 20, 25, 32, 165; conversos, 49
Abudiente, Moshe, 74
Abulafia, Hayyim, 89–92
Abulafia, Yitzhak, 191–92
Activism and change, 138–44
Aderbi, Yitzhak, 21
Adret, Shelomo ben, of Barcelona, 3
Aguilar, Grace, 152–55, 159; *The Jewish Faith: Its Spiritual Consolation, Moral Guidance, and Immortal Hope*, 153; *The Spirit of Judaism*, 152
Ahasuerus, 47
Akiba, 13, 15, 92
Alashkar, Moshe, 36
Alevy, Moshe, 167
Alfasi, Yitzhak, 1–2
Algazi, Shelomo, 89
Alkabets, Shelomo, 30–31, 38–39, 41
Alkalai, Yehudah, activism and change, 138–44; blood libels, 146, 148–49; *Shema Yisrael*, 139; Zionism, 205–207
Alliance Israélite Universelle, 152, 159, 166; modernization of education, 180–81, 186; Mortara case, 148
Almohads, conquest of Spain, 2
Almosnino, Moshe, 12, 18, 22–26, 35
Alsheikh, Moshe, 38
Altmann, Alexander, 54
La America (newspaper), 172–75
Amigo, Abraham, 89

Amsterdam, Sephardic exiles, 7, 56, 60–62, 64–65
Andalusia, expulsion of Jews, 4
Anti-Judaism: abduction of child, Mortara case, 147–48; attacks from Christian preachers, 42–43; blood libels, 144–49; crypto-Judaism, 45–48; Inquisitions in Spain and Portugal, 44–50
Antinomianism and salvation, 70, 77
Anti-Semitism: see Anti-Judaism
Apostasy, 16th century Iberia, 42–55
Aragon, conversos in, 2; massacre of Jews, 3
Arba Turim, 36
Arditti and Castro (publishers), 168
Arditti, Isaac, 168
Aristotle, 22, 25
Aryeh, Gabriel, 166
Asher ben Yehiel of Toledo, 3
Ashkenazy, Abraham, 186
Ashkenazy, Abraham Nathan, 72, 75–77
Ashkenazy, Elisha Hayyim, 72
Assaf, Simhah, 50
Assimilation, Israel and the nations, 197–207
Auto da-fé, and Spanish Inquisition, 48
Azikri, Eliezer, 39; *Sefer Hereidim*, 40–41, 123, 128
Azulai, Hayyim Yosef David, 77, 113, 116, 135, 192; ethical literature, 118, 120–24, 127–29, 131, 134; Jewish homeland, 89, 92, 94–95

Bacrat, Abraham ben Shelomo Halevy, 6
Baer, Yitzhak, 48, 88
Barcelona: conversos in, 3; murder of Jews, 3
Bar Kokhba, 92
Barrios, Daniel Levi de, *De un Pecador Arrepentido*, 53
Behar, Abraham, 169

Behar, Nissim, 180–81; Jewish education, 180–81

Benamozegh, Eliyahu, 193, 200–202; *In Ethical Paths*, 156; *Israel and Humanity*, 200–201; Sephardic Haskalah and Jewish ethics, 155–57, 159

Benardete, Mair José, 65–66; *The Hispanic Culture and Character of the Sephardic Jews*, 172

Benattar, Hayyim, 91–94; ethical literature, 118, 122, 125–26, 128, 131, 134; *Or ha-Hayyim*, 10, 92–93, 134

Ben Diouan, Amram, 94, 95

Bengualid, Yitzhak, 182–83, 189–90

Benguiat, Alexander, 164

Ben Ish Hai, 191

Benoliel, Jose, 172

Benveniste, Ezra, 164

Benveniste Hayyim, 74–75

Berav, Yaacov, 34, 36, 53, 139

Berdugo, Raphael, ethical literature, 118, 121, 130–31

Blood libels, 144–49, 198–200

B'nai B'rith and blood libels, 147

Board of Delegates of American Israelites, Mortara case, 148

Board of Deputies of British Jews, 147

The Book of Splendor (Zohar), 3, 121

Boton, Yitzhak de, 176

Braudel, Fernand, 66

La Buena Esperansa, 164

Capon, Laura Papo, 176

Cappon, Abraham, 179

Capsali, Eliyahu, 6

Cardoso, Abraham, 75–78, 81

Cardoso, Isaac, 64–65, 76; *Las excelencias de los Hebreos, (Excellencies of the Hebrews)*, 65, 81

Carmona, Elia, 164; *Como nacio Elia Carmona* ("Elia Carmona's Upbringing"), 166, 169; *Los dos hermanicos*, 169–70; *La novia agunah*, 170

Carmona, Hayyim, 164

Carvallo, J., 148

Castile, Jews in, 2

Castro, Hayyim de, 164

Castro, Yitzhak Orobio, 64

Catholicism: abduction of Jewish child, Mortara case, 147–48; Spanish Inquisition and persecution of Jews, 3–4

Chouraqui, Andre, 116

Christiani, Pablo, 3, 42

Christians, discrimination against Jewish "New Christians," 44–45

Clement IV, Spanish Inquisition, 3

Clement VII, 48

Como nacio Elia Carmona ("Elia Carmona's Upbringing"), 166, 169

Confanton, Yitzhak, 36–37

Consolation for the Tribulations of Israel, 15

Conversion: Christian militancy in 16th century Iberia, 42–55; and intermarriage, 204

Cordoba, Jewish cultural center, 1

Cordovero, Moshe, 38–40, 70–71, 117

Costa, Uriel da, 60

Cremieux, Adolfe, 145

Crypto-Jews, emigration and settlement, 56, 67

Curaçao, Sephardic exiles, 8

Dan, Joseph, 38–40, 117, 119

Danon, Abraham, 172

De un Pecador Arrepentido, 53

Dialoghi d'Amore, 25

Drachman, Bernard, 161

Dreyfus, Alfred, 165

Education, modernization of, 180

El Conciliador, 60

El Instructor, 167

El Jugeton, 166, 169

El Telegrafo, 167

El Tiempo, 167

Enlightenment, religion and modernity, 179–96

Ergas, Yosef, 79

Españoles sin patria ("Spaniards Without a Country"), 171

Esther, Queen of Ahasuerus, 47

The Ethics of the Fathers, 177, 187

Excellencies of the Hebrews, 81

Federation of American Zionists, 161

Ferdinand and Isabella, expulsion of Jews, 1, 4, 45

Franco, Moshe, 180

Fresco, David, 164, 167, 169

Gabbai, Isaac, 164

Gabbai, Meir ben, 22, 24–26

Gabbai, Shemtov, 91

Gabbai, Yehezkel Effendi, 164

Gabison, Abraham, 12

Gadol, Moise Salomon, 164, 172–75

Galante, Abraham, 40, 118, 164–65, 172; modernization of education, 180; *Rinu*, 165–66

Galante, Moshe, 77, 86–87, 89

Gaon, M. D., 176

Garden of Eden story, 37–38
Garson, Yosef, 37, 49
Gerona, murder of Jews, 3
Gerondi, Yonah, 117
Geronimo de Santa Fé, 42
Goitein, S. D., 8
Granada, expulsion of Jews, 12
Guerin, Victor, 198

Habib, Moshe, 96
Ha-Cohen, Eliyahu: ethical literature, 118, 120, 124–29, 132–33; *Midrash Talpiot*, 114; *Shevet Musar*, 134
Hacohen, Moshe, 31
Hacohen, Yosef, 5; *The Valley of Tears*, 15
Haggiag, Abraham, 186
Hagiz, Moshe, 77–84; 136; ethical literature, 118, 120; Jewish homeland, 88–89, 95, 99; *Mishnat Hakhamim*, 80–81; *Sefat Emet*, 88
Hagiz, Yaacov, 70, 77, 87, 89
Hai Gaon, 183
Halakhah (Jewish legalism) vs. Kabbalah (Jewish mysticism), 15
Halevy, Abraham, 31, 40
Halevy, Eliezer, 31
Halevy, Yehudah, 2, *Kuzari*, 63
Ha-Nagid, Shemuel, 2, 20
Ha-Nagid, Yosef, 2
Hasan, David, 91
Hasdei Hashem, 10, 24
Hayon, Nehemiah Hiya, 78–79, 81
Hayun, Yosef, 34
Hazan, Eliyahu, 184–86, 191–93, 195–96; blood libel, 198–200; conversion and intermarriage, 204; modernization of education, 184–86, 191–93, 195–96
Hazan, Israel Moshe, enlightenment, 157–59, 183; *Nahalah le-Yisrael*, 158; Sephardic Haskalah, 157–59
Hazan, Yosef, *Hikrei Lev*, 189
Hazan, Yosef Refael, 157
Hebrew Immigrant Aid Society, 173
Hemdat Yamim, 77, 118, 120, 131
Heresy, challenge to rabbinic tradition, 70
Herrera, Abraham Cohen, 65
Herzl, Theodor, 139, 205
Hikrei Lev, 189
The Hispanic Culture and Character of the Sephardic Jews, 172
Horowitz, Hayyim Leibush, 199
Hovot ha-Levavot, 117, 121
Huli, Yaacov, 77, 103, 118; *Me'am Lo'ez*, 103–104, 106, 111; principles of Judaism, 103–110

Humanitarianism, Sephardic Haskalah, 150–63

Ibn Abi Zimra, David, 52, 59–61, 102
Ibn Ezra, Abraham, 2
Ibn Ezra, Moshe, 2
Ibn Gabirol, Shelomo, 2
Ibn Migash, Abraham, 21
Ibn Pakuda, Bahya, 2; *Hovot ha-Levavot*, 117, 121
Ibn Shaprut, Hasdai, 1
In Ethical Paths, 156
Intermarriage and conversion, 204
Isolation, Israel and the nations, 197–207
Israel, Abraham, 99
Israel Baal Shem Tov, 93; Jewish literature, 133–34
Israel, Eliyahu, 99, 102, 115–16
Israel and Humanity, 200–201
Israel, Michael Yaacov, 99, 146
Israel, Moshe, 96–97, 99, 102, 115; *Masat Moshe*, 96
Israel, Moshe II, 102
Israel, Reuben Eliyahu, 187–88; *The Ethics of the Fathers*, 177, 187

The Jewish Faith: Its Spiritual Consolation, Moral Guidance, and Immortal Hope, 153
Jewish homeland, 85–100
Jewish literature: ethical teachings, 117–34; Sephardic classic texts, 58–66
Jewish state as religious ideal, 141–43
Jewish Theological Seminary of America, 160
Judaism: crypto-Judaism in 16th century Iberia, 45–49; intermarriage and conversion, 204; new Christians returning to, 56–67; *see also* Anti-Judaism

Kabbalah: ethics in Jewish literature, 117–34; (Jewish mysticism) and halakhah (Jewish legalism), 15; mysticism and philosophy, 68–84
Kaf ha-Hayyim, 191
Kaf Haketoret, 32
Karo, Yosef, 34, 36, 38; 52; *Beit Yosef*, 36; *Maggid Mesharim*, 38; *Shulhan Arukh*, 36, 38
Katz, Jacob, 68
Kol Sakhal, 61
Kook, Abraham Yitzhak, 194
Kovo, Yaacov, 182
Kuzari, 63

Leeser, Isaac, 152–53, 155
Lehem Yehudah, 21
Leon, Yehudah, 95
Leon, Moshe de, *Zohar,* 3, 121
Levi ben Habib, 34, 36, 53
Lexington School for the Deaf, 161
Los dos hermanicos, 169–70
Luria, Yitzhak, 38–41, 69, 71, 90, 112; ethical literature, 119, 130, 133–34
Luzzatto, Moshe Hayyim, 78; ethical literature, 118, 120, 122–23, 127–29, 134; *Mesillat Yesharim,* 120, 134

Maggid Mesharim, 38
Maimonides, 2–3; *Mishneh Torah (Mishneh le-Melekh),* 103, 109; on rationalism, 20–21, 28; *Shemonah Perakim,* 117
Mainstral, Shelomo, 86
Malki, Ezra, 102
Manoel, King of Portugal, 45
Masat Moshe, 96
Mateh Dan, 63
Me'am Lo'ez, 103–104, 106, 111
Medina, Shemuel de, 35–36, 52–53, 58, 102
Medini, Hayyim Hizkiah, *Sedei Hemed,* 191
Mehemed Effendi (Sabbatai Sevi), 74
Menasseh ben Israel, 50; 69; *El Conciliador,* 60; *Thesouro dos Dinim,* 60
Mendelssohn, Moses, 150
Mendes, Abraham, 160
Mendes, Henry Pereira, 160–62, 174, 205
Mesillat Yesharim, 134
Messianic hope, 19, 32–35; in ethical literature, 118–19; in 16th century Iberia, 48–49; 51; restoration of Jewish sovereignty, 139–43; Sabbatai Sevi, 68–84; world to come and Musar teachings, 124–33; Zionism and migration to Israel, 205–207
Midrash Talpiot, 114
Mishnat Hakhamim, 80–81
Mitrani, Barukh, 176
Modena, Leone de, 69
Modernity: Israel and the nations, 197–207; modernization of education, 180
Molho, Michael, 116
Molho, Solomon (Diogo Pires), 48
Montalto, Eliyahu, 69
Montefiore Hospital, 160–61
Montefiore, Moses, 142, 145, 147
Morais, Sabato, 160
Mortara, Edgardo, abduction of child, 147–48

Mortara, Mordecai Halevi, 159
Mortera, Saul Levi, 54
Moshe ben Nahman (Nachmanides), 3, 19–20, 42, 117
Moslems and Jewish exiles, 1–2; banishment from Portugal, 45; conditions for civil rights and privileges, 8–9; yellow badge for Jews, 8
Mysticism and philosophy, era of Sabbatai Sevi, 68–84

Nahalah le-Yisrael, 158
Nahmias, David, 36
Nahmias, Samuel, 36
Nasi, Gracia, 90, cultural contributions of women, 110–11
Nasi, Yosef, 34, 90, 139
Navon, E. of Istanbul, 176
Navon, Ephraim, 95
Nehama, Yehudah Yaacov, Sephardic Haskalah, 159–60, 182
New York Board of Jewish Ministers, 161
Nieto, Haham David, 62–64; 136; *Mateh Dan,* 63
Ninth of Ab, Sabbatai Sevi abolishing fast of, 73, 75–76
Nissim, Shelomo, 159
Nomologia, 62, 81
La novia agunah, 170

Oral Torah and rabbinic authority, 61–64
Or ha-Hayyim, 10, 134
Orobio de Castro, Yitzhak, 64
Orot Elim, 135
Otolenghi, Moshe Yaacov, 181–82

Palache, Hayyim, 186, 188
Papo, Eliezer, 118, 122, 124, 126–27, 129–30, 132, 134, 135–38, 146; *Orot Elim,* 135; *Pele Yoets,* 124, 134–35; *Sefer Hassidim,* 135
Papo, M., 176
Papo, Menahem, 135
Papo, Yehudah, 135
Pele Yoets, 124, 134–35
Perez, Alexandro, 176
Peri Hadash, 89
Persecution, 15th century Spain, 1–15
Philosophic principles in Jewish literature, 117–34
Philosophy: Sephardic Haskalah, 150–63; and religious faith, 16–17, 31
Piety and world to come, 135
Pirkei Avot, 177
Pius IX, abduction of child, Mortara case, 147–48
Plato, 25

Pool, David de Sola, 174
Portugal: banishment of Jews and Moslems, 45; Inquisition and Judaism, 45–46, 48; Sephardic exiles, 7
Puerta del Cielo, 65
Pulido, Angel, 171–72; *Españoles sin patria* ("Spaniards Without a Country"), 171

Rabbinic authority and Oral Torah, 61–64
Rabbinic ethics in Jewish literature, 117–34
Reason and experience, Sephardic Haskalah, 150–63
Religious piety, diaspora Sephardim, 58–59
Reshit Hokhmah, 40
Resurrection, 33
Reubeni, David, 48–49
Rinu, 165–66
Rosanes, Solomon, 172
Rosanes, Yehudah, *Mishneh Torah (Mishneh le-Melekh)*, 103, 109
Roth, Cecil, 50
Rovigo, Abraham, 78

Saba, Abraham, 34
Salem, S., 176
Saporta, Hayyim Barukh, 95
Sarug, Israel, *Puerta del cielo*, 65
Sasportas, Yaacov, 51; and kabbalah, 73–74, 76
Scholarship, customs and community, 101–16
Scholem, Gershom, 69
Sedei Hemed, 191
Sefat Emet, 88
Sefer Hareidim, 40–41, 123, 128
Sefer ha-Rokeah, 121
Sefer Hassidim, 121
Seventeenth of Tammuz, Sabbatai Sevi abolishing fast of, 73, 75–76
Shaltiel, Joseph, 31
Shelomo le-Bet ha-Levi, 21
Shema Yisrael, 139
Shemonah Perakim, 117
Shevet Musar, 134
Shimon bar Yohai, 3
Silva, Hizkiah de, *Peri Hadash*, 89
Simhah ben Joshua of Zalozhtsy, 113–14
Slavery, Jewish women and children sold into, 3
Social progress and Sephardic Haskalah, 150–63
Sofer, Yaacov, *Kaf ha-Hayyim*, 191
Spain: anti-Jewish riots, 43; expulsion of Jews, 1–15

Spanish Inquisition, 44–48
Spinoza, Barukh, 61, 80
The Spirit of Judaism, 152
State of Israel, messianic hope and Jewish homeland, 85–100

Taitatsak, Yosef, 21, 36
Taragano, A., 176
Tarica, Yedidiah Shemuel, 102
Theodicy, dilemma of good and evil, 22–23
Thesouro dos Dinim, 60
Toledano, Yaacov Moshe, 195
Toledo, Christian conquest of, 2
Tradition: Sephardic Haskalah, 150–63; and will of God, 136
Turiel, Shelomo, 37

Union of Orthodox Jewish Congregations of America, 160–61
Usque, Samuel, *Consolation for the Tribulations of Israel*, 15
Uziel, Benzion, 194–96, 202–207
Uziel, Raphael, 164
Uziel, Yosef, 176

The Valley of Tears, 15
Victor Emmanuel, King of Italy, 187
Vidas, Eliyahu de, 14, 38, 117; *Reshit Hokhmah*, 40–41
Vital, Hayyim, 38

Werblowsky, Zwi, 38
Women, cultural contributions by, 110–11
World to come, 124–33
World Zionist Organization, 161

Yaacov ben Asher, *Arba Turim*, 36
Yaavets, Yosef, 10, 16–19, 24–26; *Hasdei Hashem*, 10, 24; *Or ha-Hayyim*, 10
Yerushalmi, Yosef H., 14, 65
Yisrael ben Meir, 52
Yisurin, acceptance of suffering, 11
Yitzhak Aderbi, 21
Yitzhak the Blind, 3
Yitzhaki, Abraham, *Zera Abraham*, 96
Yosef ben Yahia, 34
Young Women's Hebrew Association in New York, 160

Zarco, Yehudah, *Lehem Yehudah*, 21
Zera Abraham, 96
Zimmels, H. J., 36
Zin, Mahari, 115
Zionism, messianic hope and migration to Israel, 205–207
Zohar (The Book of Splendor), 3, 121